DON'T GO THERE

FROM CHERNOBYL TO NORTH KOREA—ONE
MAN'S QUEST TO LOSE HIMSELF AND FIND
EVERYONE ELSE IN THE WORLD'S STRANGEST
PLACES

ADAM FLETCHER

DISCLAIMER

I've changed the names of many of the people in this book because I've said questionable things about them. I don't want them to find and punch me. I've a very delicate disposition that does not respond well to punching. I've also changed the order of a few trips to make things less chaotic and nonsensical than real life has a regrettable habit of being. Please forgive this neatening of history.

1

ISTANBUL, TURKEY: "HOW COULD YOU BE SO STUPID?"

Erdoğan, (un)relaxing city breaks, Crippling Englishness, Gezi Park

The first hint this wasn't going to be a relaxing city break in Istanbul came immediately upon landing. Wheeling my suitcase through the airport, I looked down at my phone to find the following SMS:

Ada: "Hi Adam. Public transport has been shut down. It's a bit crazy here. Get the taxi driver to call me. Okay?"

Ada was our Airbnb host. My German girlfriend, Annett, and I had prepared for backgammon, ferry rides, tea, and eating large slabs of foreign cake. Not for craziness.

Me: "Who shut it down? Getting in a taxi now..."

Ada: "Who do you think shut it down? Get the taxi driver to call me."

I had no idea who had shut it down. It wasn't like there was a master public transport switch you could just turn off, right? It's not a floor lamp.

Me: "The taxi driver says he knows the address. See you in a bit."

Ada: "Get him to call me anyway. I'll tell him what roads are still open."

Me: "Why are the roads closed?"

Ada: "Do you watch the news? There are big protests here."

I did not watch the news. I avoided the news like other people avoided cholesterol. But that's not something you admit. Ignorance is not a virtue.

The other reason I didn't want to ask the taxi driver to call Ada was that I suffer from a hereditary disease called Crippling Englishness (CE). This renders me incapable of inconveniencing people, however mildly. Asking our taxi driver to call someone? Madness. Finding a specific address and reaching it in a motor vehicle was the man's entire job. He was a logistics professional. I looked across at him from the passenger seat. He was in his early forties, balding, and attempting to compensate for this by allowing the frizzy hair from the sides of his head to grow free from the confines of good taste. He looked more than familiar with the art of scowling—his eyebrows sunk deep into his eyelids, reminding me of imprints in a well-worn sofa. His off-white T-shirt was flecked with recent lunches eaten at the wheel. He was muttering to himself.

So he was a shabby, irritable example of a logistics professional, but a logistics professional nonetheless. I would not call that into question by suggesting he would not be fully abreast of the latest road closures in this, *his* city.

The next time I looked at my watch an hour had passed. "Are we nearly there?" I asked. We'd just turned onto a hilly street to find it blocked by a barricade of trash, wood, and two upside-down shopping trolleys. Around us flowed a mass of young people in homemade riot gear. It looked as if there were to be a reunion party for the hit 1970s band Village People. It was the third such do-it-yourself barricade to hinder our progress in ten minutes.

"Fucking idiots," said the taxi driver. He didn't seem to be abreast of any of this. He crunched the gear stick into reverse, turned around, and tried to steer us back to the road we'd just come from.

"What are they protesting about?" I asked.

"Protesting, yes," he said, his reversing manoeuvre complete. He scowled at two women carrying a large gay pride flag. "Fucking Terrorists."

He didn't seem like a very nice man. The few English words he had mustered during the journey had been spat aggressively in my direction. Turkish words, I suspect of an adult nature, went the other direction, out of the driver-side window and into the faces of pedestrians, other drivers, and any inanimate objects brazen enough to be in our way. Inanimate objects he seemed to find particularly irksome.

"These people don't look like terrorists," I said.

"Terrorists, yes."

I wanted to debate this further but I held back—mostly because he was driving as if we were in a go-kart and he'd eaten a special mushroom giving him infinite lives. I looked out the windscreen at a group of protesters, at their face paint, dyed hair, ripped jeans, and multicoloured vests. I was pretty sure these were not terrorists, and were even, probably, The Good Guys. Protesters are almost always the good guys, right? Because protesting is was more effort than not.

If people can be bothered to organise a demo, write songs, paint signs, and march through the streets holding those signs and singing those songs, outraged, you can be pretty sure they'll have a valid point. On the rare occasion they don't, there will likely be an even bigger protest-protest against them. You don't see the people doing the bad things out chanting: "What do we want? MORE TYRANNY! When do we want it? Well, that's up to us really, isn't it?" No, you don't see those people because those people have already won.

The taxi driver pulled into yet another side street, was confronted by yet another home-made barricade, and said, yet again, "Fuck."

"Did you know about any of this?" I asked Annett, the trip's instigator. She looked at me, tutted, sighed, frowned, and rolled her eyes, all at once. When it came to communication, she was a quantity person cruelly stuck in a quality world. She took a breath to compose herself. "About the protests? You betcha I knew. It was in the news. But I didn't know it was this big or that we were anywhere near it. Or in it, which it kinda seems like we are now." She looked around. "We're in it, right?" She twitched her nose.

We were in it.

I'd made the mistake of sitting in the front of the taxi, a rare mistake of personal initiative that meant I was now responsible for liaising with the taxi driver. I hated responsibility. I hated solving. I wanted to be back home, on my couch, ignoring all of life's problems while eating biscuits.

The next street the driver tried had a somewhat familiar feel to it. I think, perhaps, because it was the third time he'd tried it. I pinched the bridge of my nose, fought off some CE, got out my phone, called Ada, and passed the phone to the driver. Ten minutes later, and five floors higher, we found ourselves standing in front of a pink door.

That door opened and a short girl in fluffy unicorn slippers wrapped me in a warm hug. The sort of hug that suggested a far deeper friendship than the simple apartment-for-money economic exchange that was actually occurring. *Ada.*

"I wasn't sure you would come. Were you not scared?"

Annett and I exchanged a blank look that said we'd have been perfectly willing to be scared if only someone had told us what about. "Scared about the protests?" Annett asked as she stepped into the apartment's hallway. "We have a lot of protests in Berlin as well."

"Really?" said Ada, leading us past her small green-tiled kitchen. "This one is quite violent. The police are behaving like animals. You should be careful."

"We won't get involved," I assured her, as we arrived in the living room. "We're just here for tourist stuff."

We spread out on the living room's giant navy corner couch. I began to relax. This was better. This was like home even, only with a little more rainbow iconography. "What is the protest about?" I asked, as Ada poured tea from a shiny red teapot. "That's complicated," she said. "Specific things and also general things. I think, mostly, the feeling that Erdoğan is trying to make the country into an Islamic state like Saudi Arabia. They even tried to ban kissing in public!"

She handed us our cups. "You know about Erdoğan, right?"

"Yes, of course," I lied. I knew he existed. Was that enough?

Ada was in her late twenties. She had short hair, shaved completely on one side. Each ear was pierced six times, and her neck was branded with a tattoo of a goldfish. Even when saying nothing she screamed *counterculture*. When her apartment was rented, she would stay with her girlfriend, a chef who owned a restaurant nearby. She would fit into an Islamic state about as well as I would an Italian nunnery. I could see why she was protesting. She had a lot to lose.

Her phone beeped. "Oh, shit. I have to go," she said, cruelly orphaning the remainder of her tea. "I've been sleeping in Gezi Park with friends. There are developments there." There was an ominousness to the way she said the word *developments*. "Come by later if you like?"

We made noises that emphasised the possibility of this while simultaneously hinting at its underlying impossibility.

Ada left, her face noticeably whiter than when we'd arrived. We celebrated our new-found aloneness by placing more of our limbs on her sofa. It was comfortable. Which was how I liked it. A short time later, there was a really loud banging noise from outside, like the early, enthusiastic thrashings of a rhythmless drummer. The sound got louder and louder the closer we got to the balcony. From that balcony we had a stunning view sweeping down the hillside. We could see at least a hundred balconies from this vantage point, and people emerging onto them to hit saucepans with wooden spoons: a kind of kitchenware orchestra. It was a remarkable spectacle. Simple, effective, lo-fi dissent. A Mexican Saucepan Wave. In the flat diagonally underneath Ada's, a small girl of no more than five came outside armed with a spatula. Her mother bent over to hold a saucepan at the right height, so she could swipe enthusiastically at it. Occasionally she even hit it. It was utterly adorable.

"Should we join in?" I asked Annett.

"I don't know. We don't really know what they are banging for."

I didn't want to tell Annett about my "protesters are always right" theory because she'd been known to argue using facts, while I came from more of an anecdotal background.

We didn't join in, but we did watch with great delight and awe and a light peppering of positive adjectives. Later we learned this was a traditional form of protest in Turkey and that it always takes place at 9pm, the time Mustafa Kemal Atatürk was said to have founded the Republic of Turkey, in 1923.

Finally, bereft of entertainment and hungry, we headed out.

"Should we go check out the park?" Annett asked.

I scratched at my beard. "That sounds pretty intense. Do you want to?"

"Yeah. It's the most interesting option we have right now."

I swapped to my neck. "Hmm. I think I mostly want to have dinner."

She shrugged. "I can live with that, I guess. Or I'm willing to try to anyway. So shall we wander down the back streets then and find somewhere quiet where we can sit outside?"

It was clear from the first few minutes of that walk just how much of life in Istanbul happens on its streets. Kids play football, hitting parked cars and running away as their angry owners appear, shaking their fists. Elderly people pass buckets on ropes down from high apartment windows to more sprightly neighbours who fill them with vegetables and fruits. People ride their mopeds up to the entrances of restaurants and a second later are air-kissing friends' cheeks and taking puffs of shisha. I guess there's a relaxedness here in summer that comes from knowing tomorrow is going to be warm. The day after that? Looking pretty good as well.

We navigated some quiet backstreets using the popular tourist method: Which Street Looks Prettiest? After turning a corner, and spotting in the distance a promising little cafe with blue mosaic table-tops, I felt a burning sensation in my throat. "What's that smell?" Annett asked through a cough. Suddenly a group of protesters ran around the bend, one pausing briefly to splash his face with some kind of milk-like substance. We backed into a door frame to let them pass. Four policemen in riot gear chased them. We were pinned against the wall. A policeman threw a hissing canister towards the protesters—tear gas. It landed a few metres to our right, bouncing off a wall. The police passed us, moving uneasily with their clunky gear, shields, and gas masks. The cloud of gas spread quickly, taking just a few seconds to catch within our throats, setting them alight.

Adrenaline surged through us. *Go. Move. Where? Who cares. Now...*

We ran away from the protesters and police officers. At the next corner was another small cluster of police officers. A protester in the distance threw a rock at them, and so by extension, at us.

Not that way then.

We turned and ran, which is difficult when trying not to breathe. On our left we saw a courtyard with its gate open. Annett pointed and we dashed inside, slamming the door behind us. It was a courtyard shared by three buildings. We collapsed, coughing and spluttering, against the iron railings at its rear.

I viewed the world through the tiny blurred slits that were my eyes. "Oh God... This is..." *cough, cough, wheeze* "...horrible."

"Shit." Annett mopped her face with her sleeve. "Ow. Fuck. *Tear gas?*"

I'd never been tear-gassed before. It's hard when you leave the house as little as I do. It is a deeply unpleasant experience that feels like a mixture of both drowning and being on fire. "Must be," I said, rubbing my face in my shirt.

"It earns its name."

Some other protesters appeared, in the same dishevelled, spluttering state, before closing the gate and entering the building behind us. Keen to be inside, where the air might be less noxious, we followed their lead. It was a bar. On seeing us its barman, now a makeshift field nurse, rushed over and squirted some of the mystery, milky liquid into our faces.

"This would help," he said, in somewhat broken English. It did help. The flood of liquid leaking from our eyes and noses dammed, we were able to properly see the bar for the first time. A dark, alternative bar, the walls full of handwritten messages and heavy purple curtains that perfectly hid the politics erupting outside.

"I think we'd better have some strong drinks," I said to our nurse, who had taken his place behind the bar.

He turned and unscrewed a bottle of raki.

"I'm not sure what tastes worse, this or the tear gas," Annett said, after her first sip. She put the drink down. A protester from a nearby table took a call, stood up, and ran out into the courtyard. The rest of the people at her table were staring up at a TV. It was a news report about the protests. The reporter stood on one of the streets we'd taken to get here.

We'd thought we were on a relaxing city break. Things had escalated quickly.

"Can you tell me what's happening?" I asked the barman. He put his phone down and came and sat on the barstool next to us.

"The police try to clear Gezi Park. There was big camp there."

He whistled to get the attention of a girl sitting two tables over. She wore knee-high brown boots, a Che Guevara T-shirt, and had wrapped herself in a thick blanket of self-confidence.

"She speak better English," he said. She introduced herself as Dora and explained that the protester camp had been getting bigger and bigger. Hundreds had been sleeping there, and thousands more had been turning up each day to protest with them—against the park becoming a shopping mall, against the country's becoming increasingly Islamic, and autocratic. In the past hour the government had cracked the whip. Police had been sent in with one clear objective: to take back control of the park. The protesters were resisting. It had gotten violent. Skirmishes had spread out to the surrounding streets, such as the one we had accidentally stumbled onto.

"How do you think it's going to end?" I asked.

She weighed her words. "We will win. Turkey has always been secular. But it will cost."

"How you getting on with the raki?" Annett asked.

I coughed. "Wonderful. Shall we go?"

She nodded. We stood up, thanked the barman, and said goodbye to the protesters. Annett poked her head out the bar's door and sniffed at the air.

"Breathable?" I asked.

"I think so."

"What do you want to do?"

"I say we risk it," Annett said. "I've lost my appetite anyway.

Which is a first. Hopefully a last. Shall we just go back to the apartment and lick our wounds?"

"Fine by me."

Two turns later, we walked into a barricade that was on fire. A police van rushed towards it. We turned back, planning to loop the long way round. Lost, and entirely by chance, we exited a lane onto İstiklal Street. İstiklal is one of the main shopping thoroughfares of Beyoğlu, an artery feeding directly into Taksim Square. A square that leads to Gezi Park. We found İstiklal awash with protesters assembling in small groups, getting kitted up in their home-made riot gear of hard hats, goggles, hazard masks, and anti-tear-gas milkshakes. From there they'd move towards Taksim, confront the police, get teargassed, fall back, rest, and then go again. Shops were frantically pulling down their protective awnings, fearing a full-scale riot. A young man appeared next to us carrying a large cardboard box.

"Gas masks," he shouted. "Gas Masks!" I laughed at this enterprising display of pop-up capitalism. "It's always like this in the Middle East," he said. "Business comes first."

We bought a mask each. They weren't really gas masks, more the sort of white hazard masks you might wear while painting, engaged in DIY, or, if you were particularly unlucky, taking a relaxing city break.

We looked on in a mixture of awe, fear, and uncertainty. We weren't the only ones. Others had been out doing normal everyday human things—shopping, eating, *not* protesting their democratically elected government—and had also gotten caught up and were equally unsure how to get out again.

I looked at Annett, standing there in her mask, checking her map. "I don't want to state the obvious, but this is not going very well," she said, her voice muffled by her mask and the sounds of sirens and chanting. The whites of her eyes no longer were. That smell returned.

People began moving quickly in our direction. I paced back and forth.

"I've no idea which way is safe," she said, "but I checked before we came out and there's supposed to be a meetup happening on

İstiklal, above that restaurant with the blue sign. It's a Couchsurfing thing. Wanna go there and wait it out?"

I had no better idea. It would get us off the street. And we'd often had good nights at Couchsurfing events, where travellers and locals meet up in bars around the world to swap stories. At the address, we found a dented metal door with the bar's name on it. The bar was on the third floor. There were about twenty people inside. It was one of those deliberately shabby bars that tries really hard, and absolutely unsuccessfully, to look as if it isn't trying at all. The furniture didn't match. Reggae music played. The Couchsurfing group were huddled around three large windows that offered uninterrupted views of the theatre of discontent playing out on İstiklal, directly below us.

A block of protesters was being pushed away from the park by a wall of overlapping riot shields. Over that wall came a jet of water and more tear gas. A protester picked up one of the still steaming cans and lobbed it back over into the throng of police.

"I can't believe this," said a girl from India. "It's like a movie scene out there."

"What are the protests about? I mean, I know they're anti-Erdigen," asked a Canadian in a red baseball cap.

"*Erdoğan*," corrected a wiry, bearded local, who introduced himself as Ahmed. He had a small ace tattooed on his right index finger. He was digging his nails into his thigh. "Erdoğan's a..." He turned to his friend, a Turkish girl in thick red-rimmed glasses. She helped with the translation. "A *tyrant*," he said. "In the beginning, he wanted to change Gezi Park into another stupid shopping mall—"

"It started before that though," the girl interjected. "He is trying to change the parliamentary system to stay in power, and ban abortion. He's awful."

Annett and I spent the next few hours at those windows, watching, talking to the Couchsurfers, drinking to calm our nerves, and being deeply impressed by the bravery and conviction of the protesters below—conviction to run deliberately into a battle with armed police, knowing full well they were going to be tear-gassed, sprayed with water, arrested, beaten up, or maybe even shot with a rubber bullet.

We witnessed many small, absurd moments, such as the cloud of smoke being punctured by a child in its pushchair, being frantically steering by its mother. They wore matching hard hats, hazard masks, and safety goggles. The child's hard hat was an adult size and swallowed almost all of his head. He held it up with one hand, his little eyes peeking out from under it, and seemed totally calm, as if he were heading back from a trip to the zoo.

I guess, in a way, he was—the Human Zoo.

As the day darkened to night, it was harder to see what was happening outside. Someone below the windows set fire to an old armchair, and three or four protesters danced around it in triumph. "That's not it, man," said Ahmed. "We have to protest nice. Otherwise we're no better than *them*."

A man clutching shopping bags appeared next to the on-fire sofa, as if he'd been in one of the new shopping malls and had gotten lost on the way to the parking garage. He whipped out his smartphone and took selfies in front of the fire, throwing gangster signs.

"Ouch, the *fremdschämen*," said Annett, rubbing at her forehead. *Fremdschämen* is a German word for the untranslatable but instantly recognisable emotion of feeling shame on someone's behalf. A kind of embarrassment once removed.

"These people are crazy," said Andrea, an Argentinian man sharing our window. There was a quiet but commendable intensity to him. He looked long and plunged deep. If he blinked, he did so in secret. Weirdly, he seemed the most affected by what we were seeing. I resolved to buy him another drink after I'd gotten back from the toilet, hoping this might help loosen him up. My adrenaline had dropped, yet I was in a surprisingly good mood up in the safety of the bar. I was impressed by the protesters, and what they were willing to endure to stand up for what they believed in. What they thought would make their country better.

The three narrow, rectangular windows in the toilet were broken and letting in the toxic air from outside. I still had the hazard mask around my neck. I sniffed each of the three cubicles to see which would be the least toxic to my health before snapping my mask back in place. My throat stung as I stood there, relieving myself to the sounds of the protest outside. I felt very present in that moment. The background faded out. I felt... interested, part of something, even. Not at home relaxing, as per usual.

Turkey was a place where you didn't have to go looking for politics—it found you. To my surprise, having being apolitical most of life, I was suddenly enjoying the sensation of being found. Maybe life was better when we didn't all just "agree to disagree," as I'd been raised to do in England.

Back in the bar, I handed out drinks. Andrea nodded a wordless thank you. Opened his mouth. Closed it again. Nodded some more. Took a swig of beer. Scratched his head. Frowned. Looked deep into our souls and found us lacking. "I don't get it, man," he said, finally. He gestured towards the window. "I don't get this. Any of it. This country. Politics. All the fighting. Argentina, even. You're from Germany, right? Germany has taken part in two world wars and lost them both. Argentina has been in *zero*. Yet today, Germany is one of the strongest economies in the world... and... we're *nothing*. We fight amongst ourselves, we fight with our politicians, just like here. Just like Turkey. You know?"

I nodded.

"Why aren't *we* Germany, while *you're* Argentina? Or Turkey? Or Azerbaijan? Or North Korea? Why do some countries work when the rest are just chaos?"

It was a good question. I thought about it at the window over the next hour or two. It wasn't the sort of question you could actually answer because it was really a thousand questions shoved into a too-small box of intrigue. He was right about one thing though: for every popular exhibit in the Human Zoo—every New York, Rome, Great Pyramid, Great Wall, Great Barrier Reef—that gets 99 percent of the attention, admiration, and tourism, there are dozens of countries, thousands of cities, hundreds of millions of people living way off over *there*, far away, in places you rarely hear about. Places where the normal equation of *People + Resources / Time = Functional Society* has gone badly askew, creating results far away from the prosperity, freedom, and (comparative) equality that Annett and I experienced in Germany.

It was past midnight now, there were fewer protesters out, and so, proportionally, it felt as though the police had grown more successful at rounding up and arresting those too slow to get away. An extensive amount of tear gas was being used. I'd seen many of the protesters scooping up the empty canisters and taking them, presumably as souvenirs. Below the window a skirmish took place. A police officer in a gas mask threw a canister at a small group of retreating protesters. It bounced off a wall and nestled behind an overflowing bin, on the opposite side of İstiklal. No one seemed to notice it.

The next time we checked our watches, it was 1:30am. Wired from all the adrenaline, we'd long forgotten about the dinner we'd never got around to having. Annett and I stood side by side at the window. There was a lull in the pandemonium. "Should we make a run for it?" Annett asked. I chewed at my lip. "The problem," I said, authoritatively, "is that by now the police just assume anyone that's out there is involved, and crossing İstiklal is the way home, and İstiklal is, well, lively. I don't think we can cross it."

"Yeah, we'll have to find another way around."

I nodded. "I'm willing if you are. We can do a big loop around and try and get there another way."

Apprehensively we stood and said goodbye to the rest of the group. They made disapproving faces and waved arms in gestures of no-ness.

"Sit down," Ahmed said. "Wait it out."

We thanked them for their concern, told them we'd be safe, said another round of goodbyes, and then headed for the exit. We found the door locked. The barman came out from behind the bar and made exactly the same "stop right there" gestures.

"Not safe," he said.

"We know."

He pointed back inside. "Stay here."

I pointed away from İstiklal. "It's okay, we'll go away from the trouble."

He seemed genuinely concerned in a manner that was touching. Since we'd arrived in Istanbul everyone had been extremely kind and accommodating—well, apart from the people who tear-gassed us or set things near us on fire, but we were sure this was nothing personal.

"Thanks, but we know the risks," Annett said. "We'll be safe."

The man's gaze dropped to the floor. "Okay," he said, "but, go that way."

"Yes, that way," I confirmed, mirroring the direction of his outstretched finger, away from İstiklal.

The stairwell wore the day's spicy perfume—*eau de rébellion*. Back on the street, I felt my adrenaline surge. We turned left, away from İstiklal.

"Hang on," I shouted at Annett, through the smoke of a nearby wheelie-bin fire.

She lifted her mask. "What?"

I twisted to look the other way. "Wait here. I'll be one minute."

Before she had the chance to object I began running back towards İstiklal. At the street corner I took a quick glance left and right. To my left there was a police van, about one hundred metres away. The air was thick with smoke and my eyes watered, blurring my vision. I knew what I was doing was stupid, but for some reason I kept doing it anyway; I wanted that tear-gas canister. The one behind the bin on the far side of the street. Deciding it was safe enough I darted out towards it, coughing, the air a toxic soup. I saw the bin just a few metres away.

Next to it a metal object gleamed. I wheezed. My lungs screamed in anger. I reached out to steady myself on the bin. Bending behind it, I felt the cool of metal against my grip. It was still there. I had it. I wasn't exactly sure why I wanted it so badly, but there would be time for that later, in regret's post-mortem. I lifted the canister. I blinked. Nothing happened. I blinked some more. My lungs were filling with liquid. I coughed violently, spitting onto the street. The can had a familiar blue-and-silver design.

No. It couldn't be, could it?

I'd just risked potential arrest and my health and for...

Nobody could be that stupid, could they?

I lifted it closer to my face.

It was... wrong.

It was... too narrow.

It was... not a tear-gas canister.

It was... *a can of Red Bull.*

I threw it to the ground in disgust. This was a new low. I began moving back the way I'd come. I saw Annett standing there, hands on her hips, head cocked. We were most of the way across İstiklal now; we could take the next left and be pretty much home, five or six minutes at the most. I pointed that way. She turned and began to run. With squinted, streaming eyes and wet cheeks we ran. A few steps later two policemen appeared from that side street, chasing a protester.

Annett swerved off to the right, back towards the bar, as I followed. Knowing the door was locked we ran on past it. Incredibly, just seven or eight doors down from it, a fruit and veg shop seemed to be open. Four or five people were inside. We tried to open the door but found it locked. I bent over, coughing violently. A man in his sixties with a trim grey beard unlocked it. He found two small blue plastic stools for us to sit on. The protesters inside offered us some more protester milkshake. The man quickly arrived with tea. You had to do very little to be given tea here. They dispensed it without provocation.

It was 1:45am.

Annett's face was red, her nostrils flaring as she sat opposite me, her hands balled into fists. "I can't believe you left me!"

I wiped at my leaking eyes. It didn't help. "I'm sorry. From the bar I saw a tear-gas canister behind that bin. I know it's stupid but I wanted it as a souvenir."

She let this sink in for a few seconds. It didn't seem to sit well. "Why? What? Why!" She shook her head furiously. "How could you be so stupid? That's just... incredibly dumb." She took her face in her hands. "Oh, the stupidity, it burns."

"I know," I said, avoiding her gaze with the help of the floor. She looked around me. "So where is the stupid bloody can then?"

"It was a..." I paused. "A..." I laughed. "Oh, God." I laughed some more. Wiped my eyes. "A..." Chuckled. She watched on from her stool, her teeth gritted as my laughing fit spiralled out of control. She tried to remain mad but as I lost control, she did too. Before long her whole tetchy facade collapsed and we were both wiping away tears, and milk and tea from the holes in our faces, even though only one of us knew why.

"It was a... Red Bull can," I stammered.

She balled a fist, put it to her mouth, took it away, turned her head, tried to speak, stopped, turned back, and punched me in the arm. "Idiot."

The black comedy continued as the owner of the shop appeared behind us, holding a cucumber aloft. "Now would be a really fine time to pick up some cucumbers and tomatoes for tomorrow's salad, wouldn't it?" He said.

Business in the Middle East, it never stops.

We thanked him for the tea and headed back out into the throng, tomato- and cucumber-less. It really wasn't the right time to think about tomorrow's salad. Plus, it was already tomorrow. With the help of our map, we took a big detour home. It was 3am before we got there, still too wired to sleep. We watched the twenty-four-hour-news channels. It felt strange to *be* the news for a change.

2

AN INTERLUDE: THE NIGHT BEFORE ISTANBUL

People always say *comfort zone* like it's a bad thing, a thing from which one should endeavour to escape. I've never understood this. Sure, *zone* is ambiguous: time zone, war zone, primary erogenous zone. Zone can go both ways. But comfort? Just try and make that negative. Not possible. Even "comfort tyranny" just sounds like a promising new folk band.

I was thinking about this while lying in the very comfortable zone offered by my living room's couch in Berlin. I heard the front door open. A loud "Hey!" emanated from within the dark hallway—dark because the light bulb had blown and I'd fully intended to exchange it that very day but had been soundly defeated by said couch's said comfort. Annett barged into the room sending the door knocking against the wall, which was pockmarked as a result of all the previous times she'd done exactly this. Annett is to subtlety and restraint what badgers are to calligraphy. She was dressed in a variety of high-visibility clothing and looked as if she'd just finished guiding small children across a busy junction while holding a lollipop.

She began her trademark high-speed talking. "Jesus what a day non-bloody stop out there it was if it's not one thing it's something else idiots most of them I told that to my work wife and then Judith called me and you wouldn't believe what's going on with Simon and tomorrow the whole meetings and staff problems and tra la la circus starts again—"

She paused, noticing my heightened state of relaxation. "Another tough day, I see?"

I nodded. "Hectic."

She removed the last of her luminous cycle-safety clothing and climbed aboard the couch. We'd purposely purchased the largest in the shop. "Evening plans?"

I gestured at my laptop. "You're looking at them."

Her face scrunched like faces shouldn't. "Let's do something! I was thinking of maybe meeting Rob and Sarah for a drink later. Wanna join?"

A spontaneity siren sounded in my head. "Later tonight? As in, pretty much *now* later?"

"Later tonight," she confirmed. "After dinner later."

Well this was certainly the biggest decision I'd had to make since the morning's Apple vs Banana Conundrum. I'd chosen the apple. It had been a close call; the banana lost due to mild exterior bruising.

"Come on, it'll be fun, and it'll get you out of the house."

That's another one for the list. Why is being in the house always considered a bad thing? Houses are a comfort zone of Internet, sofas, cushions, toast. They're really an embarrassment of riches in a cruel, indifferent, and largely toast-less world. "Yeah, I think I'm going to pass. It's always awkward when we meet them because I can't ever remember what we talked about last time, or what Rob does for a living, or, really, anything about him. Then when he remembers stuff about me I look like a bad friend."

Annett sighed. "You *are* a bad friend. We know them for a year already! He works for the Arbeitsamt."

"I thought it was one of those Amts. Nah, I guess I'm just not feeling it with them."

Eyes were rolled. Not my eyes. "Oh no. They're not about to get your defriending email template are they? I like them. Sarah's a great laugh."

"You can go. Just tell them I'm busy."

"Busy with what? Making spam websites? Googling yourself? Avoiding anything that looks like a responsibility? Taking the easy way out? Did you reply to Dan about his wedding?"

"I don't want to go," I said, breaking eye contact. Dan and I had been best friends for ten years, all through school. He still lived in my small home town, Thetford, back in England.

"I want to go! It sounds fun. Don't you think it's strange that we've been dating for six years and yet I've never even been to Thetford?"

Six years, damn. Time flies when you're on the couch. "We've been there, don't exaggerate."

"Yeah, we've picked up your nan and then driven straight out. That's it."

"Trust me—for my home town, that's more than enough."

Her voice grew louder. "I think you're in a rut. All you do is sit about the house eating chocolate and watching documentaries. I get why not really having to work was fun at the start, and it's still amazing to me that those websites work without you, but isn't it enough now?" Her mouth twisted at the edge. "Don't you want to get back out in the world and do something?"

That sounded like almost certainly the worst idea ever. I sucked in my cheeks. "I'm in the world. Sometimes."

"You're not. You just sit around taking me and just about everything else for granted. I'm going to meet them tonight and I want you to get off Planet Adam and come with me, okay?"

I shrugged and decided this was a good moment to become really interested in a nearby plant. She tutted, slipped on her green headphones, and became personable with her laptop. Their relationship still burnt with the fire and intensity of heady, early moments of infatuation.

An hour later she tried again.

"You're not coming are you?"

I shook my head. Wordlessly she got up, put on her shoes, and left, the door slamming behind her. I stayed in, on my beloved couch.

I fully intended to change that light bulb but fell just short. I took consolation in some light googling of myself.

It would be fine. We were going to Istanbul tomorrow (her idea). There would be plenty of relaxed, quality "us time" there. I hoped there would be couches.

3

ISTANBUL TO BERLIN: "I FEAR THIS ENDS IN SOME KIND OF EAT PRAY LOVE EPIPHANY."

Flights, Eat Pray Love, *also-rans*

As we sat on the plane hurtling back to Berlin spewing toxic fumes from its rear, carbon hastening the demise of Maldivian islands and panda-grazing habitats, I felt odd. Not myself, but like a ghost haunting myself. Surprisingly, what with all the difficulty we'd been having breathing, I was sad to leave Istanbul. A ridiculously attractive and charismatic city. A seductive, best-of blend of Asia and Europe, tradition and modernity, petulance and serenity.

The intensity did drop in our final days there, but not by much. We sat with the protesters in Gezi Park when it felt safe to do so. We felt the heat and rip of tear gas upon our nervous systems several more times. Over the whole ten days of unrest, more than 8000 people were injured, 4900 were arrested, and 5 were killed. There were 150,000 tear-gas canisters used. None of which came home with us. We saw Ada a few more times. Several of her friends had been beaten up, arrested, or both, fates her and her girlfriend managed to avoid.

It had been a great trip, made so by the energy of the protesters. We'd met so many interesting people standing up for what they believed in, what they thought would make their country better. In some small, insignificant way, we'd joined them.

It felt good.

Annett was in the aisle seat watching something on her laptop. I tapped her on the arm. Begrudgingly, she removed her headphones. "What?"

My pulse quickened. I groped for the right words. None came.

"Yeesss?"

"Do... *do* you think I'm one of the good guys?"

She frowned. "What kind of a question is that? What does *good* even mean?"

"Well, everything that happened in Istanbul has got me thinking. If some higher power came down, some kind of karma accountant..."

She rolled her eyes. "This is quite an elaborate scenario you're painting here."

"I'm not saying it's imminent. But if it did happen, do you think he'd find me to have been an above-average human?"

Annett's grimace showed that the line of questioning annoyed her. It was not an Annett line of questioning because it was pointless and unanswerable and she lived in a perfect realm of practicality. There was nothing she wouldn't optimise. Everything had a specific place. Our apartment was covered in Post-it notes with specific instructions for the systems she'd concocted to organise our shoes, batteries, towels, light bulbs. She even numbered the juice cartons in the fridge to stop me opening them out of order. She logged every single financial transaction she made, even chewing gum, into a MASTER FINANCE spreadsheet so detailed the mere sight of it gave me a migraine. She'd nailed adulthood and its responsibilities. I ignored it and hoped it would go away.

She finished pondering my pointless, unanswerable question. "You don't volunteer, you don't donate to charity, you only vote when I arrange everything for you and tell you who to vote for. You'd sell your own mother for five euros. You think a principle is something that leads a school. As far as humanity is concerned, I'd say you're pretty much a *Mitläufer*. What's the English for *Mitläufer*?"

"I'm not sure I want to know."

She tilted her head. "*Also-ran*, maybe? *Hanger-on*?"

I winced. "Ouch."

"My *Mitläufer*," she added, taking my hand in hers. "But a *Mitläufer* nonetheless."

The fasten seat belt light came on. I didn't fasten my seat belt. I was done fastening seat belts. It was time for a new me. A better me. I sat straighter in my chair, looked her square in the face, and said, "I'm done being a *Mitläufer*. I think. Hmm. I don't know. Ugh."

It wasn't much, but it was a start, possibly, or a premature end, perhaps. I sank back.

She nudged her glasses back into position. "You interrupted me to make that bold statement?"

"Yeah, I guess so." I fastened my seat belt. There was new and then there was reckless. She turned back to her screen. I cleared my throat. I was losing her because I was delaying saying my least favourite words in any language.

"You're right..." I hated saying those words, but she was. "I've been in a rut. I've let my life get too easy and comfortable. On this trip, rather than some perfect, sanitised tourist experience, we got a glimpse of something raw, something being built-or destroyed; I'm still not quite sure about that. But I am sure it was messy, alive, uncertain, and there was something at stake. I remember what that feels like now and I think I'd like to feel it some more."

"Oh no," she said, covering her eyes. "I fear this ends in some kind of *Eat Pray Love* epiphany. Do you want to go find yourself?"

I shrugged. "I don't know. Maybe. Or just get lost a little in parts of the world other tourists ignore. Which leads me to my question. I know you were excited about a trip to Italy in November, but—"

She tapped her lip. "But you want to cancel it and go somewhere more challenging?"

"Would that be okay with you?"

Her eyes widened. "Ooh yes! Let's get you out of that rut, mister. And I think I even know where we should go next."

4

CHINA: "IT'S UGLY IN HERE. AND MURDERY."

Chinese New Year, John Wang, never-ending bus rides

"*Cesou, cesou, cesou*," practised Annett, as we climbed the three steps into the warm night bus, shaking the snow off our new winter clothes.

"*Cesou*? You can't possibly need the toilet," I said, walking behind her down the aisle, scanning for our bunks. "We only went a minute ago."

She kicked her bag roughly under a bunk. "Don't underestimate me."

We had just boarded the fourteen-hour night bus from the small town of Tangkou to the megacity of Wuhan. We bought these bus tickets not because we enjoyed long night-bus rides, or had any desire to go to the industrial city of Wuhan, but because a mixture of Chinese New Year and the worst weather in fifty years had made this the only option that would move us in the (general) direction of Xi'an. It had thousands of terracotta warriors standing around in a big hangar, for our enjoyment. We really wanted to go to Xi'an.

~

"You want to change?" Annett had said just a month before, as we walked through a park in Berlin. "You want to struggle. I'll give you struggle, buster. I'll give you change. A billion humans' worth of it. We should go to China."

I groaned. "China? That feels quite deep end. Maybe we could splash about in the shallow end a bit first, country wise? Canada? Chile?"

She skipped a step. "Noooooo way. You've been shallow too long, my friend."

My admitting she'd been right about my early-thirties life crisis had only galvanised her. I had become a project. The ultimate delusion is the delusion you can change your partner. I'd re-awoken that delusion. Perhaps the bigger surprise was how it had also seduced me. Two cheap, last-minute flights later, we'd come face to face with the Asian dragon strutting through Chinese New Year. We'd thought this would mean fireworks, dancing under paper dragons, and drinking mao-tais while enjoying benign displays of patriotism. Instead we'd actually plunged ourselves, in unsuitable clothing and complete cultural ignorance, into sub-zero temperatures and the largest human migration on earth. During Chinese New Year, seven hundred million people are on the move.

This year, seven hundred million... and two.

In Tangkou we'd climbed a mountain in a blizzard. Before I'd climbed a mountain in a blizzard, I would have said it was impossible. Having just about survived doing it, I could now say it was merely not recommendable.

The bus had three rows of metal bunks, two bunks high. These bunks were a reasonable size, assuming you, by Chinese standards, reasonably sized. I was not. I cramped just looking at what was to be my home for the night—left aisle, bottom bunk, number 13. A good omen, no doubt. To my right was a window offering an intimate view of the blizzard. Total visibility: five centimetres. I climbed into my bunk, adopting an innovative mixture of the foetal and brace-brace positions.

Suddenly, there was a loud, guttural *HWKKKWWHHH* sound

from the bunk above Annett's new home, next to mine, in the middle aisle.

"Ugh," she said, leaning out into the aisle so she could get a look up at the elderly Chinese bunking above her. That sound, we deduced, was the man reaching deep within himself and returning an offering of his phlegm, which he'd spat into a small carrier bag. He was attaching this bag to the corner of his bunk. A spit bag.

"China is disgusting," Annett said, rolling over to face away from me. There's a "better out than in" belief in China, so it's totally okay to spit, burp, and fart at will. We'd been trying to let go of our Western "it's better in than out" philosophy, but it had proved stubborn to shift. Much more stubborn than this man's phlegm, anyway.

Fourteen hours to go. I put my head on my pillow, trying to ignore its smell of smoke, closed my eyes, and groped for sleep.

I was brought abruptly back to consciousness by the loud sound of another fluid exodus. "Hey!" shrieked Annett. I found her on her back kicking at the bunk above her.

"What happened?"

"He is... argh, yuck." Steam rushed from her ears. The man peered down at her. "You missed!" she said, pointing at a trickle of phlegm running down the side of his spit bag, down the bed frame, and onto her bed. The man smiled a mostly toothless grin, adjusted his spit bag, and lay down again.

"I hate it here," she said. "It's disgusting. The weather is horrible. Everything we've tried has gone wrong. I hope you're getting something out of it, because I'm not sure I am."

"I am. I think," I said, not feeling brave enough to risk an all-out difference of opinion. I didn't hate it. It was alive and bustling and weird and exciting. Every day was full of challenges. The weather was relentlessly bleak, though. I was with her on that.

One hour of our journey had passed. Thirteen to go.

At the front of the bus, the crew talked loudly. We had a crew of four. I had no idea why a bus needed a crew of four. I think most likely because this was China and owning a bucket was considered a three-person job.

There seemed to be a one-size-fits-all problem solving solution here that I'd summarize as *keep throwing people at it until it goes away*. The bus pulled to a halt. Out the window was a thick, fluffy blanket of white.

I closed my eyes again.

An hour later, I was still awake, and we were still stationary. I climbed out of my bunk and ambled to the front of the bus to stretch my giant, impractical, European legs. We were in front of a bridge. Through the windscreen and falling globs of snow I could make out an electronic road sign flashing a big *X* at us. Behind that sign was a barrier, and that barrier was down. Traditionally speaking, that's not how you want your barrier. That's when barriers are being no fun.

The crew were deep in discussion as I approached. The leader was obviously the man sitting in the driver's seat. He had a thick head of ruffled hair, parted to one side and combed forward in a moppish, Beatlesesque manner. His toned, lithe body had commendable posture, and the belt holding up his faded jeans—jeans faded through wear, not the whims of fashion—had a large metal buckle. He chewed between words, like a cow chewing on grass. The steel in his gaze could have been mined for millennia. He reminded me of a Chinese John Wayne, a John Wang, if you will. The crew turned as I approached, as if I might be about to say something, which I wasn't, because I couldn't, because we shared no language. A small bottle of whisky passed between two of them. I stared. They stared back, before turning and resuming their conversation. I ambled back towards my seat. I imagined John saying: *Team, we have a situation here. The bridge is closed and we have two Westerners on the bus tonight. One is from England. England is the size of a large melon. The longest journey he will have done is twelve minutes, when he circumnavigated his entire tiny island. I'm concerned if we don't get to Wuhan on schedule he's going to die of travel fatigue. We need a plan.*

Although it was probably more like: *Team, we have a situation here. We're running very low on whisky. The bridge is closed, and I have absolutely no clue where the fuck we are, and, therefore, where we can buy more whisky.*

We settled in for our first night on the stationary bus. That night was long, every second cursed with the heft of ten. The bridge stayed closed. We stayed in front of it. The X continued to flash. The skies continued to release clumps of frozen water. Night put up a good fight before finally surrendering to its nemesis, morning. Out the window I could still see nothing but snow. Popular consensus is that China is overpopulated. Actually, vast chunks of China are as barren as the moon. The cities feel overcrowded, so much so that they're building cities they don't even need yet. Backup cities. Reserve cities. B-side cities. Cities full of empty homes. Sixty-four million homes stand completely empty. There's plenty of space yet beyond their cities' borders.

Ten hours had passed.

I apologised to my angry limbs. They'd called a meeting and were threatening to evict me. My back was particularly outspoken. It was having a miserable time in my too-small bunk. It wanted change. Morning became mid-morning. Because Annett and I had believed this was just going to be a fourteen-hour journey, and overnight, the only sustenance we'd thought to pack was one five-hundred-millilitre bottle of water and two croissants. We shared one of these for breakfast, and as we were doing so, something in our fearless leader snapped. He fired up the engine, turned us around, and drove frenetically down the hard shoulder, away from the bridge, past all the waiting cars.

"Holy shit, we're moving!" said Annett, sitting up in her bunk. We high-fived across the aisle.

Hooooock, tsst.

Annett's bunkmate was harvesting saliva once more. She snarled up at him. His bag had gotten quite full overnight.

Fifteen hours had passed.

At two in the afternoon, the bus skidded to a halt once more. From my window we could see, some twenty metres in the distance, two wooden shacks.

"Wuhan's let itself go," I said. Annett climbed from her bunk and looked for her shoes. "It's a *cesou* break, I think,"

There had been unofficial toilet breaks during our first night at

Hotel Barrier Down. People had gotten off whenever and relieved themselves by the side of the road. There was no privacy, but in this part of the world, privacy was a fairly novel concept, like Blockchain or the Higgs boson.

We got off and headed for the shacks, the icy wind whipping our faces. I was excited to pee in private for a change. Reaching them, I saw that they had no doors. In their place was a chicane of intersecting wooden walls that led, unceremoniously, to a large ditch dug out of the dirt floor. The sort of ditch where, had this been a Mafia movie, someone would bury a police informant.

The person in front of me walked up to it and swiftly began relieving himself into its centre. I wasn't sure if I was supposed to wait, or join him. I shifted back a step towards the entrance. The rest of the driver's crew and some passengers arrived, knocking into my back, confused as to why I was blocking the non-door door. They nudged past me and crowded the edges of the hole. What followed was a lot like the dancing fountains you find in theme parks, only the liquid was a different colour, and had no discernible rhythm, and was accompanied by spit. I looked on but mostly down in a mixture of horror and disbelief. In normal life we're pretty good at believing we're highly evolved because we've invented things like laser eye surgery, crème brûlée, and Istanbul. But there are some experiences —getting stuck in traffic, giving birth, being hungry—when you realise how flimsy civilisation really is. That reveal us as the shaved monkeys we are. Watching eight men urinate into a hole is one of these experiences. I waited for all of them to leave, then took my spot at the edge of the pit, where I tried to pee, alone, confused, and mildly disoriented, only to remember I was dehydrated and had no spare fluid to offer it.

Outside, I found Annett crouched over, washing her hands in the snow.

"How was it in there?" I asked.

She looked haunted. "Let's never talk about it."

I stooped to wash my hands as well. "The men's was just a big pit."

She glanced back over her shoulder towards the women's. "The sound was the worst." She sighed, forgetting she wasn't supposed to be talking about it. She had a strangely calm tone, as if it had happened to someone else who just happened to share her body. "They were doing multiple things, simultaneously. No bodily fluid was left behind. On the plus side I think all my inhibitions just died. I could go to the toilet right here now, in front of you, if you want?" She reached for the buckle of her jeans. "Just say the word, buster, and I'll do it."

I didn't say the word. We returned to the warmth of the bus.

Seventeen hours had passed.

"We should have arrived ages ago," I said, as we settled back into our bunks.

"I know, right. Do you think we're going back to Tangkou?"

I shrugged. It wasn't like we could ask anyone. Deflated, sore, I pulled the blanket up to my face. It too smelt of cigarettes. We knew that, broadly speaking, there was a no-public-affection rule in China, but we were feeling rebellious and so held hands across the aisle anyway. We didn't say much, because there wasn't much to say. We were stuck. But we were stuck together. The previous year we'd gone on an all-inclusive holiday to Mallorca. How quickly things changed. An easy thing to conclude in China. No other place on earth was changing faster. It's easy to automatically think that progress must be positive. I wanted to progress too, didn't I? To put myself in new situations, with the hope that how I behaved would surprise me, as it had in Istanbul. Perhaps this was a little too much change, too quickly.

Day two dusked, and we settled in for a second night of queuing —probably at the same bridge we'd queued at the previous night. Then we'd been at its front. Today we were at its back. We'd spent the day going less than nowhere. The atmosphere on the bus was calm. No one seemed in the slightest bit concerned that we'd all gotten on a vehicle one evening and instead of getting off it the next day, hadn't. There was no mutiny, or even a hint of dissent. No one challenged the crew's authority. Everyone just sat quietly in their bunks. China has only one political party: the Chinese Communist Party (CCP). It carefully controls, through its Propaganda Department, what people say about it and who gets to say anything at all. Fortunately, in Germany, Annett and I didn't have to work within such strict margins, and had been raised to believe that our opinions were important. That our government owed us, not the other way round. In the UK or Germany, if one of the peoples' buses had stopped moving, I don't think that it would have been twenty-three hours and fifty-five minutes before we rebelled, or cobbled together a passable mutiny.

The second night arrived.

"How hungry are you? Like on a scale from one to ten?" I asked Annett.

"I was hungry, about six hours ago. Then I was an eleven. Now I'm just kind of... five?"

"I feel the same. It's like because my body knows there's no food, it's stopped bothering to bug me for it."

She began cycling her legs in the air to keep her blood flowing, "Yeah, it's weird, isn't it? I thought you got hungrier and hungrier until you could think about nothing else and then went out hunting and gathering, or whatever."

"Back home I used to think I'd get a headache if I didn't eat some mid-morning chocolate. Doing a trip like this does remind you you're much more flexible than you imagine. That's something I've learned." I wasn't cycling anything anywhere.

She considered this. Squinted. Sucked in her cheeks. She wanted to agree. Was trying hard to, even. "Yeah... well... given the choice I'd pick to be inflexible, but in possession of coffee and cake."

"Do you regret this trip?"

She chewed her lip. "Yes. At least at this moment. Which is not a good moment really, all in all, I find."

"Do you blame me?"

"Of course! Yes! Entirely! We could have been in Italy. Okay, it was my idea to go to China, but for you, not me, and I was busy with work and so I didn't do the research I would normally have done about why it's a really, really bad idea to do China in January. But let's not get distracted from who's at fault here, which is you. You would not want to know what I've been doing to you in my imagination lately. It's ugly in here. And murdery."

"Murdery is not—"

"Shut up. I will hurt you."

I turned back towards the window. If there really was a new me, maybe it wasn't too late to return him for a refund?

Twenty-four hours had passed.

I spent the second night rotating like kebab meat, trying to find some part of my body that wasn't sore and a position that would allow me a few minutes of precious, glorious sleep. My tongue was swollen from dehydration. I'd eaten only half a croissant and drunk only half a bottle of water. One solitary tear trickled down my cheek from frustration. I was miserable. *HWWKKWKKWKKW TTCHCHC*, said the man in the bunk above Annett.

It was the most sensible thing anyone had said in hours.

The next morning we found the crew conspiring once more. It was still snowing, albeit a little less than the day before. The flashing yellow *X* was a public scoreboard testifying to our continued defeat at the sport of travel. There was a mad glint in John Wang's eyes. Sure, Project Spend-the-first-night-queuing-in-front-of-a-bridge-give-up-drive-all-day-and-end-up-back-at-the-same-bridge hadn't proved a master stroke. But his bow had many strings, which made it closer to a harp. Upon that harp he planned to play a tune of great ingenuity, I just knew it. An elderly lady in the bunk in front of mine coughed furiously, perhaps in encouragement, perhaps in resignation.

Even if John Wang had wanted to, we couldn't just abandon this queue as we had the day before because the road's hard shoulder was now blocked with cars. We were boxed in. The queue stretched far behind us, far further than we could see. Another hour passed. "Shit," said Annett, kicking the end of her bunk in frustration. She'd abandoned forming actual sentences, I guess in order to conserve energy. I punched my pillow.

A sudden whoosh of cold air rushed in; the front door was open. Two of John's crack team were outside. *Why? What? When? Action. We had action!*

One of the crew walked to the vehicle in front of us. He asked that vehicle's driver to squish up close to the next car. The second crew member got the vehicle on our right to drive into the new space before us. This freed up further space on our right, for the vehicle behind us to take. Which created a space for us to reverse into, which created space in front of us, and the whole glorious process repeated. It truly was a master stroke. John thumped the steering wheel in existential delight as he slowly reversed the bus back through the queue and away from the closed bridge. Car by car, by car, we were moving. For the first time in a long time, we were moving. The sullen atmosphere lifted. People began chatting with their bunkmates. Annett and I celebrated with the last half a croissant, and a few swigs of water. It was a good time, the best of times.

Thirty-six hours had passed.

We neared the back of the queue, which was crowded with vehicles waiting for the bridge to reopen, the fools. I could see empty road behind us. We were nearly out. The bus began a three-point turn to freedom. We could almost taste it. Then, in the distance, approaching quickly, was a set of flashing blue lights.

Annett had gone to the back of the bus for a better view. "It's the police."

"Shit," I said, mirroring her newly constrained language. The police car pulled up behind us as we were at a forty-five-degree angle, poking out from the bottom of the queue. John opened the door and leapt out to talk to the policeman, who was calm, and wearing sunglasses. This was absurd. John would not be reasoned with by a man wearing sunglasses in a blizzard. Who was this chump? Did he not understand that people on this bus were suffering?

Thirty-seven completed hours of suffering.

John spat theatrically at the ground. With a mixture of loud grunts and flailing arms he gestured towards the queue, and to the bus, and back out behind us—to the empty road. The policeman smoked, watched, but remained unmoved. Fifty thousand cigarettes are smoked every second in China. That's a remarkable statistic.

While you read that, another hundred thousand were smoked. There goes another hundred thousand.

The policeman shook his head. John spat once more and climbed gingerly back into the bus, his head sloped forward. He'd been outside only a few minutes, but as he retook his seat at the wheel, and brushed the snow off himself, it looked as if he'd aged five years. Instead of continuing the three-point turn, he was forced to steer, dejectedly, back into the queue. We'd been near the front. Now we were at the very, very rear.

Somewhere up in the distance, a big yellow *X* continued to flash.

"Is there any water left?" Annett asked. Two sips later there wasn't.

The mood was sombre over the next three hours. We went to dark places, mentally. Annett and I avoided eye contact with each other. There was nothing to say, nothing to do. We tried to sleep, mostly. I did a little quiet seething.

Thirty-eight hours had passed.

Suddenly, there was a murmur of something a few bunks over; a game of cards paused. The crew grew suddenly animated. Then, the most beautiful sound of all: the engine spluttered into life. A space had opened up in front of us.

Could it mean?

Surely not?

Yes.

We edged forward.

Then again.

Really?

Yes. The bridge had reopened. The snow had stopped. Hallelujah. It took an hour before we passed the barrier onto the bridge. A loud cheer broke out as we crossed it. I looked down at the frozen river below.

"Do you think it's nearly over?" I dared to ask.

Annett squinted. "I don't know. I don't want to let myself think that it might be."

"If we end up queuing for another bridge, I'm going to throw myself off of it."

We did get across that bridge, a bridge that we'd been queuing in front of for forty hours. The next few hours we were able to drive unhindered, breaking twenty kilometres per hour on several occasions, an almost dizzying speed. Annett found a small container of Pringles hidden at the bottom of her bag. We celebrated like (carbohydrate) lottery winners.

We saw the first road sign for Wuhan. The end was not exactly in sight, but certainly within the day's driving distance. The bus sighed with collective relief. We threw off the stress we'd all been carrying and took turns stamping on it.

Then, as innocuously as it had begun, the ordeal was over. We breached the city limits of Wuhan. Shacks rose into tall towers of concrete rigidity. Single-lane roads multiplied outwards until they were eight wide and scarred with bright advertising boards for tablets and smartphones. The bus shuddered to a halt in front of a garage displaying the bus firm's logo. We grabbed our stuff and skipped to the front of the vehicle. As we reached it, one of the crew waved us back.

"What?" I said. "We're here, right? W-U-H-A-N?"

He shook his head, and continued to wave us back towards our bunks.

No one else was getting off. Annett looked both disappointed and pale at a ratio of ten to one.

"Well, we waited this long," I said, turning around. Annett put her face in her hands. Solemnly, we trudged back down the aisle to our bunks. I felt like a death-row prisoner told I'd been released only to be rearrested in the car park on a misdemeanour driving charge and returned to my cell.

The crew disembarked and began changing tyres and removing the heavy chains that had helped us through the snow. Why the tyre change couldn't have waited until after they'd dropped us off, I didn't know, and they couldn't explain.

After forty-five minutes, they were finished. This must be it? The end of the saga? But then, out of nowhere, a small puppy ran out from the restaurant opposite us and took refuge under the bus. The dog's owner ran out after it, brandishing a stick. This had to be a metaphor: the bus was life, the stick was fate, we were all the puppy.

The sight of a man in a dirty apron running around the sides of the bus and lunging with a stick at a hiding, yapping puppy was just too much for me. I began thumping and kicking at my bunk in frustration. The levy that held all my usual indifference and self-control cracked and split. Before long I was crying tears of frustration. I hadn't cried in years. I don't know where I found the water. Annett got caught up in it as well. It morphed at some point, and without our knowing, into a new form of extremely aggressive, angry laughter. It was, in many ways, a beautiful moment. The sort of moment, I imagine, that people go travelling for. One of complete presence. A moment that will play longer in the theatre of the mind than a hundred nights of Netflix on the couch, a thousand boring business meetings, ten thousand uneventful commutes. A moment that you sense, while in it, will become one of *your* stories. A track on your anecdote Greatest Hits playlist. Part of your identity.

Did I tell you the one about the blizzard? No, well, sit down...

Forty-two hours had passed.

John and his crew, fresh from the success of their tyre change, waved the stick-wielding maniac away. They huddled in a corner of the garage and strategised how to get the puppy out.

"Oh, this is going to be good," Annett said, having joined me at my bunk to watch.

"I wouldn't be surprised if their plan is just to wait until the puppy becomes an adult, and no longer fits under there," I said.

She puffed out her chest. "No way. That's way too practical for these goons."

One of them went to a different corner and rummaged in some boxes. He returned with a large cloth sack and several fishing poles. He gave the bag to John Wang. The group walked back towards the bus. John moved near to its door. The rest split up around the bus and lowered their poles beneath it. Their new plan—perhaps an annex to the currently failing one—was to use the poles to drive the dog into one corner of the undercarriage, where, finding itself with no other way to avoid all the poles people kept thrusting at it, it would enter the cement bag of its own youthful volition.

John crouched and shook the bag. The others thrashed with their sticks.

Every time a pole went under the bus, the dog barked furiously and tried to bite it. Being poked with large poles by strange men didn't seem to reinforce in him that all was well and he should probably come out of hiding to enter a dark cloth bag.

Several minutes passed. John stood up and wiped the snow from his face.

A girl looked on from the pavement. She was in her mid-twenties, and wrapped snuggly in a puffy white jacket, white bobble hat, and red scarf. Her arms were clamped so tightly around her middle it looked as though she were attempting to hug herself. I could see a lot of sympathy for the dog in her face. She told the men off and waved them away from the bus. Then she crouched under it and said what I'm sure was the mandarin equivalent of *here boy, here boy, cute little doggy, aren't you a good boy, you're a little cutie, oh yes you are.*

The dog ran straight out and into her open arms. The long-rumoured female touch? She scooped him up, stood, turned, and handed him back to the restaurant owner in the dirty apron. And then she walked away. The dog had been double-crossed. Classic femme fatale. The poor dog would never trust another woman for as long as it lived, which would be a fortnight, at most. The owner pinched it by the back of its neck, swinging it left and right like a conductor's baton as he walked back across the road to the restaurant.

The crew climbed back aboard. The engine turned over. The new, chainless tyres simply turned. We were on the move once more. Annett and I hugged in relief.

We trundled further into Wuhan. It looked like every other Chinese city we'd seen; a maze of high-rise and nondescript; a tribute to right angles; as if designed for practicality and haste, not style and longevity; as if aiming to inflict as much visual shock as possible on the millions swapping their lives in the countryside for its promise of shiny, neon, urban progress.

We arrived in what we assumed to be its centre. Everyone rushed up from their bunks and towards the door.

All except two people: Annett and I.

This bus had cried wolf too often. We'd just cried. Something else was going to go wrong, surely? Waiting out there would be poles and cement sacks and we'd be hoisted up and unceremoniously dumped back into our bunks once more.

The front door opened. The first passengers disembarked. The crew formed a row from the driver's seat to the door and shook hands with the disembarking, dishevelled passengers. This hadn't been a normal journey for them, either.

"I think this is really it," Annett said, as we collected up our stuff and sloped down the aisle.

"It can't be. It just can't be. Can it?"

John held out his hand to me. I had a sudden, strange urge to thank him. It arrived unexpected, at the back door of my mind, like a burglar. What did I have to thank him for? I investigated the feeling. It was a new feeling. It felt good to be having new feelings. Even if they were just vague and confusing.

I tried to assemble the feeling into a shape. In Berlin I tutted and stamped my feet and cursed the heavens if I arrived at an underground station and the screen said I'd have to wait five minutes for the next train. Here, with minimal complaint, no entertainment, and almost nothing to eat or drink, I'd spent forty-three hours. This experience and so, by extension, John, *had* taught me a lot. I now knew that I could sleep in a space little bigger than a matchbox, that I could live on half a pastry a day, that I could pee in an open pit, that I didn't need the soft furnishings of home, that I rose to challenges, rather than ducking, covering, and lightly whimpering in their presence.

I grasped his hand. It felt like leather. We shook. I nodded at him. It wasn't much. I hoped it was enough.

Stepping out into the street, I looked down at my watch for the final time.

Forty-four hours had passed.

We were mobbed by sellers. Despite the simplistic, out of date stories they tell themselves of being socialists, capitalism hunts you down here, shouts its prices at you, harangues you into looking at all its trinkets. We bought everything. We bought it all. Water, cookies, pot noodles, fruit. With our hungry eyes and empty bellies we indulged. Oh, did we indulge.

The little old lady from the bunk in front of me hobbled past, twisted over her wooden walking stick, her back worn down by the abrasives of time and gravity. I wondered what those forty-four hours had been like for her. They were outliers for Annett and I because we were used to things just working. We expected things to be easy, comfortable, reliable, safe because that was how our lives had always been until now.

Distance, time, hardship—it all existed on a different scale here. I doubted that this journey would make it into any book of her life, not compared to what she'd lived through here. What was forty-four hours of mild inconvenience when you'd already spent thirty years trapped in a high-speed vehicle of political change with an even less clear destination, no possibility to get off, and the view from the windows showing a dizzying, relentless blur of progress—of indoor plumbing, skyscrapers, cars, scooters. Everything getting bigger, wider, faster, then smaller, flatter, shinier and congested as cities gobbled like Pac-Man at the surrounding farmland. Did she think she still lived in a Communist country? That long after Chairman Mao some formula was amended, some missing zero was added and the code of Communism finally clicked into place and transformed a nation where everyone was supposed to be equal into a nation with the fourth-highest level of inequality in the world? That was a lot of change for one lifetime. I didn't envy her having to try to make sense of it.

We checked into the first Western chain hotel we could find. It was gloriously generic; its shiny, marble lobby spoke to the standards of luxury it would offer us. Our days of peeing in a pit were over. In our room, wrapped up in our complimentary fluffy dressing gowns, we ordered room service and guzzled water. Our bathroom had a door. I felt almost guilty about the decadence. We were bus people no more.

Climbing out of the shower, having set a new world record for longest time spent in one, I found Annett sitting up in bed, reading a book. "Do we have to do the full three weeks?" she asked.

"You want to go home early?"

She rested the book on her lap. "Don't you? Are you having fun? Because I'm not, really. It's just blizzard, chaos, travel breakdowns, a bit more blizzard. And once this is over I have to go back to work. You don't. I'm actually looking forward to work because it won't be this."

I took a moment to try to convince myself I was having fun. "I'm not sure you go to China for fun," I conceded, having failed to do so.

"Well why are we here then? You certainly go on holidays for fun."

"Forget the why. We're here now. Again, your idea—let's make it work. It can't get much worse than that bus trip, right?"

"It had better not," she said, picking up her book.

We did make it to Xi'an, where we narrowly missed being in a car crash on icy roads. Our car spun in a circle before clipping a metal pole. We saw the terracotta warriors created to protect Qin Shi Huang, China's first emperor, in the afterlife. An idea that is absurd (terracotta figures go to the afterlife?), nonsensical (pottery can fight?), and unnecessary (what's the worst that can happen there— you die again?). Yet, to the emperor's credit, it was a madcap act of mass ceramicism executed with commendable zeal (eight thousand soldiers' worth).

A short (thousand-kilometre) train ride later we reached Beijing, where we climbed a certain famous wall while learning about Mongolian hordes. A wall that robs you of your breath, replacing it with awe and disbelief that mere humans could build something this expansive just to stop other humans from killing and enslaving them. The cold never let up. Travelling was a grind; simple tasks such as buying train tickets sometimes took half a day because of language breakdowns and insurmountable cultural divides regarding personal space, queuing, and politeness. Menus were perennial lucky dips. By Beijing I was both flu-ridden and a nervous wreck. Aside from rousing myself for the Great Wall, I spent all my time admiring the four Average Walls of our hostel room. I got up only to eat soup and use the bathroom.

We lasted the three weeks, just.

On the plane home we jigged down the aisles, happy knowing we'd never have to endure another Chinese winter. Or China, in general. Not that I regretted anything. I wanted more holidays like this, full of adventure, excitement, uncertainty, and struggle. We had wanted weird and strange and different. Actually, maybe *I* had wanted these things and Annett had wanted to give them to me. Regardless, China had delivered them. But it hadn't delivered enjoyment. The longer we'd stayed the more convinced I'd become that enjoyment wasn't the point of China. People go there because they know one day China will be in charge. That this day may already have arrived. They go to see what kind of a guardian it will be. They go because its present is frenzied and complex and dissonant from what it tells itself. They go because the planet's future almost certainly depends on China's. There are more than enough reasons to visit—just nowhere near enough to make that visit in January.

5
_____

KISSI, GHANA: "IT'S NOT REALLY FUN IN THE CLASSICAL SENSE OF FUN."

The Gospel of Green Tea, clickshakes, moonshine

"I know where I want to go next," I said, as we sat at our kitchen table eating a pasta dish I'd prepared and which had been unfairly criticised as "lacking in passion."

"Okay. Where?"

I made jazz hands. "Aaaff-rica."

"If you even think about *Lion Kinging*, I'm leaving you."

I put down my jazz hands.

"Africa is kinda large. You got somewhere specific in mind?"

My eyes widened. "I was thinking... *Ghana*."

"Why Ghana?"

"Well, firstly, because it's in Africa and we've never been there. And Ghana is kind of a weird one since it's English-speaking, safe, and has good weather but isn't anyone's definition of a tourist hotspot. I'd kinda like to know why."

She pushed her glasses up. "And we have a contact there."

"Exactly."

That contact was a genuine, bona fide, enormous Ghanaian called Djarbah. I'd met him in Berlin once to eat falafel. We had mutual friends with whom he ran Future Hope People, a charity building schools in rural Ghana.

Annett nudged at some of her impossibly delicious pasta. "I'll buy the Lonely Planet," she said, moving to get up. I looked down at her half-empty plate. "Don't you want to finish your pasta first?"

Her forehead rumpled. "What makes you think I haven't?"

Not wanting to repeat the fiasco of China, and wanting to prove to Annett that I could be organised too, I emailed Djarbah many questions. None of which he answered.

Hello Adams,

Thanks so much for your mail but the connection is so bad today so i will answer it tomorrow.

Djarbah

I didn't hear anything for the next few weeks, and felt this was stretching the accepted definition of *tomorrow*. I asked one of our mutual friends, Manuel, if Djarbah's sporadic communication style was normal, and he explained that Djarbah only had Internet access when he travelled thirty minutes to the nearby town, and that the Internet cafe operated via a hotspot running from a single mobile phone. As a result, it could take up to fifteen minutes to open an email. Knowing that, I wished I'd put a bit more effort into mine. It must be extra infuriating to spend such a long amount of time opening something only to discover that it's incorrectly punctuated. By the time I got answers to my questions we were already in the capital, Accra, and so didn't need them.

"Djarbah?" I said, trying out my new Ghanaian SIM card in the shadiest corner of the hostel's courtyard, hiding from the humidity smothering me like a pillow.

A booming voice overwhelmed the phone's puny speaker. "ADAMSSS?"

"Djarbah! We made it, we're in Accra!"

"Oooh, very fine. How do you like it?" Djarbah has a majestic way of speaking. His words stroll out like well-dressed senior citizens on an afternoon walk.

I wiped a trickle of sweat from my forehead. I'd finished showering only ninety seconds before. I intended to shower again ninety seconds after the call. "It's... er..." I skipped the part about the constant power cuts and oppressive heat. "*Great.*"

"Good, good," he said. "When are you coming to Kissi?"

"In two days. Tuesday. Is that okay for you? If not we can stay longer here..."

"Tuesday? Oh, very fine. Take the bus to Takoradi and tell the driver you want to get off at Kissi. Call me when you get here."

It sounded so easy. And then, Tuesday morning, we arrived at what everyone assured us was the bus station. Seconds after leaving the taxi, we were engulfed in a swirling tornado of humanity. A giant, frenetic melee of capitalism. People hawked fruit, water, car parts, entire cars, entire chickens, and parts of a cow. There were no buses.

"This is a bit full on," I said to Annett, as a scooter swerved and missed my foot by a single-digit number of centimetres. She stood on tiptoes, trying to see over a nearby stall selling mobile-phone credit. Probably to be used by people caught in the centre of the melee frantically calling out for help. A curious thing about Ghanaian melees is that they have no discernible beginning or end. They just suddenly appear, like a sand storm, and then before you have time to resist, you find yourself, inexplicably, in the dead centre of one, confused and disorientated. It had happened to us several times over the previous days.

She scanned the horizon. "There must be some kind of system, right?"

The core of Annett's world view is that, underneath it all, everything is striving to be logical and efficient. This belief cannot be dented by evidence to the contrary.

We were looking at overwhelming evidence to the contrary.

Eventually, more through luck than judgement, we found the part of the melee that had the buses in it. It was about a hundred metres past the rusted-car parts area, down the end of a narrow alley of carcasses on hooks, sharing an entrance with both the Bible and assorted brooming paraphernalia stalls.

Obvious, in hindsight.

Two long hours later the last seat on our bus was sold (no timetables here) and we could leave. As the vehicle began to slowly excavate itself from the melee, a man who had been crouching next to me in the aisle sprang to life. I thought he was going to offer us a sermon. We'd seen this often—someone getting on a vehicle to bless the journey and remind everyone taking it of God's love for them. They did this on a no-obligation, pro-bono (the legal term not the singer), voluntary, discretionary, gratis—*oh, you want to tip me? Really? Well, that's unexpected and absolutely in no way why I am doing this but I guess, since you insist*—basis.

Instead, this man reached down to the plastic bag at his feet and removed a dark-green rectangular box of tea.

"Good afternoon, ladies and gentleman," he said, confidently, as if he'd been specifically booked as the bus's keynote speaker. "This is a-powerful tea, brothers and sisters." His tone was firm and measured, that of someone born to sell packages of beverage on a moving vehicle. With one hand he gripped the overhead luggage rack, and rocked himself back and forth, while holding the green tea packet aloft triumphantly with his other hand.

"It's not like your normal *a-tea-ah*. Your fruit *a-tea-ah*. OOOH NO-AAH! It is *a-strong*. You put it in, you stir, and you take it *a-out*. You do not leave it in. No! It's *a-powerful*. Ladies and gentleman, sir and madam, the benefits, the BEN-A-FITS of this A-TEA-AH..." And here he paused for dramatic effect, bowing his head slightly, before returning it towards the heavens.

"WOW... *A-WOW*."

During our days in Accra, in the rare moments that we'd been blessed with electricity, we'd tried to watch as much TV as possible, though what we found always left us in a state of shock: God TV, Praise TV, Hallelujah TV. About 50 percent of the channels were religious, and featured men who looked almost exactly like this man. They seemed so used to this proselytising style of selling that it was now how they sold everything, even the Gospel of Green Tea.

"It's good for the digestion, GOOD for the headache, GOOD for *a-so* many health benefits, SO MANY. Men, it's also good for your... you know." He winked. "Ah *hmm. Yep.* And... *ladies and gentleman...* it's also good against *THE CANCER!*"

After twenty minutes of high-tempo, high-energy salesmanship, and with four packets sold, the man got off. The journey felt uneventful in his absence. The most fun was looking out the window and enjoying Ghanaian business names. In Ghana, people's religious inclinations are woven into everything they do, and so the naming of businesses is a perfect chance to try to outdo each other in sanctity and devotion. My Redeemer Lives Fast Food was an early favourite, before we spotted Clap for Jesus Fishes, which had the crown for forty-five minutes until we discovered Thank you Jesus Plastic Chairs.

After four hours, one hour longer than expected, Annett prodded me.

"Can you go and check with the driver again?"

"Why do I always have to go?"

"Just go."

I clenched my fists. "Aren't you supposed to be a feminist?"

"There is no 'supposed to be,' mister. *I am* a feminist."

"Then why are certain tasks automatically mine? Talking to strangers, investigating scary sounds in the middle of the night, erm... *emptying bins.*"

She flicked her wrist. "I don't think you understand feminism. Ask the bus driver about it while you're up there."

"Hello sir," I said, approaching the driver. "Just checking—you will tell us when we reach Kissi, yes?"

The man turned to face me as the bus collapsed into a generously sized pothole. "Yes sir, yes, not far now. Ten minutes, perhaps. Yes?"

I wasn't sure why this was a question. "Erm. Wonderful, thank you."

I briefly considered asking him about feminism, but what with trying to snake the bus through the thin slivers of flat road, he already had enough to do. It looked as though the country were at war with moles.

It was losing.

I headed back down the aisle to my seat. Heavy blows from the mole army upon the vehicle's suspension knocked me into the lap of an elderly man in a brown-striped corduroy suit.

"Ten minutes, apparently," I said, collapsing, winded, into my seat.

Annett frowned at her phone's screen. "He said that the last time, one hour ago."

I shrugged. "Ghanaians don't seem all that great with time."

Eventually, it wasn't the driver but a neighbour (and a soon-to-be-cancer-free green-tea purchaser) who alerted us that we were now approaching Kissi. Another saw us getting up and shouted to the driver that he should stop, which he did in an unsafe manner that involved screeching brakes and minor passenger whiplash.

Disembarked, we found ourselves in front of a petrol station. The heat hugged us like a jilted ex-lover who just wouldn't take the hint. We took solace under a nearby tree. I called Djarbah. He also claimed he'd be there in "ten minutes."

Twenty-five minutes later—laudably punctual by Ghanaian standards—a battered Toyota pulled up next to us, blaring German hip-hop. I recognised the man driving it. Firstly, because he was dressed in a luminous yellow Borussia Dortmund football jersey and hat. How common could Dortmund fans be in these parts? Secondly, because the man was gigantic. Behind the wheel he looked like an elephant in a golf cart. I know that today doing something as innocuous as wearing a silly hat, or expressing a minority political opinion, might be enough to get you labelled "larger than life." Well, when I say that Djarbah is larger than life, I mean it in the original sense of the phrase. He's a two-metre tall, seven-metre wide wall of muscle.

"Adams!" he said, leaping out and attempting a handshake, which because of the size of his hands, and the muscles of the frame manipulating them, ended up more like a wrestling move that crushed my arm as if it were a grape. He ended this affectionate mauling with a click of two of his giant bear fingers. My arm was returned to me, limp, confused and having lost most of its market value.

"You made it," he said, turning to embrace Annett. "How was your journey?"

She seemed to fare slightly better with the hug she received, perhaps due to her years of boxing training. "It was fine," she said.

I shook out my arm, trying to resuscitate it. "The bus driver didn't seem to know where Kissi was, though. He kept saying it was ten minutes, for two hours."

Djarbah laughed. A deep, heavy, booming laugh. The ground shook. Some leaves fell from the tree we were sheltering under. Surfers in Papua New Guinea reported larger than usual wave activity. "Ghanians are not so good with time. I think maybe that we do not require it like you do. We are not a nation of precision."

It would be an understatement to say that this was an understatement. We'd already noticed back in Accra that if you stopped people and asked for directions, not only would they not know the answer, your having asked them the question seemed to make them also suddenly uncertain of where they were. They were like cartoon characters running off a cliff, able to keep running just as long as you didn't make them look down.

The car groaned as we turned off the main road onto a smaller dirt path so uneven we bounced down it in first gear, which felt oddly in keeping with the hip-hop music blaring out from the stereo. I felt as if I were in an MTV video from the early nineties. Djarbah acknowledged every person we passed. A short man in an imitation Barcelona kit shouted something at him, making him howl with laughter. An under-construction skyscraper in Abu Dhabi imploded. At one point the road got so bad, and we were driving so slowly, that a friend of Djarbah's was able to shake hands with him through the window as we passed. No doubt regretting it straight after. Again, the handshake ended with the click finish—the Ghanaian clickshake.

Timidly, but now in second gear, we turned left into the town of Kissi. Kind people would describe Kissi's dirt roads, unnamed streets, and waterlogged football pitch—goats munched on the centre circle's last blades of grass—as "unspoilt," "rustic," or "picturesque." I'm a moderately kind person and will commit to only "authentic," "has potential," and "exists."

The car stopped in front of a large brick building at least three times the size of any we'd passed. "We have arrived, Adams." Djarbah's home was imposing. It served as Future Hope People HQ, and so needed spare rooms for the NGO's volunteers. During our visit it would just be Djarbah, his wife, Monica, their four children, and us. Djarbah went to the boot and removed all our luggage, which he carried with just one hand, as if it were a punnet of strawberries. Monica was waiting on the large veranda and preparing fufu (a substance made from yams smashed repeatedly with a giant wooden club).

"You, sit," Monica said, pointing to some plastic chairs. "Welcome." She compensated for a lack of English vocabulary with an abundance of enthusiasm, never once letting her wide smile slip. It could have eclipsed the sun. She did big well. In Ghana, big is beautiful, because big implies wealth, suggests you've calories to waste. I had no doubt Monica received admiring looks while out buying further unnecessary calories. While we waited for that fufu, I thought about how weird a human quirk it is that we consider whatever is exotic or mostly unachievable beautiful. So while we Europeans are heading out to the tanning salon to get darker skin and sweating our way round laps of the park to lose weight, there are Asian people covering their faces to keep their complexions white while the citizens of Ghana double down on fried chicken to try to stay un-trim. We just love to make it hard for ourselves. We are, in many ways, quite ridiculous.

A few minutes of veranda relaxation later, three miniature

humans appeared at the home's gate, dressed in school uniform. These were the family's three oldest children: Nana, their son, and daughters Julia and Judith. Nana was nine. Their youngest, Theresa, just two, was already playing at our feet. No sooner had they arrived than Nana had a broom in his hand and was busy sweeping the already immaculate living room. I cornered him and practised my clickshake on him. He was kind enough to only laugh quite hard at the poorness of my technique.

"You're surprisingly calm," I said to Annett, as we climbed into bed that night. A dozen sharp mattress springs protruded into the flesh of my back. "Ow."

"What?"

"Nothing."

"You expected me to be freaking out by now?"

"Well... maybe, a bit. Or at least optimising their kitchen drawers."

She rolled to face me. "Do you think I'm some kind of princess? That I can't survive somewhere like this? I'm more rock and roll than you, Mr Couch Potato."

"I don't think you're a princess," I said, attempting to extricate myself from both the bed springs and the hole I'd begun digging. "But at home, if the Internet goes down for even thirty minutes our relationship is in serious jeopardy. Here we haven't been online in four days. We're barely eating, sleeping, washing—and it's still sort of fine."

"I know what you mean," she said. "Earlier when I went to the toilet, the door fell off. Then I flushed the toilet forgetting that I couldn't because there's no water. Then I came back to bed, and it was so dark, because there's also no electricity, that I walked into the bedroom door and banged my head, which fortunately didn't fall off. The door, I mean. I didn't even get that annoyed, for me. And I do annoyed well. I guess in Berlin, my expectations for how things should be are just so different, there's no way I'd be able to stay calm. But here in Ghana, you sort of go into challenge mode."

"Uh-huh." I nodded. "It's not really fun in the classical sense of fun. The enjoyable sense. The let's do this again sense."

"No. In fact, I might need another holiday after to recover from it. Which is a problem, since I actually have a job, whereas you only have a hobby that's gotten out of control."

"Yeah, maybe because my normal life is such a holiday these days I want my vacations to feel like work."

The next day Djarbah drove us to the local school. "Is this a private school or a government school?" I asked, as we ascended another fracture in the road that made him jump in his seat and knock his head against the car's roof. The roof felt it; he didn't. "This is a little bit complicated, Adams. In theory the government is supposed to provide education. But, well, the money never quite makes it to the school."

"What happens to it then?"

He shrugged. "Corruption happens, Adams. The government school we are going to see now, Future Hope People built much of it."

The school was four large rectangular concrete buildings set around a field, or what was probably once a field. Now it was an expanse of space. An ex-field. It was break time, and about a hundred kids were out playing, all dressed neatly in green-and-white uniforms. Above each of the classrooms, in white paint, was the name of the class.

"Are you ever going to tell him that your name is not Adams?" whispered Annett, getting out of the car.

"No. It's too awkward now. Call me Adams as well, please, Annetts."

Djarbah was one of his man-mountain strides ahead of us. We could just about see him. "I will take you now to meet the headmaster," he said, "I'm sure you have some questions for him."

Saying "I'm sure you" has to be the absolute fastest way of

creating uncertainty in another human. Annett and I looked at each other with trepidation.

The headmaster was a small man with a round face and black circular glasses. It looked as though he usually lived underground and had popped up to check things out but wasn't sure if he liked them yet. He greeted us enthusiastically in his office. His window looked out over the playing children. The clock on the wall was ornamental, I noticed. The air was a soup of thick dust. He sat on the other side of a large desk, flanked on either side by a woman. One wore a shiny silver shirt just the wrong side of form-fitting. The other wore an expression of subtle disappointment. The women were not introduced. Annett and I took a seat opposite the desk.

It felt like an interview for a job we hadn't applied for. Djarbah stood near the door, I think because it was simply impossible that the furniture would have been sturdy enough to contain his bulk.

The headmaster looked reverently towards him. "Djarbah is a big man in these parts." Ah, more of that great Ghanaian understatement. Djarbah belonged at the top of a beanstalk. "A great man. A great friend to the school. So you two are also from Future Hope?"

Annett and I traded glances, unsure where we were from and why exactly we were no longer there. I waited for her to say something. She waited for me.

"Are you volunteers, maybe?" he tried. This only worked to heighten our uncertainties about all the things we were not.

Annett shrugged. "No, we're just on holiday."

The man looked at each of the women in turn. The women looked at the man. Djarbah looked out at the ex-field. The headmaster chuckled to himself. The women chuckled. Djarbah excused himself and stepped outside.

"Probably you have some questions?" asked the headmaster. I looked at Annett. She looked at me. I looked at the headmaster. He looked at me. Then I looked at the women. They looked at me. I looked at Annett. She looked at me.

"Questions, right," I stammered. "Hmm... umm..." I tried to think of any kind of question; any normal human question. "What... errm... hmmm... *How many* students are there here at the school?"

Brilliant. Insightful. Relevant. Nailed it.

He'd almost certainly never heard this question before. He said an answer which I didn't listen to because I was too busy constructing a follow-up question. This question was just as good, although, were one being critical, one might have perhaps noticed that, in many respects, it was exactly the same question but with the word *students* swapped for *teachers*. Five or six questions in, I ran out of steam. I nudged Annett with my foot. She didn't acknowledge this. I nudged her again. This didn't seem to help. I kicked her in the side of the foot.

"*Ow.* Why are you—"

"Annetts," I said, "I'm guessing you have some questions as well, right?"

She gave me a you'll-pay-for-this-later glance of death, and cleared her throat. "Djarbah said there is a problem with corruption in the school system?"

The headmaster nodded sympathetically. The women nodded too. The headmaster made a *mmm-hhhhm* sound. They echoed it. "There is *more* than enough money," he said. "More than enough! But before us is the regional council, then the local council, and the board of education. As you can imagine, that's many fingers. So, sadly, we are reliant on outside benefactors *like yourselves*."

The two women nodded. One *mmm-hhhm*ed. They were a slick operation.

My stomach fluttered. We were "outside benefactors"? I thought we were confused, naive tourists? Fortunately Djarbah returned just in time, ending both our identity and question crises.

"Adams, Annett, maybe you would like a tour?" he asked.

"Good idea," replied the headmaster.

Mmmm-hhhm.

The headmaster asked one of the women to go get Mrs Ansah. Mrs Ansah promptly arrived. She was also quite blessed, calorifically, her top half seeming to rather overwhelm her bottom half, causing her to stoop like a collapsing wedding cake.

"How do you do!" she said, in what was supposed to be a question but was delivered as a statement of fact. She was very personable and seemed delighted to have company, perhaps deciding we'd be better behaved than the kids in her class. We weren't sure exactly what we were going to be shown, because we were pretty sure we'd already seen everything.

She took us to the junior class, Basic 1. Twenty kids sat behind tiny wooden desks. She walked us to the front of the class, near the blackboard. It had the letters of the alphabet scrawled across it.

"Children!" They snapped to attention. "Children, today we have special guests, from Germany." *Special guests.* That title we could live with. It was suitably ambiguous.

The class stood up. A chair in the back row tumbled over. "Welcome, sir! Welcome, madam!" they shouted. "How are you?"

Annett and I smirked at each other. This was unexpected, and a bit awkward. I waited for Annett to speak. She waited for me to speak. We really needed some kind of system. I was beginning to suspect we had one, albeit poorly defined, and that system was Adam-talks-first.

"Hello, class," I said, trying to sound confident and like I regularly addressed Ghanaian children, or children, or people in general.

"We're..." I gulped. "Good. Thank you. And *err*, how are you all?"

Without the slightest hesitation, they shouted, "We are fine."

With this they sat back down.

Then no one talked.

Then we just stood there.

I had no questions.

Annett had no questions.

The kids had no questions.

They stared at us, some daring a whisper to a neighbour. I felt their little, innocent eyes piercing me. Probably they'd met many Westerners before from NGOs—kind, empathetic people here to help them, and to work with them to improve their country. I was not one of these people. I buy light bulbs from Amazon to save walking one street. I don't take my organic waste out of its plastic bag before tossing it in the bin. I wasn't even sure I believed in most aid work. I was here on some poorly defined inner quest. I was not one of the good guys. They could see this, I was sure. I looked to Mrs Ansah. She smiled. I looked to the teacher, who was reading something at his desk. He looked up, gave a brisk nod, and returned to his book.

We had no questions.

After what felt like an age, but was probably only thirty seconds, Annett gestured with her hand towards the exit. Mrs Ansah nodded, relieved. We walked back towards the exit. Another potentially tricky social situation had been navigated. I stepped down from the classroom to the dry earth of the ex-field, wiping at the river of sweat on my brow. That had been intense. But soon this school visit would be over and we could get back to playing the card game Mau Mau with Djarbah on his veranda. We took a couple of steps back towards the car. Mrs Ansah, however, didn't.

"This way," she said, gesturing behind her. "Basic 2."

Who had said anything about Basic 2? Yet she already had one foot inside its classroom. There didn't seem to be a way out, not without causing offence. So we walked to Basic 2. And before long we were back in front of a class again. "Class, we have special guests, from Germany..."

"Welcome, sir! Welcome, madam! How are you?"

"We are fine. How are you?"

"We are fine." It was word for word the same.

And then we stood there again. In silence. Question bereft. Twenty kids staring at us. I mumbled something about it being a very nice class and then tried to make for the exit. Outside, we took a few steps towards the car.

"So, Basic 3," Mrs Ansah said, and ushered us into the class next door. "How many classes are there?" Annett whispered. Since they were so clearly marked in white paint on the outside, it was easy to tell. There were another six. The awkwardness was almost overwhelming. We were frauds. Frauds on display. Frauds not here to help. Frauds not volunteering. Frauds without questions. Poverty tourists. Rubberneckers. *Mitläufer*. For the next twenty-five minutes we toured the remaining classes to choruses of "We are fine."

A skip in our steps, we stepped down from the last classroom and back across the field, to the computer centre, to collect Djarbah. We found him on its veranda, talking to a teacher.

"Our tour is over, Djarbah," Annett said. "Everyone is fine."

"Fine, fine, very good, yes."

"So..." She nudged her head in the direction of the car.

"Ah, yes, Adams and Annett, I have some errands to complete. I have asked some of the older boys to give you a tour of the town."

Two boys appeared, like rabbits pulled from the situation's hat. I have no idea where they came from. Possibly a pothole.

"They're good kids," said Djarbah. "Boys, make sure you show them where they make the moonshine."

"Don't the boys have class?" I asked. Djarbah shrugged. He didn't seem to view the next hour or two as being make or break in their education. He turned, smiled at the boys, and thudded off towards the car. Seismographs the world over recorded sudden tectonic activity.

The two boys grinned at us. They were some of the school's older students, perhaps thirteen or fourteen years old. "Hello, sir," said the first, shaking my hand enthusiastically. "My name is Kofi." He had an unusually soft voice and projected a strong *it's going to be fine* aura. The second had a round face accentuated by a thick pudding of hair. He was called Michael. He fumbled for my hand, unsuccessfully.

"How are you doing today?" I asked.

"We're fine," they answered. This did not come as a surprise.

"What are you doing in Ghana?" asked Kofi.

"We're on holiday," said Annett.

They laughed. "In *Ghana*?"

With our new chaperons, somewhat hesitantly, we headed away from the school and back out towards town, avoiding the sun wherever possible, which was nowhere. Before long three other schoolboys, friends of Kofi and Michael, had joined us on the dusty dirt road to town. They were a funny, rambunctious group. Ghanaians have a playful, easy-going way about them. And they talk to each other everywhere. Which is important if you have few other ways of getting information. A sense of humour and a small ego are probably quite helpful when whatever it is you're trying to do that day isn't working, again. Since you can't rely on the state for much, everything becomes a negotiation with someone. This makes mastering the dark art of conversation very useful—profitable even. Everywhere we looked we saw Ghanaians sitting, or leaning on things, and gently joking with each other. The pace of life was slow. I'd never been anywhere where there appeared to be so many people, doing so little, so harmoniously.

"How many churches are there in Kissi?" Annett asked the boys. Now she had questions! The children began counting. They could agree on nine, although one swore it was ten. Ten churches for a town of just 1500? A town that didn't even have paved roads, reliable electricity, or grass? It was easy to conclude there'd been a mismanagement of priorities. We passed an under-construction church, the tenth. They then took us out into the fields to the north of the village, where we stopped at a tin shack hidden back in the brush. Stooping to enter, I saw five men, three sitting along the left wall, two to the right, on red plastic chairs. Behind them, across the centre of the shack, was a large metal trough, like you might use to feed animals. In the back half of the dwelling were various drums with tubes running between them. One on my right was releasing a clear liquid into the trough.

A strong smell of ethanol stripped the whites of my eyes and split the hairs of my nose. All the men were either asleep or dead.

"I think we've found the moonshine."

Annett coughed her agreement.

Kofi said something to the custodians of this rural craft brewing enterprise.

It didn't wake them up.

He said it again, louder.

It didn't wake them up.

He shouted it.

The man to our left rocked back on his chair, which thudded against the wall of the shack. He grunted. His face was flat, as if his features had withdrawn from the world. Then he rubbed his sunken eyes and got to his feet, swaying slightly. He and Kofi exchanged a few words in a local language.

I smiled nervously at the man, feeling guilty for having ruined his slumber. It was quite obvious to me from his gaunt face and bulging red eyes that he was having his cake and eating it, dipping his toe in his own pond, and getting high on his own supply.

He wiped at the grime on his face with a rag from his back pocket and exhaled loudly before beginning an explanation of the brewing process. Kofi translated, pointing to the barrels at the back of the shack. "In here goes the water. Then... what's that word in English?" He looked to the other boys. They shrugged.

Michael kicked his foot in frustration at not knowing the word. "Hmm... *chemicals*?"

Kofi nodded. "Yes, *chemicals* are added. Then it's made warm."

It wasn't clear if the man couldn't explain what he did for a living, or if Kofi couldn't translate it. I suspected a little of both. The man bent down to run his fingers through the liquid in the trough, and said something to Kofi, who accepted it warmly.

"Alcohol comes out." I had no doubt that alcohol came out. I also had no doubt that quite a lot of it went into the mouths of the men around me, at least when they were awake. I thanked the man and edged back towards the door, wanting to let him return to his mid-morning nap.

"Would you like to try it?" Michael asked Annett and me. This excited the boys greatly. It excited my internal organs less. The boys crowded in. The man reached for a dirty orange plastic pot at his feet. He swilled it out onto the floor with water, dipped it into the trough, and held it out to me. I looked at his face. The lights were still on but the property was long vacant. As advertising for a product went, this was like being sold contact lenses by a blind man.

Offend people or drink the moonshine? It was a difficult decision, mostly because so many eyes watched me as I made it. This drink was obviously not good for humans—nothing made in the woods in a metal trough is. Yet this man had consumed rather a lot of it and he seemed fine. He passed his days asleep on a plastic chair in a tin shack. His eyes were the colour of nuclear winter, but he was still alive, mostly, I think.

I had to drink it. Or pretend to drink it. I nodded, took the pot from him, held it to my lips, and took the smallest sip that I thought socially acceptable. The liquid charred my tongue and spread south like an out-of-control bush fire. The boys laughed.

"It's..." *cough, cough* "Good." I now had the smoky, smooth baritone of a soul singer. I'd describe the moonshine's taste as science. The drink had only one job to do, one function, and it was sure as hell going to do it. That job? Make you forget whatever awful thing had happened in your life that, by comparison, made drinking this moonshine seem like a good idea.

I thanked the man generously, complimenting him on the fastidious, albeit illicit, job he was doing. He smiled back. I noticed he was no longer burdened by teeth. I assumed this was because he was now powered exclusively by moonshine, and so no longer needed them. Evolution in action. As we turned to leave the shack, there was a loud bang at its rear. Then a second bang. I turned back to find liquid gushing from one of the drums on the far wall. This barrel caught fire. Flames shot up towards the roof. The man leapt into action, shouting at his colleagues to help as he darted to the back of the hut. "Run," he shouted, proving he knew at least one English word. The kids sprinted for the exit with us in close pursuit. I turned just before the door to see the man frantically turning valves and trying to calm the fire before the shack blew up. The other four men? They didn't even stir.

By the time Annett and I made it out of the brush and onto the dirt road, the boys were already halfway back to town, giggling manically. We never found out if he got the flames under control, but back on the veranda, we saw no signs of fire in the village or the sky. We played some more Mau Mau, and Djarbah won with such regularity that accusations of foul play were levelled.

I shuffled the deck. "A lot of people blame white people for having messed up Africa. What do you think about that?"

His eyebrows rose like flags. "Blame? What should we blame them for?"

"Don't you think Ghana would be more developed today if the British had never colonised it?"

"There is no one to blame for Ghana but Ghanaians. But why blame? Things are good here. Go to Togo, or *Nigeria*."

I stopped shuffling. "I thought Nigeria was quite developed? They have all that oil and Nollywood?"

"No. *Noooo!* Adams, go to Nigeria. *Pur-lease.* You won't make it out in one piece. I was there for tennis. Never. Never. Never again! Ghana is nothing like that. *We* are the African success story."

The kids were sitting with us on the veranda, their schoolbooks spread out on the floor. "Dad, what's the difference between me and God?" asked Nana, in English, the language in which they studied.

Djarbah pondered this question, stroking at his goatee for inspiration. "Let me see your book."

Nana carried it over, his steps measured. He was a quiet boy who radiated thoughtfulness. Djarbah looked at it; scratched the back of his head; turned back a page; read a bit; stroked his beard; flipped a few pages forward; read a bit more and then, suddenly, his eyes widening, clapped. Several nearby houses fell over. "Easy, son," he said, clasping Nana on the shoulder. "The difference between you and God is that you are a sinner!"

Annett's mouth fell open. I cocked my head. This was madness. Nana broomed far, far too much to be anyone's definition of a sinner. "God is not a sinner," Djarbah continued. "You are a sinner. That's the difference between you and God. *Write that.*"

I asked to see Nana's workbook.

It looked like a regular schoolbook; and it covered English grammar, multiplication, the structure of an atom, etc. But then, smuggled into every fourth or fifth page, were things that didn't seem, well, all that academically rigorous—God, Hell, the wonders of the church, miracles, creationism.

I handed it to Annett, who flicked through it tutting and sighing and then handed it back pointing at the "donated by the Church of Pentecost" text on the cover. This explained so much about the country. They really were getting them while they were young. "Are all the schoolbooks donated by the churches, Djarbah?"

He thought about this for a moment, scratching at some more of his XXL body parts. "Yes, I think so."

"Do you think that's problematic?"

"Problematic, Adams? Why would it be so? The churches do much good here and if they didn't provide the books, who would?"

"The state?"

He collapsed back into his wicker chair, chuckling.

"As lovely as Djarbah and his family are," said Annett, as we were in bed that night, "I can't wait to go home." This wasn't how you were supposed to feel at the end of a holiday. "It's not the heat, or the lack of electricity, or the bad roads, or the food, or that there's not all that much to do. It's seeing so many people investing energy in something you're absolutely, absolutely certain is a dead end."

I rolled over to look at her. "I don't know. I can see why it's an attractive message here. To think that there might be more than this life."

"That's the point though! If they weren't wasting time giving money to these groups they could invest it in making things better. Religion is the exact opposite of what they need. Which is to focus on *now*."

Rather unexpectedly, since this wasn't a Hollywood movie, the ripped, muscular, shirtless torso of a Ghanaian superhero appeared at our bedroom door.

"Adams, we must go immediately to the hospital. Something is very wrong with Monica." I scrambled to locate my clothes, hopping in one trouser leg towards the living room. There I found Djarbah trying to steer Monica in the direction of the front door. She was in a nightie, covered in sweat, resisting him, and muttering unintelligibly in a trance. Her expression was blank.

"Help me get her into the car," he shouted from under one of her armpits. I ducked under the other and together we attempted to hoist her down the small hill to the car. "Annett, you're in charge," he yelled over his shoulder. "Look after the kids."

"What?" she shrieked. "How do I do that?"

Annett is not into children in the same way people are not into being hit with rocks. She's aware that they exist and that there's nothing she can do to prevent this, but feels no desire to enjoy their existence any more than that. Perhaps because they're so uninterested in being efficient. Fortunately, Djarbah's children were well behaved to the point of being faulty.

Tottering on the descending dirt path, ten metres from the car, we were just about managing to keep Monica upright. She was mumbling incoherently and foaming at the mouth as we folded her in half and pushed her into the back of the car.

It was, all in all, completely terrifying.

Djarbah hit at the steering wheel in frustration, cursing every crater and crevice, as we bounced down the road in first gear. Looking at my feet, I noticed I'd left in such a rush that I'd forgotten to put on shoes. I looked to Djarbah's; he was also barefoot. Heading out of town, we turned down a road I'd not spotted before, which curved up a slight incline, then stopped in front of a dark rectangular building: the hospital. The wheels had barely stopped rotating before we sprang out. I opened the rear door on my side and threw myself at Monica, trying to push her out the opposite door, where Djarbah stood, pulling. Eventually we freed her and were under her arms again, steering her as if she were a late-night drunk.

I've never seen a hospital with so few lights on and people in it. A nurse pointed us to a room with three beds. We took the closest, wrestling Monica, rear end first, onto it. She was still in a semi-lucid mummy-like state as we grabbed at her arms and legs and heaved her up and flat onto the hospital bed, wheezing from the exertion.

Djarbah disappeared to find a doctor. I had a moment to take the room in. There were no sheets on the beds. The next bed over held the sparrow-like frame of an extremely old woman, her skin like tree bark. Her breathing laboured and sporadic and causing her to vibrate with the exertion of it. I'd heard the term death rattle, but until that moment I'd never actually heard one. It sliced through all my cynicism and indifference. That would be me one day. Just as it would be all the people I will ever love. A young woman cried softly as she stroked the dying lady's hand. A nurse entered the room and pushed some pills into Monica's mouth. Djarbah watched on from the door frame, his face awash in fear and worry.

I waited in the hallway, feeling concerned for Monica and awkward that there was nothing I could do to help. It's nice that human society has reached a level of sophistication and development that we don't have to spend our time bent over in fields encouraging food to appear from the ground. However, now that we've all become yoga teachers, graphic designers, and writers, it's easy to forget how spectacularly bereft we are of actual life skills, how flimsy our qualifications are in the things that really count: life and death things. If there was a zombie uprising and society broke down, what could I do? What could I offer? *Metaphors?* Probably the polite thing would be just to sacrifice myself to the waiting hordes in the hope that it might buy enough time for a doctor, physicist, or professional footballer to sneak out the back door to safety.

Djarbah reappeared, snapping me back to the here and now. He seemed smaller in this moment, shrunk in the wash of panic that had brought us here. He took a seat beside me, on the wooden bench outside Monica's room. "She is a little better now," he said. "They gave her something and she is sleeping. I will drive you back, and we can tell the children not to worry."

"Does the doctor know what it is?"

"No. It is beyond the complexity of this place. I will have to take her to a nearby city for some tests once she is better."

Thankfully, Monica was discharged the next day. Annett and I saw her briefly before it was time to leave. We discussed the trip on the bus ride back to Accra.

"Are you excited to go home?" I asked, while rustling through my bag looking for chewing gum. I handed her a stick.

"Oh yes. So much. You?"

I paused between chews. "No... not really. There's not all that much there for me at the moment. Not in comparison to moonshine and blizzards and tear gas, anyway. I want more experiences like this."

The bus lurched past three teenage boys who had been filling in potholes then begging for money for their labour, or feigned labour, since for every pothole they'd filled I could see another dozen ignored.

"I'm glad you've got some of your old zest back," she said. "But if you don't feel lucky or can't enjoy the incredibly sweet life you've got, well, there's something wrong with you."

I nodded. "I'm working on that thing."

"That's good. But my life already has enough stress in it."

"Uh-huh." I glanced out the window, already knowing where this was going.

"I can't drop everything any time you want to go somewhere that's only got water half the day, and electricity even less than that."

"Uh-huh."

"And where the most popular form of entertainment is drinking alcohol from a sock. Or some crazy dictator has changed the days of the week to his own name."

"Uh-huh."

She pushed me on the shoulder. "Hey. Are you listening to me?"

"Uh-huh."

"Stop saying *uh-huh*. I'm just asking that you also think about my needs as well, okay?"

"That might set a dangerous precedent."

She tutted. "Yeah, wouldn't it just."

~

Thankfully, Monica recovered. The tests revealed she has a mild form of epilepsy, and she now has medication for it.

Back in Germany, I tried to make something of the Ghana experience. Was I surprised its charms hadn't attracted more of the global tourist masses? I thought back to the bustle, diesel, and disorder of its capital, Accra. I remembered the starchy, bland food. The long, bumpy journeys. The trash covering the beaches. The omnipresence of organised religion. Sleepy evenings spent walking unlit roads looking for something to do to pass the time.

No, not especially.

But I also appreciated that Ghana doesn't try to be something it isn't, either. It doesn't show off for you. Mostly, it doesn't understand why you've come or what you want from it, and it's not going to put on airs and graces trying to find out. I'd come around to Djarbah's way of thinking. Not every country is trying to become Germany. There's more to life than efficiency. Change can come, sure, but it didn't have to come at breakneck China speeds. I tried to remember that for myself and my own project of reinvention.

Ghana is what it is. It's its own thing. It's an African success story.

6

TEL AVIV AND JERUSALEM, ISRAEL: "CAN YOU FEEL THE FIRE?"

Pre-Renaissance men, wine monsters, novelty ties, conspiracy nuts

I arrived at Berlin Schönefeld early, since I'd heard security can be pretty overzealous when you're heading to Israel, or are in Israel, or if you've ever been to Israel and want to go somewhere that isn't. I was alone. Annett was coming on the trip but staying two weeks less and so had taken a different flight from the city's other airport. In the departure hall, a small bearded EL AL (Israel's national airline) employee collected me at the outer ring of the system of pre-check-in counters. This was new. The man had heavy black eyebrows and thin metal glasses with circular frames.

"Good morning. My name is Levi," he said, grinning and taking my passport. Some people fit snugly into their environment—the humourless accountant, the nerdy scientist, the heavily tattooed tattoo artist. Levi was not one of these people. He was like a small Jewish cheerleader, his face permanently failing to restrain the sheer wonder that was his own existence. I found him a delightfully positive presence in the sterile, depressing, authoritarian environment of airport security. During all the weird things that were about to happen to me, that face always said, "I'm totally on your side, buddy" (no matter how firmly the rest of his body said, "YOU SHALL NOT PASS!").

"Now, Adam," he began. "Israel, is, err, as you may know..." His eyes darted diagonally upwards in search of suitably delicate wording. His tone was that of a teacher explaining basic arithmetic to the class idiot. "We're, *well*, a little bit *special*. So there will be some extra questions today. But if there are no problems, then you can proceed to the check-in counter. Okay?" He gestured to the counter over his left shoulder. A bored-looking woman sat there, waiting for someone to correctly answer enough questions to win her audience.

"Sure, no problem," I said, because I had both no choice and nothing to hide. As for Israel being special, I already knew that; it was why I was going there. China and Ghana had been memorable, without being enjoyable, and I knew that unless I wanted to travel alone, I needed to find somewhere that struck a better balance between delight, danger, and drudgery. Many of our friends had raved about Israel, which promised trash-free beaches, great food, interesting people, and intensity. After Ghana, I wanted to see somewhere with even less separation between religion and state. You don't choose Judaism, you are simply born Jewish. They are their religion. It's a country that's all politics, all the time.

"Why are you flying from Germany and not from England?" Levi asked.

"Because I live here in Berlin."

"How long have you lived here in Berlin?"

"Three years, I think."

"You think?"

I cleared my throat. "Three years."

Levi's eye twinkled. "You know, you look a little bit Israeli?"

I didn't know what to say to this because I didn't really know what the average Israeli looked like. I'd only ever met one. Levi flicked through my stamps. He lingered on the ones I'd collected from Muslim countries that Israel doesn't like. Which is all of them.

"Thank you, Adam. Please just wait here a second. I'll return shortly."

I relaxed. It was over and I could now enjoy an interesting holiday. Levi approached a scary-looking man standing to the side of the check-in counter. This man had the appearance of a nightclub bouncer. He was wearing an earpiece, the cord of which disappeared into his tight blue EL AL shirt. The shirt looked stressed in its attempts to retain all of the man's muscles. He had at least three times as many as I did and had successfully exercised all of them to tautness. He didn't have a face like thunder—he had a face that seemed able to produce thunder, amongst other bad weather, all of which could be unleashed upon you at his discretion.

Levi approached him warily, like Oliver Twist asking for more gruel. The buff man eyed me like a lion might a badly wounded gazelle. The two exchanged words, and the man shook his head, slowly, keeping it perfectly level. Levi returned, smiling, as if absolutely everything was perfect and this was, in many ways, the best day of his life.

"Fantastic. Thank you for waiting," he said, as if I'd had a choice. "I'm going to need to ask you a few more questions today. Is that okay?" My shoulders slumped forward. "Can you tell me what your occupation is, Adam?"

This was a difficult question. I prided myself on my ability to function as a human without anything resembling an occupation. You may have heard of the concept of a Renaissance man. Well, I'm a pre-Renaissance man, stubbornly devoid of any skills. Technically, I could have said "journalist" or "writer." However, admitting to these professions is like uttering a special secret password to Travel Hell. No one wants journalists or writers in their country because they have a habit of writing things, and sometimes these things are even true.

"I'm a small business owner," I said. "I have a few different websites." Which was true and paid the bills better than any of my flirtations with the written word.

"What do these websites do?"

"I have one called The Hipstery, where I sell products, and one called TheTeeDirectory where I recommend them."

He cocked his head. "*This* is your job?"

"I know, right? But, yeah, it is."

"Do you intend to work on these websites while in Israel?"

"No. I barely work on them while I'm here in Berlin, to be honest."

He folded his arms. "*Huh.* Fascinating. I'm here all day in the airport asking questions, and some people are just living from their websites. The world is pretty strange, isn't it? Do you think you'd be able to show me these websites?"

"Sure," I replied. BECAUSE I HAD NO CHOICE IF I WANTED TO GO ON HOLIDAY. Levi walked me in the direction of the Hulk. Hulk watched me closely. I thought I saw him lick his lips. I showed Levi my websites on a special EL AL Laptop of Extravagant Paranoia sitting on the countertop near Hulk. Levi went to consult Hulk again, and Hulk shook his head again. I felt as if I were taking part in a game show—The Game of Nations—where everything I said triggered a loud "Wrong!" sound. Levi skipped merrily back to me, a wide grin on his face, as though it were my birthday and he'd prepared strawberry sponge cake.

"Just a few more questions."

I sighed. I'd heard that Israelis were paranoid, but I didn't know they were this paranoid. I just wanted to go on holiday.

"Don't sigh," he said, hurt. "You're doing just fine. We're nearly there. Next question. Where will you stay?"

I retrieved the Airbnb booking from my bag. He held it as if it were sacred. "It says here that the accommodation is for *two* people." He exhaled theatrically, pointing. His face cracked like an egg thrown from a roof terrace.

Gotcha #1. "You told me you were travelling alone!"

We were a team. He had my back. But now... this... Hulk wasn't going to like this. He wasn't going to like this at all.

"I did?" I shifted on the spot. "Well I am *travelling* alone. My girlfriend is on a different flight."

An *egh-ugh* buzzer sounded.

"We're coming back at different times. She's on the Lufthansa flight that left a few hours ago."

He wrote down her name, and took it to Hulk. Hulk didn't move. Trees don't move, either. Neither do walls. Levi bounced back across on the front of his feet. There'd been a few speed bumps on the Yellow Brick Road to check-in, sure, but nothing we couldn't manage if we just worked together and told each other the truth.

"Everything is going great," he lied. "Just one or two more questions. Do you know anyone in Israel? Do you intend to visit the occupied territories?"

I tried to excavate myself from the box marked *irregularity*. "I do not, nor will I. A friend from Tel Aviv did send me a list of recommendations. My girlfriend and I will probably just work through that."

Gotcha #2. The colour drained from his face. "You said you don't know anyone in Israel, yet now I'm hearing you have a list of recommendations from an Israeli friend?!?!"

"I, err, don't..." I stammered. "Well..." I tried to continue. "Erm. The other day I met a girl at a conference. We got talking and I told her I was about to go to Israel and so she sent me this list." I unfolded a piece of A4 paper and handed it to him.

"What is this girl's name?"

I could only remember her first name. This seemed to upset him on a very deep, personal level. I didn't tell him I was actually only 62 percent certain that this was even her first name. The list itself was just a collection of bars and restaurants, with comments like "Be sure to try the eggs Benedict!" I might as well have printed out an Internet listicle called "Seventeen ways to Tel you're in love with Tel Aviv."

Levi checked every word on the list closely, as if deciphering a secret code. He then took the list, the Airbnb booking, and my passport back to Hulk. Hulk shook his head once again.

Seriously? Was I that atypical? With my slightly Israeli face, lack of job, invisible girlfriend, and first-name-only eggs Benedict conference contact?

Levi bounded back like a lamb in a summer's meadow. "We've decided to send you for advanced luggage screening," he said, making it sound as if I'd won an Airport Oscar. "It's nothing to worry about, of course."

It's funny how often people say "it's nothing to worry about" precisely when it's exactly a point in your life deserving of concern. It's like they're trying to convince themselves. It's right up there with other classic human self-denial statements such as "It's just a small lump," "I'll get around to fixing that soon," and, "What you don't know can't hurt you."

Hulk certainly could hurt me. His glances had already been quite bruising; one long, piercing stare had left me winded. Levi disco danced alongside me across the check-in area and over to a metal chair outside an ominous, unmarked door. We were about twenty metres from the—now quite full—check-in area. I was trying to remain calm but found I no longer knew how. I went to where calm was normally stored within me, but everyone there said they'd never heard of it. They recommended I try something called anguish instead. Levi left me on a chair and entered the room.

My brain scurried around unlocking the vaults of my memory, searching through all the things I'd ever done wrong, presumably, so it could confess to these upfront before the waterboarding really got going. It was a long list: I stole a pencil sharpener from a shop when I was twelve; I pretend to be a real journalist to attend sold-out events; I illegally download. Okay, that's quite a short list, but that's only because I've suppressed all the really damning stuff.

Levi returned, retaining his the-Queen-will-see-you-now demeanour. I followed him into the small, windowless space. Inside, a hairy man on an office swivel chair met my gaze as he snapped on a pair of rubber gloves.

"You do that when everyone walks in, right?"

He jutted out his chin and narrowed his eyes.

"I'll just be outside," said Levi jovially, as if dropping off his kid at playschool. "Good luck."

Wait, why would I need luck?

The door closed with a click.

I laughed at the absurdity of all of this.

"Remove your clothes," the man said.

I stopped laughing. "A-all my clothes?"

"No. You can leave your underwear on."

Oh, the kindness. I stripped down to my boxer shorts. The man looked in my mouth, made me cough, and swept everything I owned with some kind of futuristic anti-terror RoboCop wand.

"Can you demonstrate your phone to me?" he asked. "Take a photo, maybe?"

While not a professional photographer, I turned, instinctively, to take a photo of the computer in the corner, behind us. It wasn't the roof of the Sistine Chapel, sure, but it was the only thing worthy of framing in this drab room. The man lunged for the phone. "Not that," he shouted. "It's classified."

This whole experience was only serving to remind me that there is no limit to the number of things you can do wrong, just as long as you're trying to do right. I got dressed and was told to wait outside. About twenty minutes passed. The door opened, and the man shouted across to Levi. Levi waltzed over, his enthusiasm for life making him as conspicuous as an Inuit on a camel in space. He disappeared into the unmarked room. The door closed. The lock clicked.

I sat heavily in my chair. A few minutes later he returned, holding my laptop. It was the illegal downloads, I knew it. They'd found the pirated copy of the new Lego movie. I was done for. "The screen appears to be loose," he said, grasping it.

"Yeah, it's a bit broken. I've taped it."

"The battery also appears to be taped?"

"Yeah, that's also broken. I'll get around to fixing it soon."

Another lie. I was a pre-Renaissance man, after all.

The check-in area had now emptied and just one or two late-arriving passengers remained. The final boarding call had been made. The whole process had taken just short of two hours. I was stressed, thirsty, and tired of being an object of unrelenting suspicion. Levi visited Hulk again. I couldn't look, unable to take any more rejection. He returned giddy as ever. "Great, Mr Fletcher, we're finished with the security check now! I hope it was not too invasive."

Was it really over? I didn't believe it. It was the night bus to Wuhan all over again. Any second a puppy was going to appear.

"It was pretty invasive," I grumbled. Levi rocked back on his heels. "It was? Oh... well... sorry about that. My colleague will take you to the boarding area soon. Enjoy your stay in Israel."

With no puppy in sight, I let out my own little yelp of relief. A stocky woman strutted over to me. "Stand up," she said, addressing me as you would a dog that had climbed on the couch and needed to be put back in its place. "I will escort you to security."

Off we walked. At first in sync, then I fell a step or two behind because we walked past a newsagent and I got distracted by all the things in it made of chocolate. I always want chocolate when stressed, and even more when not.

She spun around to face me. "DO NOT walk behind me."

"I'm sorry?"

Her voice lowered. "You MUST walk IN FRONT of me."

I swatted the air. "Come on! This is just ridiculous now."

She clamped her hands onto her hips. "You think international security is ridiculous?" She held the pose. It was not a new pose for her. I cleared my throat. Decided words wouldn't help. Stepped past her. Wordlessly we moved towards the security gate. I was a pace ahead. I hated this woman. I hated flying. I hated Israel, which was a bold opinion to hold considering at this point I'd never actually been to Israel. But that wasn't my fault. I was trying. I was doing my bit. She escorted me all the way to the plane door. I collapsed in my seat and began quietly seething, an activity that kept me busy for the whole four-hour-long flight, during which I avoided looking at anyone, since the other passengers probably assumed I was one of Osama Bin Laden's inner circle.

Annett was waiting for me in the arrivals area of Ben Gurion Airport. She looked much more relaxed than I did. Possibly for the first time ever. I told her the story in the taxi, on our way to the city.

She was crying genuine tears of laughter by the time I reached the strip search. "I'm never flying EL AL again," I said.

"Well, it doesn't sound like they'd let you anyway."

Fortunately, the intensity level did drop once we reached Tel Aviv. For brief moments it even felt as if we were on holiday, and had not merely reached a new place where I was to be ritually humiliated.

Broadly speaking, Tel Aviv should be a relaxed place. Its standard of living would be remarkable were it not for its cost of living. Holding up a pot of yoghurt in the supermarket, I could only conclude it had been priced deliberately to antagonise me. A short note from capitalism: "Fuck you, Adam."

There were also guns. Lots of guns. That didn't really help with the relaxation. Especially since these weapons were being carried around by people so young you wanted to stop them, point at the machine gun on their shoulder, and ask, "Do your parents know you have that?" These heavily armed people were soldiers on compulsory military service, two years and eight months for men, two years for women. The city felt full of them.

The other thing that let the city down, relaxation-wise, was all the people who lived in it. It's only logical that living under the existential pressure that haunts every Israeli, every day of his or her life, will have an effect on your disposition. It's simple cause and effect. If you think, at any moment, that you're going to be vaporised by a weapon from Iran or Saudi Arabia, you're probably going to stop holding your tongue. If you think you're going to go out anyway, you might as well go out with a bang, or a drink, or a smoke, or some sex, or a raging street argument with some guy in a car who didn't wait long enough for you to cross the road. It seemed to me that the country's real currency was not the shekel but *the heckle*: a quick release of frustration in a small, overcrowded city in which the traffic sucks, the buildings are long past their peak, everything costs three times the price that it should, and the devout have to live directly on top of liberals, atheists, agnostics, and people more interested in the stock market than the Torah.

Sipping offensively priced pomegranate juice on the chairs of a street cafe, as the first perfect day began to dusk, we saw this friction playing out again and again: an Orthodox Jew on a bright orange mountain bike whizzed down the hill, his long beard flapping in the breeze as a car overtook him, leaving insufficient room, and he began shaking his fist at the driver; a group of baby-faced armed soldiers strolled past; a young girl walked in the other direction carrying a "I wish I were a lesbian" bag; three catwalk models (sorry, I mean average Israeli women) stopped to get coffee. Thick curtains of wild curly black hair hugged their irritatingly symmetrical faces. The genetic lottery had certainly been won here. It was late summer, and people in their mid-twenties sauntered around loosely wrapped in board shorts, vests, and tank tops paired with Ray-Ban sunglasses. Some had arms and legs speckled with tribal tattoos. I'd describe the aesthetic as "I don't care how I look. *But I look good, right?*"

We were having a lovely time, even with all the guns. Next we were going to visit the famously less relaxed city of Jerusalem. Upon hearing that, our Airbnb host, Adam, offered us a little of his own opinion soup. "Don't go there. There was an attack like three hours ago. Palestinians are killing themselves just to get two minutes of media coverage. It's stupid. Like going to Jerusalem."

It was an especially sensitive time to visit the country, since there had been waves of terror attacks in the previous weeks from Palestinians crossing into Israel. There were even suggestions of a looming third intifada, a full-scale Palestinian uprising. Back home, we'd been a little nervous watching the news coverage, but since our flights to Israel were non-refundable, we'd decided to take them anyway. We weren't sure about Jerusalem now though, the place where most of the attacks were taking place. We shrugged, and told Adam we'd think about it over dinner.

That dinner was to be shared with an Israeli man called Oded. He was a friend of a friend. I knew nothing about him other than that he was a journalist for a left-wing Israeli newspaper. We hoped he'd be able to give us a second, better-informed opinion. We agreed to meet at a trendy new restaurant and microbrewery favouring exposed copper and steel.

Arriving at the restaurant, we found a thin man picking nervously at his beer mat. He had a large fluffy cloud of black curly hair that made "balding me" instantly jealous. Over three too small, too expensive, unnecessarily exotic beers, the three of us got to know each other. We asked for his opinion on our going to Jerusalem. "I was domiciled there for seven years," he said. "I visit now, occasionally, when I can muster the cour*rr*age." Israeli's roll their *r*'s in an extremely pleasing way that should come as standard with the English language, just as cars come with airbags. "Here... well... it is no picnic, sure, but there are fewer people foisting sharp objects at me. There are so many attacks now that we don't even make major stories out of them. They appear only in the daily *rrr*oundups, between adverts for insurance."

Foisting sharp objects at me. Oded had a way with words. A way in general, actually. I found him hypnotic. Sometimes you meet someone and he's such a brilliant, perfectly formed character that you can't quite believe he can exist here, in highly flawed Real Life™. It's like bumping into Hannibal Lecter in a newsagent buying Haribo. Were Oded a casserole, the ingredients would have been:

1x Eeyore
Half a cup of manically depressed Woody Allen
250g of David Foster Wallace
The hair of Robert Smith (from The Cure)

All cooked in deadpan, until lightly disorientated. I fell quickly into deep, platonic love with him. With a real-life Israeli here for my enjoyment, I began peppering him with questions. Here I had questions. I had my notepad with me because I always have a notepad with me. After the fourth question, he looked towards it and said, "I'm not *rr*really enjoying being the Israeli cor*rr*espondent."

"No?" Humans usually love any chance to confetti other humans with their opinions. Especially in Israel. We'd only been here three days, but it seemed to me that many Israelis had long stopped waiting for a question before loudly shouting its answer at you.

"Your literary endeavourrr is completely futile," he said, matter-of-factly. "It will fail. How do you explain a country? It's impossible. *Rrr*idiculous, even. It would be nothing more than a lie."

I gripped the edge of the table. "But by that logic there would be almost nothing we'd be able to speak about. We couldn't even discuss this table. I don't even know what type of wood it is."

He smirked. "Yes, so we should not. Or we should speak only of its function. It is a good table for *rrr*esting our beer upon, no? My beer feels ve*rrr*y supported upon it."

"Okay, that's the table done," I said, slapping it with my palm. "Shall we talk about the glass I'm holding next?"

Oded nodded briskly. "A good glass. I think your beer feels ve*rrr*y secure in it." A wry smile crossed his lips. His first of the night. "I'm sorry, Adam, but I don't want to be your opinion puppet. Also, I'm Is*rrr*aeli. I'm absolutely soaked in this culture. So many people have tried to explain us. It is a fool's e*rrr*and."

He was right, of course, but I reserved the right to try anyway. Narcissism is the writer's superpower. Even the very occasional writer. Three young soldiers in uniform walked past the restaurant's open front. Annett's gaze followed them. "Did you also do military service?" It was hard to imagine Oded with a gun.

He sighed. "No. I was neither for nor against it. As a seventeen-year-old, I was simply too ignorant to understand the *rrr*amifications either way. They interviewed me for four hours and decided I was 'mentally unfit to serve.'"

"Did that surprise you?" Annett asked.

He paused to consider this, stroking the bottom of his glass. "Not *rrr*eally, no. Mostly because we had spent much of those four hours discussing how depressed I was and how much I wanted to blow my own brains out. Also, the day before the interview someone had kicked a football at my head. It left me with a nervous tick in one eye. That was probably ve*rrr*y fortuitous."

Only Oded could find being hit in the head with a football fortuitous. "At the end of the interview, they did ask if I would consider a job defusing bombs. I think they thought, 'This kid wants to kill himself anyway. Let him do some good in the process.'" His wry smile returned. "I politely declined."

Oded was the blackest of black comics. Someone so fused to his trauma, so honest and self-deprecating with it, that he wore it like a bow tie. This was not a man you wanted good things to happen to; he'd have no idea what to do with them. If he found a one-hundred-shekel bill on the floor, he'd bend down to pick it up, put his back out, and run up a five-hundred-shekel medical bill. He was wonderful. I wanted to surgically attach myself to his hip. "Do many people fake being mentally ill to avoid their military service?"

"Yes. I had one friend who didn't want to serve and so every morning before roll call he would deliberately wet his bed. Eventually they let him go."

"Is there long-term stigma for people who don't serve in the military?" Annett asked, while signalling the waiter for another wine.

"In job interviews they always ask me if I served. I say I was found mentally unfit. Then they look at me and say, 'You seem fine to me.'"

Oded seemed many things, but not fine. There was a lull in the conversation. I took some gulps of my well-supported beer thinking about how we live in a world where refusing to join the army makes you mentally ill. The people not dragged kicking and screaming into battle would be the ones I'd worry about.

"Are you still depressed now, Oded?" I asked.

"No. I have a good sh*rrr*ink now. She costs a third of my income. But she's certainly worth it."

"How do you know?"

"Well, when I first went to see her, I was absolutely *drrr*owning in self-loathing. I'm not anymore. You *don't* go to a shrink, Adam?"

"No," I said raising my palms. "I won't even go to a doctor unless something is about to rot off."

"Huh," he said, with the sort of surprise one might have upon learning the new Ku Klux Klan Grand Wizard was a black lesbian immigrant with disabilities. "*All* my friends go to a shrink. I think this is the true Isrrraeli national hobby." He glanced down at my notepad. "You can put *that* in your book, if you like..." He said the word *book* as though it were something unfortunate he'd just stood in.

"Adam always thinks he knows best," Annett interjected. "He's totally un-helpable."

Oded's eyes narrowed to thin slits. "I'm ve*rrr*y surprised. You are obviously sick, Adam. You need help."

"YES!" said Annett. "I've been saying that!"

"What?" I said, slapping the tabletop. "Don't you start, Oded. I'm not sick. I'm perfectly fine. If anything, I'm swimming in *self-love*, not self-loathing."

"Exactly." He nodded. "Exactly. That's the problem. You are sick, Adam. *Verrry* sick. You should go see a sh*rrr*ink."

Annett high-fived Oded. He was so startled by this happy human gesture of camaraderie that he spilt some of his no-longer-well-supported beer down himself.

We spent the walk home trying to decide if we should go to Jerusalem.

"I think we shouldn't," Annett said. "It just seems too risky and there's plenty of other places we could go. How about Haifa?"

"Jerusalem is the main reason we wanted to come here."

"Yeah, but that was when it was calm. Comparatively speaking."

"I think we need to go. Going to Israel but not seeing Jerusalem is like going to the dentist but refusing to open your mouth."

"That's a strange analogy."

"Thanks," I said, as we waited at the curb for the light to change.

"It wasn't a compliment."

"Oh. Well, I mean, Israelis live and function amongst these kinds of dangers every day. Surely we could handle just three of them?" The light changed. We stepped out into the street. Annett said nothing for a few steps. A bicycle whizzed past, ignoring our right of way.

"The risks are far higher than within our normal lives, but I guess they're still relatively low. Compared to a job defusing bombs anyway."

I hugged her, nearly knocking her off her feet. "Great! I'm sure it will be worth it. You'll see."

The next day, our backpacks on, we headed for the train station. Two ambulances rushed past us, their sirens forcing us to put fingers in our ears. I felt a spike of adrenaline down my back. My pulse quickened. Directly ahead we saw police tape across the closed road that would have led to the station. On the ground behind the tape sat a girl crying hysterically, leaning against a railing. A metre from her was a large patch of blood. Someone approached the girl and embraced her. Whatever had happened here, had just happened here. We weren't safe in Tel Aviv either. Neither were they. It explained a lot about them.

My hands trembled occasionally during that train ride. A discouraging development. There was a lot of security at Jerusalem station when we arrived. As we waited for the public bus that would take us to our hostel, I couldn't help but eye everyone with suspicion, wondering if at any moment someone was going to pull a knife or gun. There had been numerous attacks on the buses in the previous weeks. Including at the very stop where we were waiting, which had only the frame of its glass shelter left.

"You're doing it too, right?" Annett asked, as we took our seats in the bus. I took a deep breath. "Watching everyone suspiciously like they're about to blow me up? Yes."

I felt significantly lighter once we made it to the lobby of Abraham Hostel, and not because I got to remove my rucksack. We headed immediately to the bar to inebriate ourselves. Annett barely drinks in Germany, but as soon as we're on holiday she morphs into some kind of WINE MONSTER. Especially if she's stressed. "I think I'll get another wine," she said, standing up from our table in the large communal lounge area. "I think happy hour ends soon. You want something? Wine maybe? It's two for one. I'll get four."

Abraham Hostel is the biggest and most famous hostel in

Jerusalem. I looked around at the other travellers, trying to work out who comes to Jerusalem on holiday. I heard Annett at the bar. "No, this is just two. I want two plus the two for free. Oh sod it, how about I just take the bottle? Cut out the middleman..."

As Annett rejoined me, a tall, wiry, blond American called Larry had cornered a middle-aged English couple one table over from where we were sitting. Larry had the feel of a surfer who had never quite got around to actually surfing. He wore a red T-shirt two sizes too big, as if ready and waiting for excesses his mouth had never delivered.

"I don't think there will be another election," he said. "Obama will change the constitution. He's the devil incarnate. Did you know he has a secret meeting every Thursday in the basement of the White House? Creates a kill list of people to be murdered that week."

The man squirmed in his seat. "Erm. *Hmm.* Is that so."

His wife stood up. "Well, we wanted to do *that thing*, hunny... In the room... We should get going..."

"Lovely to have met you," said the man, rushing off after his wife.

"Yeah, I'll send you some links," Larry shouted after them. He got up and approached an Asian man washing up in the kitchen area. He stopped two steps closer to him than normal social etiquette allows. "They put chemicals in the water to keep us stupid," he said. "I read it on this website—The Mind Unleashed. Do you know about The Mind Unleashed? Yeah, you won't hear anything about it from the Western imperialist media machine. *Oh no.* Puppets for murderers they are."

Larry put two fingertips into the soapy water and then rubbed them on the end of the Asian man's nose. The man was frozen to the spot, holding a purple plastic plate dripping suds onto the floor tiles. He appeared to have gotten stuck trying to work out what was happening, and more importantly, how he could make it stop. Larry brushed some locks of blond hair back behind an ear. "Some people just believe everything they're told. Me? I like to dig a little bit deeper. Find out what *they're* not telling you."

Who "they" were was not clarified before Larry walked off in the direction of the dorms. Annett waved at me from the other side of the room, where she'd been pretending to look at the hostel's library. I took my wine with me. You can't be too careful. Or drunk.

"Two seats down," she whispered into my ear. "Trainee female rabbis talking to one of the organisers of something called the Gathering."

If life were a game of Scrabble, finding trainee female rabbis would constitute a triple word score. We settled down into the free seat nearest to them, Annett hugging her wine bottle like an old friend for which her feelings were complicated and better expressed through actions rather than words. "Are there a lot of female rabbis?" the man asked. "I thought pretty much all rabbis were men?"

"The famous ones are," replied one of the trainees. She had short hair dyed red, and a soft, button nose unwilling to make a point. "But women can also be rabbis."

"Wow, fantastic," the man said. His tone that of a talented used-car salesman who knew exactly how he would close this sale. "I'm humbled by your dedication and devotion. I'm actually one of the founders of the big Christian event called the Gathering. You'll see a lot of people around here with purple wristbands. They're all Gatherers."

We *had* seen a lot of people with purple wristbands. One group of them had even broken out into an impromptu prayer circle one wine ago. Yes, it is perfectly okay to measure time in wines. I'm pretty sure that's what the Greeks did.

"The Gathering is *the* biggest Christian festival in the world. We're expecting around fifteen thousand worshippers. Every prayer is like a small call up to God, but when we band together it amplifies that sound."

"It sure does," the redhead said, authoritatively, like an experienced prayer-sound technician.

"I think we're really close to a breakthrough now. To learning what He wants from us. Tomorrow's going to be the day. The power of the Gathering is just... just amazing. After the first event in Singapore I was totally energised, just enraptured, right?"

"Right." The trainee rabbis nodded.

"So I got into a taxi and on the way home I told its driver about the power of Christ. At the end of the journey I gave him my Bible, *my personal Bible*. I wrote my phone number in it, in case he ever wanted to talk. Three years later, I get this phone call."

They inhaled sharply. "No way!"

The man winked. "Uh-huh. It was the taxi driver. He said, 'I just want you to know that you changed my life that day. Three years later, I'm still following the way of Christ.'"

"Oh, wow," said the redhead. "That's really something."

"Amen," added the other.

"*That's* the power of the Gathering," said the man.

I was reminded of something called Jerusalem Syndrome, where visitors are so overwhelmed by the religiosity of the city that they stop believing they're management consultants, golf instructors, or window cleaners and start believing they're prophets. We'd not even left the hostel, but it seemed as if all the people around us had been touched by the city in some way. Overwhelmed, we went to bed. Not because of the power of the Gathering, but because of the power of the wine. We were both still very much following the Way of the Vineyard.

We awoke to yet another beautiful day in (highly strung) paradise. It was time to visit the old city; a spiderweb of narrow passageways and caverns that entangles every visitor. It was Shabbat, the Jewish weekly lo-fi holiday, a day mostly spent at home with family. Upon arrival, we found security at each major intersection, and the police outnumbering the visitors in parts. After a final security check we stepped out for our first glimpse of the Wailing Wall, and sitting above it, the Temple Mount—perhaps the most contested piece of real estate on earth and the centre of three major religions: Islam, Christianity, and Judaism. To me, it seemed rational to conclude something from this, that maybe the major religions of the world had more similarities than differences. But, alas, humanity, in its infinite stubbornness, has elected to squabble and kill for this piece of land. As I wasn't religious, the whole thing felt particularly absurd, like watching three kids on the playground argue about whose imaginary friend had been there first.

I walked into the section reserved for male worshippers, swapping my baseball cap for a white yarmulke, and stepped down the slope towards the wall, hearing the hum of the worshippers for the first time and seeing them rocking back and forth, a motion called *shuckling* that is unique to the Jewish faith: one hand on the wall, the rest of the body convulsing to the chanting of Torah verses. I found some empty space. A man to my left chanted louder; several men joined in, their words rippling along the wall. I couldn't understand a word; it was ineffably beautiful. This wall divides, like so many others, but it also unites a whole religion and nation.

I really hoped I would feel something when I reached out to touch the wall. It didn't have to be a lot. I wasn't expecting to have a spiritual awakening from the trip. That said, experiencing just a tiny fraction of what the men around me felt would have been very welcome. The feeling that I wasn't alone, perhaps; that there was a point to all of this; a plan, and a project manager in the sky overseeing it; that I was more than just the random outcome of numerous complex, indifferent systems. Systems that I moved through each day while kidding myself about the control and agency they offered me. That I would not just be here for a short while, having a reasonably nice time, before dying to little fanfare.

Standing at the wall it seemed, suddenly, that I'd been analysing religion incorrectly. I'd been getting too hung up on the *but they're wrong*. That part isn't really important, were it even knowable. I should have been focusing on the *how does it feel to be part of that (probably wrong) thing*. Quite good, a lot of the time, I bet. You get to be a small cog in a larger combine harvester of faith. You get structure, rules, great headwear, to be one of God's chosen ones. Sure, you also have to give up a little free will, sanity, and bacon, but you get community, purpose, and sociality. I'd started this project because I realised how alone I was. How simple and easy my life had become. I was trying to change that. Trying to connect with something bigger than myself. It felt like a trade I might be willing to make.

I looked across at the man to my left. He was rocking and wailing with great intensity, his eyes closed, his head tilted slightly towards the heavens. I mimicked his stance and reached out with my palms to the cold limestone surface of the Western Wall.

I felt...

Well...

I felt something!

I felt a little bit sick, mostly. Like there was a knot in my stomach. A feeling that the things contained within it were going to hastily exit and I had little control of when that might occur. Was this a message from God? If so, it was certainly a strange one. I closed my eyes. That seemed to help. Ah, was that a clue? I opened them again. The feeling returned.

Oh.

I wasn't experiencing a religious awakening after all. People travel from all over the world to place prayers into the cracks of the Western Wall. Thousands of pieces of paper cluster in its deformities. This was the problem. I suffer from something called trypophobia, a (completely irrational) fear of clusters. Google it, but only if you want to see some pretty harrowing pictures of the insides of kiwis, melons, and beehives. Warning: it's the stuff of (my) nightmares.

This was what was making me feel queasy. God wasn't talking to me after all. It was time to leave, still Godless, alone, and burdened by existential angst. This was not my tribe. I was not one of the chosen ones. It would remain just a wall, to me.

That night, back in the hostel, Annett and I went conversation surfing once more. An American in a wide baseball cap advertising a beer talked to a Belgian dressed in specialised outdoor wear. They were playing a very popular travellers' game that I call Authentic Experience Tennis®.

The American served. "Have you been to the Wailing Wall yet?"

"Yeah, twice," the Belgian parried, without hesitation.

"Twice?" A slice-backhand response. "Well, I had a conversation with a local, bearded man today. It was just fantastic."

"Was he a rabbi?" the Belgian's forehand answered.

The American lunged towards the baseline. "No, he was a baker. He sold bread. But very authentic bread." A skilful return from a difficult position. The Belgian had not met a baker of very authentic bread. 15–0 for the American.

Annett had gone to the lobby to get closer to her God: Wi-Fi. She sent me a Skype message that suggested absurdity was taking place there and I should make haste. I joined her to find a portly blond man in a short-sleeved white shirt. A shirt that had not made the acquaintance of an iron for quite some time. He was pacing the hostel entrance, looping the beat-up sofas, half-empty vending machines, and a reception desk staffed by a volunteer not older than fifteen. Extravagant creasing was not the most attention-grabbing part of this man's get-up; that was his tie—his tie featured the Israeli flag.

It looked like the sort of novelty tie you'd buy spontaneously with your last loose change, at the airport, for your wacky Uncle George. The man didn't seem to be wearing the tie as fancy dress. It seemed to make sense to him to be wearing it. And it did, of course, in Jerusalem. But Jerusalem has a pretty low threshold for logic. I'm sure Jerusalem makes perfect sense to itself, but it leaves many others scratching their heads and pulling at their novelty ties.

The top half of the man's face asked questions the bottom couldn't answer. He went to the payphone, made a call, paced the lobby some more, muttered, sat down a few seats over from us, scratched at his arm, rubbed his temples, and then got up and did the whole thing again. While doing this he repeated the same phrases:

"Can you imagine what it's like to not see your family for five years?"

"I have to call the embassy."

"I support the State of Israel!"

A woman entered the lobby from the street. She was short, middle-aged, squirrelly, and wore a grey shapeless smock that made her movements ghostly. "They took my family. I have to call the embassy," he said, as she sat down next to him.

Her hand flew to her chest. "Who took your family?" She looked around the lobby frantically, as if maybe they'd been bundled out the entrance, wrapped in sheets, into an unmarked van, just this minute.

"The Norwegian government!" he said, digging his nails into his arm.

She raised an eyebrow. "They took your family? Where did they take them?"

"To Norway. They kicked me out. Now I've lost my family."

She thought about this for a moment, considering how best to help. It was kind of her. To take the time. To offer assistance. Not everybody does. We've all grown so busy. Her solution was quite innovative. "Did you pray on it?" she asked.

"Yes, you bet I prayed on it."

She sat up straighter. "If you prayed on it, God will give you your family back."

Annett and I exchanged an open-mouthed *is this really happening?* glance. We'd been using this glance quite a lot since arriving in Israel. It had usurped all our normal couple glances: *you know I hate it when you do that*; *oh, it's you again*; *get me something from the kitchen that is made out of chocolate—for example, chocolate.*

The woman stood up. I thought she was going to hug the man. That would have been nice. Hugs, not drugs. Instead she leaned over him, or rather tried to, but found herself too short, even though he was sitting down. She then held one outstretched finger over his head, at a forty-five-degree angle, and began making circles.

"MMMMH..." she hummed. "Do you accept the Holy Spirit, Jesus Christ, as your Lord and Saviour?"

"Yes," he responded, without hesitation.

She circled faster. "Can you feel the fire? CAN YOU FEEL THE FIRE?"

The man's eyes met our own.

"Ooohhh Jesus Christ..." she murmured. "Our Lord, our Saviour. CAN YOU FEEL THE FIRE?"

He was feeling something. Awkwardness, mostly, I think. He looked like a man being sold an ostrich that he really wasn't sure he had a use for.

"I don't know, maybe," he said, meekly, his shoulders slumped.

"MMMMMMH... Can you feel *IT*! Praise Jesus! Can you FEEL the FIRRRRRE?" Her finger circled faster and faster. "Accept him. *Praise him.* Pray to the Lord Jesus. Can you feel the fire? CAN YOU FEEL THE FIRE?"

"Well..." He looked as though he really wanted to feel the fire. Would have gladly welcomed its heat. "*M-maybe,*" he said, staring down at his feet. "But then, there's a lot of fire *within* me."

The woman smiled, satisfied with this tepid response. Another job well done, another soul saved, she sat back down. "Pray to Jesus and he'll give you your family back."

To me, the obvious rebuttal to this would have been "Why did he take them in the first place?" Instead, the man chose, "I have prayed," and put his head in his hands. Presumably to do so once more.

"Not hard enough," she replied, packing up her things. "I have to go. *I have to go now.* I have to pray at the church." With this she disappeared back out into the street, the heavy glass door juddering closed behind her. The man got up and headed towards the payphone. Annett and I sat completely still, rendered mute—who were these people, and more importantly, could we book for their matinee performance?

"Oh. My. God. I love this country," I said, after recovering my powers of speech.

"Me too. There's nowhere that offers this much entertainment for your money."

"Could you imagine living here though?"

"No way in hell. Too much FIRE," she said, getting up and circling my head with her finger as she passed. "I'm going to go get some more wine. You want something? A wine, maybe? I'll get four. I think the happy hour ends soon."

Later that night we were upstairs again, enjoying the common area. Larry the conspiracy theorist had returned. He was making his rounds, proselytising his own religion—The Truth—to some traveller *sheeple* and Singaporean Christians. "I've been getting these really bad headaches lately," he told a young German couple. "So I thought maybe the government had planted a radio transmitter in my mouth."

BullshitFM: all the conspiracy theories, all the time.

"So I went to the dentist, who did a scan, but he didn't find anything. Weird right? I thought maybe I was going crazy, but then I read about this new remote mind-control technology on The Mind Unleashed. The US government created it. *No chip.* So that explains the headaches. Do you know The Mind Unleashed? I'll send you some links."

The couple got up from the table and left, saying something about Larry being a nice guy but that he believed some very strange things. I guess it's well and good unleashing your mind, but you have to be careful it doesn't wander off.

"Yeah, well, not everyone is ready for The Truth," he shouted after them, before returning to his beer. He *was* right about that, something he didn't seem to be making a habit of.

Ever since I'd seen Mr Israel Tie downstairs, I'd been hoping for one thing, and one thing only. Then it took place. It's wonderful when that happens, right? When the Universe does what you want. It almost makes you believe in...

Never mind.

Yep, Mr (Maybe) I Can Feel the Fire came upstairs, still sporting that novelty tie, and walked directly into Conspiracy Larry's den of quarter-truth. I wriggled in my seat in delight. This must have been what it was like to watch Lennon meet McCartney. These two could combine their talents to produce the Sgt Pepper of governmental conspiracy.

"They stole my family," Mr Israel Tie said, standing at the edge of Larry's table.

"Yeah, they'll do that all right," said Larry, slamming his beer bottle down on the table. "Sit down, man. Tell us about it."

"They stole my family. I have to call the embassy. I need to get them back." His shoulders collapsed forward, giving him the appearance of a neglected plant.

"Which embassy?" Larry asked.

"Norway."

"Norway stole your family?" he said, one eyebrow arched. "Why?"

"Because I believe in the State of Israel!"

Larry tucked a tuft of hair behind his ear. "Wait... this makes no sense." Yes, Larry had picked *this* moment to suspend his suspension of disbelief. Perhaps willingly, perhaps because he was under the influence of chip-less mind control. "I believe in the State of Israel as well. No one stole my family."

"Well, *Norway* stole mine. I was living there, and people from the government came one day, to see my wife."

"*Pfft.* Don't get me started on *the government*, man. Bunch of fucking terrorists."

"They said to her either she has to divorce me, or they would take our kids away from us."

Larry shook his head. "Why would they say that?"

"Because I support the State of Israel!"

"You can't force someone to get divorced like that."

You know you've fallen quite far down the well of logic when Conspiracy Larry refuses to bail you out.

"Are you calling me a liar?" Mr Israel Tie said, standing up from his chair.

"No, man. Sit down. I'm just wondering if there's a bit more to it, to make the Norwegian government deport you?"

"Because I'm a supporter of the Jewish state!" he repeated, as if this really did clear everything up.

Larry leant back in his chair. "Obviously it's a sad story and I hope you get your kids back, but it just sounds... I don't know, a bit far-fetched to me."

Mr Israel Tie flinched. "Well I'm here, aren't I. They kicked me out of the country."

"Are you Norwegian?"

"Yes, I have a Norwegian passport."

"This doesn't make any sense. They can't kick you out of your country. Even the government wouldn't do that."

This is the point where a normal person might have gotten angry, but Mr Israel Tie had simply reached the end of his tape, and so looped back to the start. "I have to go call the embassy," he said, shuffling off downstairs.

"Crackpot," quipped Larry, after Mr Israel Tie was out of hearing range. He turned to me. I may have been listening in a little bit too zealously. "Can you believe that guy?" he said. "Some people, right?"

I nodded, although actually I had no problem believing Mr Israel Tie. I also believed Larry, the Gatherers, the trainee rabbis, and the Orthodox Jews rocking out at the Wailing Wall. Not *in* their stories and beliefs, but that their stories and beliefs made perfect sense to them.

Because I felt it too. This... hole.

This *what's the point of this* hole.

This *none of this makes any sense* hole.

It's perfectly normal and rational to try to find something to fill that hole. Wasn't it why I was sitting there in the first place, in a random hostel, in a random country, surrounded by strangers? Whether it's with work, religion, drugs, hedonism, model trains, love, friendship, sex (see hedonism), or travelling to weird places (my latest drug of choice), we're all looking for something to fill that hole. It's very possible that if you meet the wrong people, or read the wrong book, or have a harrowing experience on the way, you can get very lost and end up joining ISIS, drinking spiked Kool-Aid with Jim Jones, or attending an Elton John concert. The mind is a fragile thing; life is its blunt-force trauma.

That said, I did feel a little guilty that we were watching all these people with such fascination when they were clearly lost, confused, ill, or isolated out on life's fringes. "Is it wrong how much we're enjoying this?" I asked Annett, who was furiously thumbing at her Lonely Planet on the nearby sofa.

She paused to consider it. "Disrespectful, you mean?"

"Yep."

"That we're entertained by, rather than respectful of, people of faith?"

"Uh-huh."

She shrugged. "They don't seem all that respectful of us quiet heathens either. We're just happily sitting here not starting any wars, not trying to control any minds, not wearing novelty ties."

"That's true."

She stood up. "Let's think about it over another drink," she said, heading for the bar. "I think happy hour ends soon."

The next day, we joined a special outreach program offered by a nearby synagogue. Usually Orthodox Jews interact with the secular world as little as possible. Judaism doesn't proselytise. It doesn't want new members. Jews are chosen, they don't choose. It's not a buffet. But this particular synagogue did believe in meeting outsiders to explain its way of life.

A middle-aged woman with an aquiline nose sitting under a heavy black shoulder-length wig met us in the hostel's lobby. Getty had been born in America but moved to Israel in her early twenties and was now a practising Orthodox Jew with a large family of her own. It's quite a weird thing to be in the presence of someone who thinks human life is only six thousand years old, which was one of her opening lines.

"Do you believe that in the literal or symbolic sense?" asked Julius, an Austrian theology teacher who was part of our group of six. He was in Israel doing Christian missionary work. I hoped it didn't involve handing out school textbooks.

"The literal," Getty replied. "We Jews can trace our lineage all the way back to Adam and Eve. At home I have a family tree showing that my family are direct descendants of King David."

The group shuffled nervously. People looked at their shoes. Someone coughed. This was a brave woman, coming out every week to meet people like us, to tell us things we'd think were ridiculous, all in a noble attempt to convince us they weren't.

She walked us around an Orthodox Jewish neighbourhood, took us to a synagogue so that we could see a Torah, then on to a Jewish bakery, a yeshiva, and finally a kind of Orthodox department store stocked full of all your daily, devout needs. I was surprised to discover the marketers of these products used similar techniques to that of the secular world. One prayer shawl had the snazzy tag line "The prayer shawl you've been praying for." There were prayer books in multiple colours. I pulled out a hot pink one. "Well, women have to pray too, right?" she said, blushing, ironically near a book entitled *Doesn't Anyone Blush Anymore?*

The tour ended at her home. An American called Andrew, on his first-ever trip abroad, looked towards the ceiling and said, "What's that?"

Getty followed his eyeline. "The curve of the roof?"

"No, that." He pointed.

"The design of the tile?"

"No, that object."

"That's... an air conditioner."

It was just a standard rectangular air conditioner.

"No way, really?" At this moment, we learned Andrew still blushed, too.

"You've never seen an air conditioner before?" Getty asked.

"Not one that looks like that."

"It has a heater function as well..."

"You're kidding me! Really? Man, I'm so out of my depth. I don't even know how to get hot water out of the shower at the hostel. I'm pretty sure I'm supposed to twist something but it's always cold. Then the toilet, I couldn't find the flush. There's just these two buttons. I was standing there like an idiot, afraid to press them. Why do you need two buttons?"

"For big business and small business," Julius's wife Sarah replied.

"Wow," said Andrew, exhaling in wonder. "That's the future. We've got nothing like that in America."

This felt like another perfect, surreal Jerusalem moment. Sitting in the home of a woman who believes human life is six thousand years old, that God has a plan for us all, that all Arabs have jihad on their minds, and that the Messianic Age is coming and with it we'll have peace on earth. On the surface, everyone in the room shared a language, used the same words—yet in reality, we were irreconcilably far apart in our backgrounds, experiences, and understanding of what those words meant. We were all Andrew, looking at other cultures' air conditioners, showers, and two-button toilets, bamboozled.

As Annett and I walked back to the hostel planning to fully avail ourselves of the last of its happy hour, I was feeling pretty good about myself. We'd had a really interesting few days full of extraordinary people and beliefs. The novelty in Israel didn't stop at ties. The slight skip in my step was the satisfaction I felt at having reached adulthood, broadly rational, mentally functional, with a girlfriend I could more than tolerate. I could enjoy these people and their wacky beliefs comfortable in my certainty that I wasn't one of them. I felt a little smug about that, and not paying attention to the street, I walked across two interconnected drains, swerving just in time to avoid the third.

Annett stopped abruptly. "What was that?"

"What was what?"

"Why did you swerve like that?"

I pointed back at the drains. "I nearly walked over three drains."

She looked down at the drains, back up at me, then back at the drains again. It was a hostile, wordless interrogation. She waited for me to explain myself. I felt I already had, and so waited for her to do the same. Couples spend a lot of time in such conversational deadlocks, waiting for the other to say something. A problem solved quickly in our relationship by Annett's compulsion to share every thought in her head, the second it arrives.

"What's wrong with crossing three drains?"

"Crossing three drains is bad luck, obviously. Everyone knows that."

She did a double take. "Why in the name of what the hell would it be bad luck?"

"You've never seen me avoiding three drains?"

"No! What happens if you cross them?"

I fingered my collar. "BAD THINGS."

She rolled her eyes. "This is absurd. You're just doing this to annoy me, right?" Annett was convinced that everything I did was designed deliberately to irritate her. As if it was my only joy in life (in reality, it was just my biggest).

She grabbed me by the arm and attempted to pull me back across the three rectangular harbingers of doom, unaware she was goading the wrath of the entire known universe.

"NO!" I shouted, as we began an impromptu street-wrestling match.

I managed to wriggle free. She walked forwards and backwards across the drains.

"You shouldn't do that."

She kept doing that, adopting increasing outlandish walking styles as she paraded back and forth atop the trio of drains. A flagrant expression of cosmic defiance that looked like something out of Monty Python's "Ministry of Silly Walks." She seemed desperate to unleash damnation and destruction upon herself. I had to cover my eyes.

"You're inviting some seriously bad juju onto yourself."

"Oh no!" she shouted. "Shit! I better stop..."

She didn't stop. Instead, she attempted a moonwalk. Yes, a moonwalk. The heresy. "I really don't want the God of Three Drains to smite me. Scary!"

I grabbed her arm and tried to pull her off the drains and towards safety. People were staring at us.

"You understand how irrational you're being, right?" she said. I'd been playing the three drains game ever since I was a kid. I'd never really thought about it. I suddenly felt less smug about myself. I guess we all have our own irreconcilable beliefs. Mine seemed harmless enough. We continued walking, in silence. It didn't last long. Annett broke it, as always.

7

HEBRON, PALESTINE: "I DON'T NEED SEX, THE GOVERNMENT FUCKS ME EVERY DAY."

Dual narratives, hidden atheism, the blame game

We hadn't planned on visiting Palestine during our Israel trip. However, after I arrived in Tel Aviv, my inbox was kind enough to inform me I had a missive from a heavily bearded man called Anwar. Anwar was a Couchsurfing member and lived on the Palestinian side of Hebron. He was offering to host us at his house in an adult-sleep-over type arrangement. This was nice, and unexpected. We mostly used Couchsurfing for its meetups because being really, really old, I have a back that gets angry when I sleep on anything but the finest Egyptian cottons. It's also rare for people on Couchsurfing to proactively offer to host you—usually you have to badger them with bribes of cheesecake and promises to do all the washing up. Possibly Anwar was having trouble attracting would-be sofa sleepers because of where he lived. Hebron was intense. Since 1995 it has been divided into two parts: H2, "supervised" by Israel, and H1, "belonging" to Palestine. Everything political here is a question of perspective.

We asked our Airbnb host Adam about the idea of dropping by to see Anwar, our new friend/Internet stranger. While he'd forcefully warned us against visiting Jerusalem, he didn't even dignify the

Hebron question with a response. He merely laughed and continued to clean his kitchen. We might as well have been suggesting strapping ourselves to a rocket and firing ourselves at his now gleaming fridge-freezer. Oded proved similarly doubtful. But that was a state he reserved for almost everything, including existence itself.

On the other hand—specifically, my hand—I kind of liked the idea of visiting Anwar. Since we'd arrived in Israel, everyone had been trying to convince us that the Muslims on the other side of the border were all knife-wielding jihadists bent on the destruction of Israel. Here was a chance to prove these people wrong. Palestinians are people you hear a lot about but rarely meet because they aren't free to travel. Now that we were nearby and being offered a chance to get to know one of them, it felt wrong not to at least entertain that possibility. The risks? Well, yeah, but there were always risks, right? Coming to Israel had already been a risk. What was a bit more risk? Or so I told myself. I was getting good at convincing myself I was a fearless traveller. Sofa Me of Berlin was long gone. I was a little embarrassed by him. Not that I'd become suddenly brave; merely increasingly, willingly, risk blind. Annett was less keen on the Anwar plan, however. "They have no problem with foreigners," I said, as we climbed into bed that night. "Their fight is with the Israelis. They'll be happy to have someone visit them and show an interest in the conflict."

She chewed her top lip. "Pretty words, but you've not done any actual research. You're just assuming everything will be fine, *as per usual.*"

"Okay, maybe," I confessed. "But everything has always been fine, right?"

"Yeah. But that's what everyone says until the thing that *isn't* fine."

I squished my head back into the pillow. "What do they say then? *Almost* everything has always been fine?"

Her voice lowered. "No, they can't say anything. Because they're dead."

We slept on it a night. Not the bed, the decision. Well, both really. The next morning over breakfast, looking up from the generous quantities of cream cheese she was spreading onto brown bread, she said, "I feel like you're just doing this stuff to write about it later."

I tried to find a way of not admitting this. Then I tried to find a way of not admitting that I couldn't find a way of not admitting this. "Well... there might be some truth to that," I admitted, albeit reluctantly. Not that I did much writing. I was the sort of writer who talked about writing much more than getting around to doing any of it. Like an armchair sports fan, I preferred to cheer literature on from the safety of the sidelines, where I didn't have to get myself sentence sweaty.

"I don't want to take silly risks so you can try to convince people you're some sort of adventure traveller," she continued. "You're not."

"I know," I said, munching on a mouthful of banana. "Yet, the more of this sort of travelling we do, the more I like it. I don't want to stop."

She sighed. A sure sign her defences were lowering.

Once we reached Jerusalem, we saw that the kind people of the Abraham ~~Asylum~~ Hostel were offering something called a Dual Narrative Tour of Hebron. On the tour, we'd spend the morning being led by an Israeli rabbi. Then for the second half, we'd cross into the Palestinian part of the city and hear from a local student there. The tour would be the perfect opportunity to visit Anwar. At the end of it, equipped with our new dual narratives, we'd not go back with the other (sensible) people, and instead spend a night or two with Anwar, or go explore some other cities in Palestine and make some new narratives of our own.

Annett agreed to the tour but refused to commit to visiting Anwar, saying that decision could wait until the last possible moment.

At 8am, on a Wednesday morning, we found ourselves seated in the hostel lobby. I was yawning about once per minute; mornings and I had long stopped talking, like siblings in a bitter inheritance feud. It was very quiet in the lobby. All the "touched" people who had been entertaining us so brilliantly thus far were still asleep. It was just us and the eight other risk-blind tourists willing to plunge themselves into the uncertainty of Hebron.

Our guide blew into the room fifteen minutes late, looking as if he'd been pulled through a hedge but didn't know by whom. His name was Elijah. He was about forty years old, portly, and wore a white yarmulke. Traditional curly sidelocks (*peyot*) framed his round face. Around his neck was a crumpled prayer shawl—perhaps the one he'd been praying for.

We took public bus #160 to Hebron. The bus was just like any other bus, other than the fact the driver carried a revolver on his hip, and that all its windows were bulletproof. Elijah sat just in front of us, and gave the group a crash course in Hebron's troubled history. "Funnily enough," he began, "*Hebron* actually means 'to connect' in Hebrew. Did you know that?" He smirked. "There's a certain irony there, of course."

Two police cars, their sirens wailing, overtook the bus. We all turned to look, except Elijah, who acknowledged their existence in the same way an elephant might a mosquito. "Yes. There will probably be a lot more of that, everyone. Don't be concerned. Hebron is really a microcosm of the whole Israel-Palestine conflict. You can learn more in one day in Hebron than in one year in a university." He then told us about Hebron University, which of course begged the question: *How much can you learn in one day in a university in Hebron?* A lot, most likely. Although probably still not enough to understand how the city had ended up in such a precarious state.

"A brief word about what you're going to see." He raised his voice so the people a few seats back could hear. "It is quite shocking. Not to unnerve you. Just to prepare you. It's probably quite unlike anything you've seen before. I know, also, that there's a lot of people out there in the media making out that every Jew in Hebron is a colonialist. That *we're* the bad guys."

His eyebrows lurched towards his forehead at the sheer absurdity of this notion. "Actually *we're* indigenous to Hebron. The problem is that there are too few of us left now. Those who remain, and *settler* is the wrong word for them... well... they need protection, so, at present,

Hebron does sort of resemble, security-wise, a European colonial outpost you might find in India or Africa."

The group traded nervous glances, brows furrowing into maybe-this-has-all-been-a-big-mistake creases. The nearer we got to the city, the more the security presence spiked. We crossed several military checkpoints. Sitting like urban birds' nests on the roofs of seemingly abandoned houses were numerous lookout towers. The only vehicle that passed us during the final minutes of the journey was an armoured van. It felt like we'd entered a forsaken city. But that wasn't the weirdest part. The weirdest part was seeing the Israeli flags everywhere; textile trophies of sovereignty flapping down from rooftops, out of barred windows, and draped down from lamp posts.

Looking at them, I was struck by how prone to overcompensation humans are. The more tenuous our right to power, the more stupendous the title we give ourselves to try to obfuscate that. The less safe we feel in our throne, the more bombastic the crown we cast upon our head.

We stepped down from the bus onto King David road. The only people on it were soldiers. Some sat on nearby roofs, others guarded a checkpoint. Elijah called it "the centre of the centre of the conflict." At one end, behind a checkpoint, was Palestinian Hebron. The other end, where we stood, amongst all the flags, and abandoned buildings, and bullet holes, and silence, was Israeli Hebron.

"This street is known as Apartheid Street. I guess I don't need to explain why," Elijah said, ushering us to put down our cameras and hurry along. "There might be clashes here later. We won't linger too long."

"Oh, don't worry," he said, sensing both his mistake and our apprehension. "It's just part of daily life here. There are always small skirmishes. After all, there's no bowling alleys, no bars, no clubs in Hebron. So what are the Palestinian youth going to do for fun? Well, come over here and throw some rocks at Israeli soldiers, that's what. It's a rite of passage for them. If you get arrested? Even better, more respect."

Previously, Palestinians had been allowed to walk across a small part of this road to get to a nearby school and the border to the main Palestinian part of the city. However, last week, a seventeen-year-old had come down some steps, pulled a knife, and tried to stab an Israeli soldier. The Palestinian media questioned whether he'd really had a knife, or whether one had been placed on him later. Elijah stood on the bottom of that staircase and recreated the incident for us.

"The guy, he comes down here," he said, hopping theatrically off the bottom step. He seemed in little doubt of what had happened. "He's probably on drugs, and then he takes one, two, three steps and pulls out the knife." He mimicked this action, holding out an invisible blade. Just two metres away, three soldiers watched on. Elijah thrust his invisible weapon in their direction. This didn't seem wise. He approached the soldier nearest to us. This soldier was a handsome young man with olive skin and high, wide cheekbones. He couldn't be older than twenty-two, and so a veteran by Israeli Defense Force standards. "It happened like that, right?" he asked the soldier. "I'm telling them about the attack here last week."

The soldier stood erect, chest out, chin high, like a flag made human. His face was chiselled and a little ruddy from the sun. A machine gun rested idly across his chest like a dozing lover. He looked at Elijah, but also beyond him and up the staircase into the hills, where there was a small smattering of Palestinian houses.

"It was similar to that, yes. I wasn't here, so I can't speak to the specifics." Bizarrely he had a perfect English accent, a southern accent very like my own, in fact. His r's were flat but his th's morphed into f's. "The guy who killed the terrorist, he was a good friend of mine. A really good friend. Honestly speaking, I fink it's really messed him up. Doing somefing like that, well..." He sighed. "It's not somefing we do lightly. No matter what you might hear in the media, or the Palestinians might say about us. We're not like that."

The soldier was called Gideon. He'd lived in England until he was twelve. Then his parents decided to make aliyah, and returned to Israel. The rest of his youth he'd spent here, and he was now finishing his mandatory military service.

"We don't want to 'urt anyone, not at all," he continued. "That's the last fing we want. There are protocols. Only if they freaten our lives in some way can we shoot to kill. Those who do attack us, they're usually on something. To hurt another human, knowing they'll be killed after—usually they have to take somefing first. The ones I've seen, anyway, they're not in control at that point."

In the distance came the sound of whistling and chanting. "Attacks might be about to start," said Elijah, stoking the fire of our anxieties. Gideon turned to the two other soldiers in his company. One threw down his cigarette. They moved slightly closer together but still appeared placid, as if this were just a normal part of their job. Time for the weekly team meeting. Soldier 3's turn to prepare tea and biscuits.

Elijah nudged us further up the road. We would have been just fine with that, were we not moving *towards* the sound of the protests. Instinctively we huddled a little closer together as well, and nearer to Elijah, our senses heightened. Cameras disappeared back into pockets. Very few selfies were taken. That was nice. A hundred metres from Gideon we reached Tarpat Junction, another of the border crossings into the Palestinian side. One of the soldiers guarding it strode out towards us.

"Are you with us or against us?" he asked Elijah. That's how simple it was here. *For* or *against*. Black or white. We heard a helicopter buzz overhead, and with it, the noise of the protesters increased.

"With you," Elijah answered.

We quickened our pace and headed up into the hills as the Muslim call to prayer sounded from a nearby minaret. Usually I found it beautiful, but at this moment it felt more like an incitement.

Once we'd reached the safety of the hills, and were just starting to relax, Elijah informed us that "after the Temple Mount, the hilltops of Hebron are probably the most contentious place in the whole country."

Thanks, thanks a lot, Elijah. He then showed us a small ongoing archaeological excavation which he said proved there was once an ancient Jewish city of Hebron here. "I even sneaked a Palestinian into this tour once and showed him this," he said, holding up some kind of rock. "But he wouldn't accept it. He said it must be fake, placed here by Israeli archaeologists." Elijah sighed. "I guess he just couldn't look past his own biases."

I didn't get the feeling Elijah could either. Not that any of us can. We're lucky if we can even identify what they are. Elijah alternated between being really quite nice and really quite irritating, depending on the conviction he had in whatever he was saying at any particular moment. I liked him when he was uncertain. Certainty he wore less well. Especially when that certainty was about Israel and its right to do things that seemed to me, with my pre-existing narratives, *questionable*.

"We have to get past the blame game," he added, moving this small rock back and forth in his hands before returning it respectfully to the ground.

We then visited the (alleged) tomb of Jesse and Ruth. Elijah casually dropped a lot of biblical names, as if we were all dedicated Bible scholars. I couldn't remember who Jesse and Ruth were, most likely because I'd never known. They sounded like a husband and wife breakfast-TV presenter team. I thought about asking but didn't want to look ignorant. Or, more ignorant. One of atheism's strongest selling points is that there's nothing to remember. It's a real boon for the absent-minded.

Elijah played the dog-eared "we were here first" card often. I found it hard not to roll my eyes each time. If you move the needle of history back far enough, aren't we all invaders, all foreigners, all squatting on what was once someone else's land? The first ape's climbing down from the trees was a dick move that condemned hundreds of thousands of other animals to extinction at our hands. Their sacred rights have counted for very little, thus far.

At the checkpoint, I was happy to leave Elijah behind. He was a nice person, and a good guide, but it was time to hear about the conflict from another perspective, even if that perspective turned out to be just as biased as I'd found Elijah's. The security at the crossing was actually far less invasive than that offered by EL AL in Berlin.

After we emptied our pockets, and a soldier took a cursory look inside our bags, we were through to Palestinian Hebron.

On the other side, our Palestinian guide waited with his hands in his pockets. He was a student called Jamal and in his late twenties. He had thick wavy hair brushed back from his face—a face framed by a neat, narrow goatee. He wore blue jeans, a black T-shirt, and a green zip-up hoodie. His movements were careful and precise. He was more soft-spoken than Elijah. The only time he got really animated was when he talked about his trips abroad. As a peace activist, he'd been invited to visit the UK, Switzerland, the USA, and France to give talks for UNESCO and the UN about the conflict. He'd just returned from six months in the UK. "It was shocking to return. I told my parents that I wanted to go back to the UK and have a normal life. But they said no," he said, then frowned. "Well, in the Middle East, you can't say anything against your parents, so, I'm still here..."

The streets on the other side of the barrier were just as devoid of life as those on the Israeli side. A few people passed on their way to the mosque. No one lingered. We stopped for lunch at a local family's home, just a couple of hundred metres from the border. The group was still on edge as we tore enthusiastically into a distracting, delicious lunch of lamb, hummus, vegetables, and flatbread. Since I come from England, a country with really disappointing cuisine, one of my favourite things about travelling, and globalisation in general, is how rarely I now have to eat British food. After lunch we walked through what was once Hebron's central market, which abutted the border. The single-storey market was flanked by higher buildings on the Israeli side of the city. This means that if they wanted, Israeli settlers could throw things down from their windows onto the Palestinians.

Jamal informed us that some of the Israeli settlers really did want to do this, and regularly threw trash, rocks, acid, and even their own waste at the Palestinians. It was an awful situation of utter cruelty. To stop this, the Palestinians had erected their own mesh roof the length of the market to try to protect themselves. You could see evidence of home-made missiles scattered atop it.

Because of its location, and the loss of almost all tourism, just four or five brave stall owners still came and opened up their wood-fronted shops cut into rock, reminiscent of Jerusalem's old city. There used to be hundreds.

"Just two weeks ago," said Jamal, as we walked through the market, "I was doing this tour, and a young Palestinian girl was murdered right in front of the group, at the checkpoint we just passed. We were all in shock. We didn't say anything to each other for the rest of the tour. The checkpoints here are crazy. You have no idea what's going to happen to you. It depends on the mood of the person. As long as they say you had a knife, they can do what they want with you. I believe they planted it on her."

A female judge in the popular American TV show *The Good Wife* always requires the lawyers to strictly demarcate opinion from fact. If they don't, she adds, "In your opinion" and "You believe" to the things they say. Hearing Jamal say "I believe" reminded me of how rarely we'd heard such softeners since arriving in Israel. His trustworthiness skyrocketed. Maybe it was okay that I was suddenly so uncertain about everything in my life. Perhaps uncertainty is a good trait, in line with the complexity of the world in which we live.

Jamal then took us to visit a Palestinian family's home for tea. As we sat on cushions in the living room, their young son played at our feet. Jamal told us their story. "Eleven generations of this family have lived here, in this house. The neighbours on the one side are Israeli settlers, and now they're locked in a bitter feud with them. The man offered them four million dollars to leave so he could extend his house into this one."

Sipping our tea, looking at the crumbling plaster of the bare, cracked walls, it seemed implausible. Jamal had already told us that a wage of a thousand shekels a month was good in Hebron. It would take very strong principles not to sell this home for four million dollars. I tried to imagine what it might be like to have such princi-ples, or really any principles at all. It was difficult. I felt like an otter asked to split the atom. Fortunately, Jamal distracted me with another story. Unfortunately, it was even more harrowing than all the others.

"This is actually his second wife," he said, gesturing to the woman sitting with us. She sat wide-legged on a blue computer chair. "His first wife was nine months pregnant when she went up to the top floor of the house to get something. The neighbour shot her five times. She died almost instantly. They were able to save the unborn child."

All eyes dropped to the cute little kid rolling around on the floor in the centre of the room. He sat up on his knees, perhaps detecting he now had our full attention. "No. It's not him," Jamal said, leaning forward to ruffle his hair. "That child is eleven or twelve now."

"Where is he?" a Canadian woman asked.

"That's also a sad story," he said, lowering his head. "Usually they made him stay inside, right, so he'd be safe. But then, one time, when he was five or six, he was playing outside on the street. The settlers from next door threw acid at him and blinded him. He was sent away to a special centre for the blind."

The group sat silently, our patience frayed by the insanity of this place. The stupidity of it. The ugliness of it. What can you say about something like this? The woman dabbed quietly at a tear on her cheek. Jamal tried to brush off the sadness that had befallen the room. "Oh, come on. I can tell you many stories like this," he said, jovially. "Everyone here has these stories. We live them every day."

We'd reached the end of the tour. "So..." Jamal said, as our tiny glass teacups were collected, "you've heard from both sides. I'm interested to know your opinions. What do you think the solution might be? One state or two?" He asked this nonchalantly, as if we were discussing the best way to mend a broken chair. About half of us said one state; the rest, two. I was for two. Someone asked Jamal his opinion. "One state is completely possible," he replied, without hesitation, "but this is the dream solution. The realistic solution is two states, protected by the UN. I don't think we really care about land any more. We just want to live freely. There *is* already a two-state solution. Already recognised by the UN, even. But will Israel let us have it? No."

We put on our shoes and walked down the stairs and back out

into the market. "The truth is that war is useful to governments. In wartime, all the attention is on that and not on the government. Corruption is easiest during wartime. In reality, the people in power don't want a solution, because they are the ones benefiting from war. We Palestinians *need* peace, the Israelis merely *ask for it*. That's a big difference. That's why it never happens."

In his opinion.

At the border we said our goodbyes, and the group passed back through. I looked to Annett. "I'm going to stay," I said.

She chewed the inside of her cheek. "Do you definitely know how to get to Anwar's?"

"Yeah, he gave me instructions. I'll take a cab."

Annett looked to the gate, then back at me. Then to the gate, then back at me. "Okay, I'm coming as well," she said, "but if something happens to me, know that I'm going to haunt your soul in the after-life, forever. You will not get one minute of peace from me. It'll be a constant stream of 'I told you so' for all eternity."

Jamal squeezed my shoulder in condolence. Annett and I never had to worry whether we were soulmates, since neither of us believed in souls. Similarly, it's hard to curse someone in an afterlife you know neither of you believe in. I gave her points for effort.

By now, the group had worked out that we weren't going back with them. I told them, through the gate, about Anwar's kind offer. One or two reacted with something like jealousy; the others seemed to think this was an idiotic idea. A weird thing was happening. Every-where we went, people told us not to go to the next place because it wasn't safe. Then we went to that place, and it was fine, but the people there gave us the same warnings about the next place, and so on, possibly forever, across all of the Earth.

We said a final goodbye through the railings, turned, and headed back towards the dusking market. The remaining few shops were closing up for the night. We headed towards the new city centre, and the bustling market that had replaced this dejected one. We heard chanting and shouting. Jamal flagged down a taxi for us. Some tyres were on fire nearby, the remnants of a recent skirmish. A smell of tear gas hung in the air. We knew that smell now. It was not welcome.

Away from the border, Palestinian Hebron is a functional, albeit chaotic, city. So chaotic it hasn't gotten around to introducing simple things like street names and house numbers just yet. Anwar's instructions were that we should follow an ominous white wall from the edge of the university compound, keeping it on our left-hand side, until we reached a bakery with a purple sign, next to a shoe shop with a black sign. So, when I'd told Annett that I did definitely know how to get to Anwar's, that was technically true in the slippery, wet-soap definition of *truth*. Conspiracy Larry's definition. I knew we had to find that wall. What I wasn't sure about was if we'd know *when* we'd found that wall. That part I'd left out. Quite a risk what with eternal damnation at stake.

In Arabic, Jamal relayed Anwar's instructions to the taxi driver. He did so as if they made perfect sense, which they might well have. Perhaps they regularly used walls as landmarks here. We climbed into the back of the taxi. The ride took about ten minutes, with other passengers getting in and out as we went. Taxis here were communal; you paid a set fare of 2.5 shekels per seat. People would wave the taxi down, say where they wanted to go, and the driver would either nod and stop or shake his head before driving off.

After five minutes, the taxi drew to a halt. The driver looked at me in the rear-view mirror. I made what I hoped was a *we're here?* expression, but his eyebrows dropped in incomprehension. Since I didn't speak Arabic and he didn't speak English, we were at an impasse. I repeated my facial expression. He repeated his. We got out. What else could we do? We shared no languages, not even Face.

We found ourselves on the right-hand side of a busy four-lane road. There were some walls nearby, which was nice, since they're useful for holding up roofs and whatnot. We compared these walls against the description offered by Anwar. None of them seemed like the wall we were looking for. I tried to call him, but he didn't answer. I sent an SMS, which also went unanswered. So we picked a direction using Total Guesswork™.

Annett stomped two steps behind me. She had expected Annett-level planning. I'd responded with Adam-level planning. We didn't talk much. It was dark. We were lost. We passed several shoe shops and bakeries.

"This is classic you."

I was busy looking at a shoe-shop sign, trying to convince myself its blue was really more of an ocean black. "You like classic me though, right? You spend a lot of time with that me. Or helping that me not get run over."

She cocked her head. "Yeah, but aren't you trying to change? Isn't that part of why we're here?" I threw my hands up in the air. We walked a few more laboured steps down the road towards an intersection. I stopped and turned to her. "And I am changing! Not this part of myself, maybe, but other parts."

She let out a heavy sigh. "Well, do you think you can prioritise change in the parts that don't respect my time, plans, or need for a heightened state of organisation?"

My phone beeped. *Anwar.* I let out a long breath. How had people travelled before phones? It's a wonder anyone has ever dared get far enough away from others to become lost, and that humanity doesn't just live in a big herd, like buffalo. Anwar was asking where we were. We told him we didn't know, that this was really the crux of the issue.

What about the wall?

Yeah, what about the wall, Anwar? There were so many walls. We sent him the name of some nearby shops. He told us to stay put. We stayed put. We sat on a wall. A small wall. It wasn't white.

A few minutes later, a lanky man with a long beard approached, held out his hand, and knew our names. "You made it!" he said, hugging us both. He seemed really genuinely happy about this.

"Did we?" I asked. "Are we anywhere near your place?"

"Sure. You didn't see the wall?"

We'd seen a lot of walls. This land was defined by walls.

He bounced from foot to foot. "I can't believe you're here," he said. "That's so great." His enthusiasm was a bit disconcerting. He was supposed to be reassuring us that what we were doing was spectacularly ordinary. We walked, relieved and light-footed, back down the road to his apartment. "How often do you host Couchsurfers, Anwar?"

He stopped and scratched his cheek. Something about his face shape reminded me of a piece of a toast. "I've had maybe four hundred over the years. Now it's more like one a month. And that's with me accepting every request. It's too much trouble now, I guess. You're brave, braver than most." Annett grimaced in a way that suggested maybe we were actually *stupid, stupider than most*. We found the shoe shop. We found the bakery. We found the white wall. It was simple, all so simple. Not as simple as having street names and house numbers, though. Behind the bakery, as promised, or at least strongly rumoured, was Anwar's building. The first thing we noticed upon entering his modest two-bedroom apartment was that previous guests had written on nearly every bit of wall space. Hostel Anwar put its guestbook directly onto its surfaces. "I don't need sex, the government fucks me every day" and "Think big, talk low, act loud!!!" were just a couple of the highlights. A guitar hung with them. I scanned instinctively for a picture of Bob Marley.

We opened the gin we'd brought with us. Anwar's eyes lit up, like only the eyes of a reggae-loving, alcohol enthusiast stuck in a dry city would. He quickly made up for lost time. I've noticed that people who are often in the company of strangers develop an ability to make those strangers forget that they are, in fact, strangers. It looks effort-less, which is how everything complicated and requiring a huge amount of practice always looks. Anwar was good at it. Still, despite his warm, easy-going nature, there was a certain sadness hanging over him. He told us about a conversation he'd had on the phone that day, with his father. "Oh man. It was the usual shit," he said, swigging enthusiastically from his gin tonic. 'You should get married. Why are you not married yet? Why can't you just be like everyone else? *People are talking about you...*'" He sighed. "Just that sentence: 'People are talking about you.' That tells you everything you need to know about Arabic culture, man. Fuck, people will do anything not to stand out here."

"I'm sorry," I said, with no idea why *I* was apologising. It didn't seem to be my fault, yet. Annett poured more drinks. Anwar sighed. "So I said to him, Father, I'm happy. I like my life." I raised my glass. We toasted. "Do you know what he said? 'This way you'll be even happier!' Can you believe that?"

We couldn't.

Anwar took another sip. "Crazy, man. Living here, it's like I always need to have my guard up. I don't fit in. I consider myself atheist, right? Well, agnostic, maybe. Anyway, can I tell people that here? No chance." He scoffed. "I'd get attacked. And that's why I need to have Couchsurfers around. I can't be open with anyone else."

The more we drank, the more Anwar acquainted us with his strong beliefs. I tried to not judge him for them, since I had no idea what he'd suffered to generate them. There are certainly facets of English culture that irritate me—it's part of why I left—but they're trivial compared to having to hide your agnosticism, or to being told people are talking about you because you dared to remain unmarried into your thirties.

"The occupation is a punishment for the way we are," he said, as we were two-and-a-half gins in. A gin is the same unit of time as a wine, which is three-quarters of a beer. "There are consequences for everything," he continued. "We are not organised. We might be four million, but we're not united. We fight amongst ourselves, man. All the time. If we can't free our minds, how do we expect to free our lands? I'd rather be anything else, even Jewish. Look at them... They're a small group, right? Yet they pretty much run the world. They work hard."

He put some dance music on, and some more gins passed. "I don't want to be depressing," he said, "just real with you. It's real here, I'm living it. I can't drink, can't date a girl. But at the same time, I don't want to waste my life, you know? This is not an enlightened place yet, and that's hard to fix with religion in the way. Just a week ago, two German women came to visit. We were walking around in the old town. They were speaking German with each other and a car pulled up. The driver lowered his window, spat at them, and said, 'Fuck you,

you stupid Nazis.' It was heartbreaking. I cried with them. I simply couldn't believe it. People willing to come here and see what our lives are like. People who want to experience our culture, and what do we show them? We spit at them and blame them for the mistakes of their ancestors. It's like being in jail here, man. Couchsurfing is my window."

We stayed in that night. Anwar was insistent that after dark there was absolutely nothing to do in Hebron. The next morning, he left early for work. We let ourselves out, leaving no evidence on the walls that we'd ever been there. It was hard to top "Make hummus not walls."

Getting a taxi back to Jerusalem was simple enough. We asked people where the bus station was; they kept pointing us in different (contradictory) directions until eventually we ended up in front of a man sitting on the bonnet of a recently white car. A car with Israeli licence plates.

"Jerusalem?" the man asked.

"Yes," we replied.

The price was stated. We agreed, and climbed inside. He shook his head, and called us back out again. "Two more people," he said. He *was* the bus, but the bus was a car, but the car must be full, but we were only two. It was Ghana, again.

The first hour passed quite quickly. An elderly lady hobbled into view, and agreed to take one of the last two spots. She waited inside the car while we stood out in the sun sharing biscuits with the man and some of his friends. The next thirty minutes dragged, and not only because we'd run out of biscuits. Finally we caved and bought the last place for ourselves, just so we could leave. It cost five euros.

Once we were on the road, it became clear that our driver was both a biscuit and a speed enthusiast. After twenty minutes, we'd reached the border. The car grew suddenly tense. "Do you have problems at the border?" I asked the bus driver of the car.

"Problems?" he said, turning and looking at me for far longer than necessary and recommendable while driving a car-bus. "No, no problems."

At the border, a friendly man, with a large gun, leaned into the window to collect our passports and IDs. He'd just need to press a little lever on that gun and we'd all be dead. This seemed remarkable and wrong and yet he was totally blasé about the whole thing.

Then a discussion that we didn't understand took place. The armed man looked through the passports again. We expected questioning. Why had we been in Palestine? Were we "for or against them?"

The soldier pointed to a nearby parking spot. The driver parked there. The hairs on my neck stood to attention. Two new and equally lethally equipped soldiers approached. But their eyes and suspicions lingered not on us, but on the old lady in the back, next to Annett. The soldier held her ID up, so that he could see both it and her at the same time. He called the other soldier over, and he did the same. Heads were shaken. Chins were scratched. They began to question her. She seemed to be failing the interview. Our driver intervened on her behalf, pleading her case. The soldier wagged his finger at him. He talked to his partner some more, then came back to the window, said something to the elderly lady, and, finally, waved us through. Just as soon as we'd cleared the border, the driver and the woman began laughing.

"What happened?" I asked. "You said no problems?"

The man couldn't talk, he was laughing too hard. That didn't slow him down though. The little white car rattled and groaned as we gained speed. Eventually, he'd recovered enough composure to talk. "Normally no problem, but the..." He pointed at the woman in the back seat, next to Annett.

"Lady?" I offered.

"*Lady*, yes. Lady ID not good."

"What's wrong with it?"

The old lady handed it across to me in the front seat. On it was the image of a young woman. An attractive one, at that. It couldn't be, could it? I looked back at her. *No way.* I checked it again. Could it? *Maybe...* The eyes were somewhat similar. She pointed at a date on the ID. The expiry date. The ID had expired in 1985!

Now I got the joke.

But that wasn't the end of it. The ID had been issued in 1965! No wonder they'd had such a problem identifying her—she was using a photograph that was fifty years old. "Last time with this ID, the man say," added the driver, as he recklessly overtook a lorry. "Very funny... yes?"

Back in Berlin, when we told people about the trip, they wanted us to give an opinion on the conflict. To come down on a side. Weirdly, I'd actually had a firmer opinion before we went. Having seen it up close, even as quickly and superficially as we had, I was now convinced only of the futility of trying to comprehend it. It was like holding a devoutly religious Rubik's Cube with all of the stickers deliberately torn off. As you picked it up and began trying to align the squares, two tribes of angry people ran out and shouted things at you and fought each other over whose ancestors had the cube first. Throughout the trip we'd met a lot of certain people, yet the Israel-Palestine conflict seemed to be one that could be fixed only with humility and doubt—only by forbidding talk of the past, drawing a line, and starting again. There are two tribes of humans trying to share one patch of land. Both deserve the right to self-governance. One has it, the other doesn't. That has to change.

I believe...

In many ways, Anwar's father had been right; you really don't want to have people talking about you. Throughout human history we've been mostly nice to each other, just as long as no one dares veer from the safety of the masses. We don't do minorities well. Anwar was a minority. Those of us born as majority people will never know how much of a fight it is to live as a minority, not protected by the cushioning of statistics. This is changing, but not everywhere, and not equally. I hoped that one day Anwar would get to live somewhere he could be both expressive and anonymous.

Visiting him reminded me of how incredibly lucky I was to be born a majority, part of the first-world-white-heterosexual-English-speaking-men-of-above-average-height-tribe. It's hard to fail when you've been dealt a hand like that. Intellectually I've always known this, but emotionally I'd stopped feeling it. In my head and heart, I felt it again. For how long I wasn't sure. But I felt it, and it was an upgrade.

8

HARE KRISHNA ASHRAM, ARGENTINA: "IT'S YOU WHO'S RUNNING AWAY FROM THINGS."

Yoga, reincarnation, heartbreak, ants

The bus leaving Buenos Aires got decreasingly crowded as the city's limits were breached. We began shedding passengers, breathing unpolluted air, and seeing things of a green nature. Nature, mostly. Buenos Aires had almost none of it, to its detriment.

An hour later, Annett and I heaved our heavy backpacks on as the bus pulled away spitting exhaust fumes into our faces. We found ourselves under a flyover, on the outskirts of a town called General Rodríguez. I took out the hand-drawn serviette map created for me by two women I'd met in a bar, after they'd told me, very enthusiastically, using an enormous number of positive adjectives, what a wonderful few months they'd just spent in a Hare Krishna camp.

"Serviettes don't make the best maps," I said, as I spun it round looking for anything on it that would pass for north, a flyover, a town, or pretty much any recognisable shape. The more I spun it, the more confused I became about where it was exactly that we were currently lost.

Annett groaned, shielding her eyes from the sun.

"I hope there's a General Rodríguez living here so he can answer the phone 'General Rodríguez of General Rodríguez,'" I said, attempting to distract her from my incompetence.

She sighed and gazed off into the distance. I was getting what is known colloquially as the cold shoulder, only Annett didn't do things by halves; she gave cold shoulders, plural.

I breathed in deeply. "Getting back to nature. Lovely, right?"

She continued wordlessly admiring the horizon. I decided to pretend I knew what I was doing, a technique I used every moment of my life, with limited success.

"It's that way," I lied, striding off confidently towards a field of green. She followed, a few steps behind me. We weren't supposed to be in the town of General Rodríguez. We were supposed to be in Mendoza riding bicycles and drinking wine. It had taken two days of persuasion to get Annett to change the highlighted, laminated itinerary she'd created for us, but I'd managed it. We were going to a Hare Krishna ashram. One of us willingly, even. It was another beautiful day in the southern hemisphere.

"I'm looking forward to a good detox," I said. "Giving up chocolate, wine, and meat. Aren't you?"

She said nothing.

"Earth to Annett."

Reluctantly, she lifted her gaze from the ground and turned to face me. "They're all the things I love in the world, so no, I'm not."

"I know. But sometimes the things you love don't love you back, right? Sometimes you're in an unhealthy, dependent relationship with them, like I am with Ritter Sport Knusperflakes."

Following a small trail along a rocky, unpaved road, we hit a crude white fence. I remembered the girls talking about this fence. Fake confidence had won out again. "It's just up here," I said, with yet more of it. We followed that fence towards a number of modest-looking wooden huts, now visible on the horizon, near a domed structure.

I swatted at the flies buzzing around my face. I was a little underwhelmed. "This looks lovely." Another lie.

"Hmmmh," Annett grunted. A cow stared at us, chewing mechanically. It's fortunate for cows that milk becomes cheese, the most delicious substance on our planet (other than Ritter Sport Knusperflakes). Personality-wise, they are extreme undynamic individuals.

"Look—a real-life cow! Amazing." More lies. "I love cows. Such gentle animals. We're really in nature now, right?"

"Uh-huh."

In the distance, we saw the beautiful white dome of the park's temple, which looked like the top half of an egg that was planted in the ground. It was adorned with mosaic tiles that glistened in the light. By the dome, a few people toiled in a field, bent over in a way that suggested hard labour, the worst kind of labour. "They look like they're having good, clean fun."

"Hmmm."

We opened a small white gate. On the other side of it, a border collie waited for us, wagging its tail. It jumped up, nearly knocking Annett over. Then we followed it under a few overgrown trees, over a muddy bog, across a broken bridge, along a stream, and past several cabins, two of which were on stilts and suspended four metres in the air. We stopped outside a large wooden building in the centre of the camp. A purple sign outside it said *Reception*.

We entered. No one was inside. "I love it," I said to Annett, patting the hard wooden bench as we sat down on it, waiting for the hard labour to end. "A real back-to-basics, lo-fi charm to the place." I didn't love it. But I was open to the idea of potentially loving it one day, once I'd changed my entire personality.

Annett sighed and looked at her feet.

A few minutes later a bald man arrived at the door. He held his head, at all times, five degrees off centre, as if in permanent, albeit mild, contemplation. His face was so blank, so smooth and seemingly unperturbed by the world, it looked as if he'd just got it new from a shop. I'd always associated this advanced earnestness and intense softness with Hare Krishnas. Granted, I was hazy on the specifics of their doctrine, but had often seen them singing and dancing on street corners in different parts of the world. They were basically a band, just like The Beatles, but one that didn't play at recognised venues and restricted themselves to the lyrics "Hare" and "Krishna." I needed a religion that would accommodate my poor memory. The Krishnas seemed like my people. I was still looking for a tribe, still wanting to connect with something bigger than myself. Surely meeting two American women in an Irish bar who had just become Hare Krishnas was more than mere chance? I wasn't sure if Hare Krishnas believed in fate. I wasn't sure I did either. But I had to admit it—if it did exist, and we were allowed to believe in it, this was probably it.

The man collected a clipboard, and he sat down on the wooden bench opposite us.

"Beautiful place you have here," I said.

"*Muchas gracias*," he said. He looked to Annett. She said nothing.

"Volunteers get up at 6:30am. Before the sunrise and heat. Most work in the garden. Don't worry, we'll ring a bell to wake you."

"Wonderful," I lied (again), looking at Annett. "Back to nature. Getting your hands dirty."

"*Sí*," said the man. "*Muchas gracias.*"

Annett leaned forward. "But we don't have to get up then, right? Adam assured me there was a non-manual labour option?"

"*Sí*. Are you sure, though?" he asked. "Sacrifice is a part of the process."

We chuckled.

"Many volunteers find it very rewarding," he added, perhaps in response to those chuckles. Probably not as rewarding as we found a long lie-in—on this point I was sure Annett and I were in agreement, and that didn't happen often. "We're on our annual vacation," Annett clarified. "We get up early all the other times of the year."

The man broke eye contact, lowering his gaze.

"Of course we're disappointed to miss out." The lies kept coming. "I'm sure it's very humbling. People just have so much now, you know? We're losing our connection to nature."

He looked up once more. "How long would you like to stay for?"

"Five days," I said.

"*Three* days," Annett said.

The man told us more about the camp. After four-and-a-half hours of work, the volunteers were free to enjoy their day in the tranquil surroundings. There were two sessions of yoga, and the more spiritually minded were invited to join meditation and chanting sessions in the temple afterwards. In the evenings, we'd all watch a movie together. He stood up. "I'll show you to your accommodation."

We trudged out. It had rained recently, and the compound was now a bog. We squelched our way through it, past the community centre and several other accommodation huts, to the far back of the complex. The man flicked the light switch on the porch of a wooden shack. Nothing happened. "Lovely." I'd lost count of the lies. "Very quaint."

"*Gracias*," said the man. Annett remained mute.

The man opened the door to the hut. Inside were three bedrooms, the second of which was to be ours. He inserted the key, turned it, and pushed the door. It got stuck. He pushed harder. That didn't help. "It's stuck," he said, which we knew, because we had eyes. I helped him lift it, and together we groaned and pushed and it slowly scraped over the uneven wooden floor a few inches until we could slip sideward into the room, after removing our backpacks.

The decor would be best described as frontier-chic. Aside from the bed, the only other thing in the room was one wooden chair in the corner. There wasn't space for the three of us, and the two backpacks, so the man stepped back into the doorway. "Probably best to keep the door open," he said.

"No problem." What was one more lie?

"Yeah, why not," said Annett, sarcastically, dropping her rucksack onto the bottom bunk. The man left.

"Oh God," she said.

"Oh Hari, you mean."

"Fuck you and him." She put her head in her hands. "This is not quite what I had in mind."

"What did you have in mind?" I asked.

She removed her hands and inspected the room. "Fewer ants."

"Suffering is part of the process?" I offered.

"Fuck you and your process."

At this point in our expectations-realignment therapy session, the man reappeared in the doorway. It was awkward. Couples who fought as often as we did really needed working doors to do it behind.

"Everything okay?" he asked.

"Yes," I lied. "We're settling in well."

"*Bueno,*" he said, and gestured with his thumb towards the front door. "I'm locked in. The lock on the front door is broken. You have to be careful, or you get locked in."

He really needed to take his own advice.

We learned the front door could only be opened from the outside. A significant design flaw. It was a shame mosquitoes couldn't open doors, since there were so many of them buzzing threateningly in a cloud just beyond it. We shouted from the window until two women came and let the man out. It turned out they were our neighbours, returning from yoga. They were from Canada, and had planned to stay a month but were now mulling over whether to leave a week early. We stood with them in their room. "It's fine," one of them said. "Totally fine. Lovely, peaceful people. Very little indoctrination. But there's... well... not much to do, you know? Unless you like yoga."

"And the early mornings," added the other, who had the sort of earnest, humble demeanour of someone open to religious indoctrination. She moved to sit on the room's bottom bunk. "Working in the garden *is* surprisingly tiring, and while I like yoga as much as the next person, you can have too much of a good thing. Even yoga."

"And how are you settling in?" she asked, looking up at Annett.

"I hate—"

"Very well, thank you," I said.

"I hate it here," Annett reiterated, as we crossed the compound for dinner, our shoes now caked in mud. The only cake on offer here.

"I think it's very quaint and rustic," I lied. "These people are focused on their religion. They don't need trappings like working doors and toilet seats that don't fall off when you sit on them. It's going to be very relaxing once we get used to it."

The dinner was fantastic. I didn't even have to lie about that, although I'd been more than prepared to. The quality of the meal was particularly impressive considering the Krishnas had banned almost everything worth eating. The vegetable-heavy fare, much of it grown in the garden, was delicious, as was the home-made bread. It didn't leave you feeling bloated and guilty like the bloody crime scene that was rest of Argentinian cuisine.

Annett was less enthusiastic about it. "It's *Moppelkotze*," she said, pushing at a pile of beans with her fork. I had no idea what *Moppelkotze* was. This truly was a place of learning. "*Moppelkotze* is like what they serve at hospitals when you can't chew," she clarified.

I picked up a little more bread. "You're seriously telling me you don't find this food delicious?"

She pushed her plate over to me. "That's what I'm telling you."

This meant that I got to eat more, which was great, but that Annett stayed hungry, which wasn't. After dinner we went to the community centre, took a yoga mat, pushed it against the wall, and watched a movie. It was a documentary with a long non-English name and designed to remind us how interconnected we all are. It was nice, and true, but weird to be watching it here, since we'd all come to the ashram to get disconnected.

"Did you like it?" Annett asked, as we slopped and sloshed our way back to our lodgings. We'd forgotten to bring a torch on the trip, and so were navigating by mobile-phone light.

"It was very thought-provoking," I lied.

"Liar!" she shouted, louder than she'd intended. She recalibrated her volume. "Stop trying to make the best out of everything. I hate it when you do that."

We discovered our hut had taken on the pungent aroma of a blocked-up sewage system, on account of its blocked-up sewage system. "Damn," I said, as the toilet seat slipped off, again, while I was sitting on it. An unidentified bug stared up at me from the shower basin.

"I heard you swear," Annett said when I returned. I crossed the room quickly, attempting a strategic retreat to the safety of my upper bunk.

"You didn't."

"I did. You hate it here as well."

I had the bunk's ladder in my hands. "I don't. I'm having a lovely time. I'm excited to learn more about the Hare Krishna faith. It's good to get out of the city and back to basics."

"Liar!" she said again, and rolled over to face the wall. "*Argh.* There's ants everywhere." She rolled back.

"Suffering is—"

"Fuck you!" She punched me as I fled up the ladder to my bunk. "That enough suffering for you?" One of the Canadians walked past, on her way to the bathroom. Our door was still open because it was still broken. It was awkward.

Day one was over. Just four to go. Hopefully tomorrow we'd find God.

The next morning the bell rang. We heard the Canadians getting up to do their volunteering stint. A few hours later, Annett and I sauntered over to the kitchen for our breakfast. The camp felt more like an organic farm than a place of worship. It had a generous vegetable patch and favoured wood, and was decorated with mosaics and yin-yang symbols. There was an outdoor raised wooden platform for yoga and meditation. About ten Hare Krishnas had their own accommodation on the far side of the camp, and they mostly kept to themselves. We found the rest of the camp—a dozen or so people, most American, dirty and irritable because they'd been labouring for hours. We'd strolled in fresh from the shower, yawning and waiting to be presented with the breakfast everyone else had harvested, cut, and cooked for us. No one sat with us while we ate it. We learned we were the only people paying more to avoid the volunteering. From this point on, the others viewed us as work-shy millionaires slumming it for a reality TV show.

"I hate it here," Annett said, as we took a post-breakfast stroll.

"It does take some getting used to," I conceded. "But we're here now. Let's have a full day here today, huh? Do the yoga and the new-age stuff and then see how we feel after?"

One of the volunteers, an American called Cindy, was studying to become a yoga teacher, and so there were three hours of yoga that day, instead of two. A lot for an absolute newbie like me. We collected our mats from the back of the room, found some space, and sat waiting for the session to start. Cindy was extremely enthusiastic about yoga, particularly about its healing properties. An enthusiasm shared by hands held in a prayer position. A soft soundtrack of bells and chanting played from a portable stereo. We tried to mirror the positions she demonstrated. She taught us the Sanskrit words for everything we were doing, which was commendable. Many dogs were present and downward facing. She slowly walked the room, telling us about our breathing and what we were feeling, and then invariably she would grab my hips or stomach and nudge me nearer to the desired shape. One-and-a-half hours passed quickly. It wasn't unpleasant at all. I was a convert. I wasn't sure I needed the second class, and a half-hour afternoon session, but Annett and I did it anyway, groaning through the positions as our bodies voiced concern about this sudden spike in pivoting, posturing, and prostrating.

After the second session we headed to the temple for an "orientation session," a chance to find out more about the faith. So far, just as in Israel, Palestine, and Ghana, no one here had tried to indoctrinate me. It didn't seem like any of the religions wanted to save the soul I didn't believe I had. I was starting to take it personally.

Inside the temple we found the Hare Krishna from check-in lighting candles for the subsequent chanting session. Annett and I were the only two people in the temple, looking for orientation. The man lit some incense and we breathed in deeply as we sat on the mats in the centre of the room, waiting for him to join us.

"How are you enjoying your stay?" he asked as he sat down.

"It's very nice."

"*Muchas gracias.*"

"I'm interested in learning a little more about the religion. I'm beginning from... well..." I squinted. "A rather minimal understanding of your faith. Is Hare Krishna a god, or was he a mortal?"

"A god. The one God." The man sat perfectly still, his back straight. "We believe no matter the religion, whenever someone prays to their god, they are praying to Krishna, for he is the supreme god."

Annett adjusted her crossed legs and leaned forward. "And the chanting and dancing is how you connect to Krishna?"

"*Sí.* The soul is mostly asleep, we believe. Dancing, chanting is how we awaken it."

I was happy to boogie for godhead. It was certainly better than years of Bible study. "Have you ever seen the Sufis whirl?" he asked. We both nodded. "So. It's similar."

Hare Krishnas have a talent for intense earnestness. There's a serious, otherworldly quality to the attention they give you. It's as if you're the only thing that has ever or will ever exist. This man had an abundance of focus. Meeting his gaze for too long pinched.

Annett pushed up her glasses. "And you also believe in reincarnation, right?"

"Yes. We believe that souls are immortal. Your deeds are judged after death and then you are reborn as a higher or lower life form."

"I like the idea of that," she said. "But it seems a bit, well, simplistic? Is there, like, a chart with the rules and what scores what points?"

"No," he said, between slow, measured blinks. "Just certain basic rules: chanting Hare Krishna, yoga, not eating animals, living in harmony with nature."

I cleared my throat. "What about, like, really, really bad people? Hitler, Stalin or... erm... that guy from *Gladiator*. Russell Crowe? What will they become in the next life? Dung beetles?"

"Lesser beings," the man said. "Exactly what is not known."

"Hmm." I scratched my cheek. "I think the only fair punishment for Russell Crowe would be to reincarnate him as himself."

Annett suppressed a fit of giggles. The man sat perfectly still. His face did not betray him. He would have been a hell of a poker player. "And just to be clear," she said, cocking her head. "No meat? That's a fixed thing? No wiggle room there? No sneaky 2am burger?"

The man shook his head. "No meat."

She frowned.

"Sex?" I asked.

"No sex."

Annett shrugged. This hurt. Me.

"Sex is about pleasing yourself, not pleasing Krishna."

"*Wine?*" she tried.

"No."

"Yeah... I'm out," she said, wrinkling her nose.

A redheaded woman in dungarees arrived at the door. It didn't look as though it was her first time on a farm. It was time to chant. The man beckoned her over, and we all sat together on the mats while he set up a harmonium, an instrument that looks and sounds like a mixture of an organ and an accordion. It's played using a hand pump. The man began to play.

"Hare Krishna Hare Krishna," he chanted. The woman joined in. Incense tickled my nose. "Krishna Krishna Hare Hare."

I bowed my head too, let the sound and ambiance of the temple float over me. "Hare Rāma Hare Rāma."

I felt too self-conscious to chant.

I opened my mouth. Nothing came out. I closed it again.

"Rāma Rāma Hare Hare."

"Hare Krishna Hare Krishna."

"Krishna Krishna Hare Hare."

I balled my hands into fists. I should have been joining in. I wasn't fully engaging in the experience that I had wanted. Annett had an excuse; her gods were Darwin, Dawkins, and Daiquiri. Me? I had slots open.

"Hare Rāma Hare Rāma," the man and the woman sang.

"Kṛiṣ—" I began.

"Hā—" the man interrupted.

"Hare," I repeated quickly, trying to catch up.

"Kṛiṣ—" I tried again.

"Rāma," he repeated.

Damn it. What were the odds? It seemed like even this religion had too much for me to remember. *It had three words.*

"Hare Krishna Hare Krishna."

"Rāma Rāma," I said. No one else said anything. "Krishna Krishna Hare Hare," the man continued.

I adopted a new approach—singing along but swallowing the beginning of each word until I was sure what it was then getting louder while attempting to catch up.

Annett said nothing. The room had taken on a mild *Eat Pray Love* aura. Yet if this was the peak of the indoctrination, it wasn't much at all. No one had even asked us for our credit card number yet.

After twenty minutes, the man stopped the music. He sat in silence for a minute, his head bowed, then got up, blew out the incense and candles, and left. We got up, shook out the knots in our limbs, and followed him outside.

"I'm not staying here five days," Annett said, as we walked back across the bog to our room. I stopped to fuss over one of the camp's dogs.

"Come on. The chanting was nice." The dog rolled over accommodatingly. "The Krishnas are nice. No one is trying to indoctrinate us. Which I'm a bit sad about. Are we not worth indoctrinating? How about four days?"

Annett stepped over the dog. "I'm leaving tomorrow!"

This was a regrettable development. Annett was the team's organiser, common-sense possessor, and, perhaps more importantly, Spanish speaker. The team would be greatly diminished if it became just me. It would be the sort of team you'd not want to be on, and quite possibly not even a team at all.

"Three days?" I countered, leaving the dog and chasing after her. "Let's make it into a challenge?"

"No," she said, angrily, and speeding up her steps. "I'm sick of your challenges. Why does everything have to be a challenge now?"

I followed her back to our room, where we continued to argue from the safety of our separate bunks, not wanting to risk being any nearer to each other. I bent round the side so that I could look down at her, looking up at me. She was grinding her teeth. "When we started this go-to-weird-places project, you promised me it wouldn't end in spiritual self-revelations in some temple. Well what was that, then? What's this place? Why are we here?"

I sighed. "That bit in the temple was a bit spiritual, I'll give you that. But we're out of our comfort zone. We're trying new things. Is it so bad?"

"Why are you all about getting out of the comfort zone? You've changed this past year or two. I thought it was in a good way, but now I'm not sure. I'm sick of the challenges and the retrospective fun holidays. Sick of you sending me job ads from foreign countries and trying to pressure me into leaving Berlin for one of your stupid pipe dreams. I'm happy in Berlin. I like our friends and our simple life. I don't want to move and rip all that up for no reason."

I rolled over, looked at the ceiling, reloaded, and spun back. "I like it there as well. But we're not getting any younger, right? It's better to have adventures now before we get settled again."

"I am settled. It's you who's running away from things."

"I'm not running away."

"*You are.* Every place we go you bug me to stay there. No matter how impractical."

I let my arm hang down, thinking she might take my hand. "So what now? What are you saying?"

"I'm done."

All the air left my lungs at once. "Done with what? *Us?*"

There was a pause. "That depends on you. I'm done with *this*. If you want to leave Berlin and travel to weird places for month and months"—she exhaled loudly—"well... you're on your own. I like my career. I like my friends. I like being an adult. I'm committed. If you want to go somewhere else you can, but you're going on your own. *I'm out.*"

Where there had been air in my chest there was now just indescribable heaviness. "Sometimes new is enough," I countered, meekly. "It doesn't have to be better."

"That's your problem. That's exactly it. Yes." She was suddenly energised. "You romanticise *new* in a way that makes you neglect what you already have. If we suddenly pack up a suitcase and move to a farm in Ecuador, what do you think that's going to be like? In the end, we'll have the same problems—we'll have to make friends, we'll have to find work, we'll have to eat and sleep. Same problems, different backdrop. You can't outrun your problems. Or your boredom."

I sighed. There was silence.

"We could have a pretty good go at it though, right?"

She tutted. "Typical, making jokes again. The English curse. You use jokes as a shield to not feel things. You know that, right?"

I remembered an article I'd recently read that said whatever first attracted you to a partner was always the thing you resented most at the end. Were we there already? "Well, it's easier for you," I said. "You have a career." I turned back to the ants running along the wall. Due to their collective nature and relentless commitment to *anting*, they were awful animals to be surrounded by when making a point such as this. Ants never suffer identity crises.

"I have a career because I created one. That's what you're running away from. You always wanted to be a writer. So come back, knuckle down, and write. Not the easy stuff, the important stuff. I think you're afraid to really try because as long as you never do, you can't fail. You confuse freedom with having no responsibilities. But that's not freedom. That's just selfishness."

We checked out the next morning: thirty-six hours after we'd arrived, still Godless. A frigid state of "let's agree to disagree" settled like frost atop the relationship. I stopped sending Annett exciting-looking job opportunities in Botswana. The next few trips I would take alone. Probably a good idea, because the next place I wanted to go was radioactive.

9

CHERNOBYL, UKRAINE: "IF SOMEONE ASK, YOU SCIENTISTS, OKAY?"

Reactor #4, bumper cars, Ferris wheels, hubris

In the early hours of April 26, 1986, reactor operators at the V.I. Lenin Nuclear Power Station were conducting a stress test upon reactor #4. This was a planned test and so, even though radiation readings were higher than expected, they saw no cause to worry. They wanted to learn the reactor's limits, after all. So they allowed it to get stressed. But as radiation levels climbed, the core temperature increased, flows of vital coolant water decreased, and the operators began to grow concerned. The test had run out of control and the temperature needed to come down quickly.

At 1:23am, they hit the stop switch on the test and inserted control rods into the reactor to slow down the reaction taking place within it. Only the Stop button they thought they were pressing turned out to be an accelerator. Less than a minute after they made that fateful decision, the temperature in the reactor's core surged past three thousand degrees Celsius, the water normally used to cool down the uranium became steam, that steam tried to expand, the reactor offered it no space to do so, and the resulting pressure blew the one-hundred-ton roof and let 50 million curies of radiation escape into the night sky. The equivalent of four hundred Hiroshima bombs.

What began that night as Chernobyl's problem became all of Europe's as a ten-day fire raging in reactor #4 spewed enough toxic, radioactive material to contaminate 40 percent of the continent's mainland. Some believe that if the wind had been blowing differently, all of it would have been rendered uninhabitable. Some 2,600 square kilometres have suffered this fate.

On the night of the accident, just three kilometres downwind of the ill-fated reactor, fifty thousand inhabitants of the town of Pripyat slept blissfully unaware. The next afternoon, with just an hour's notice, and still unaware of the scale of the calamity, they were forced to evacuate their homes and leave all but their most important possessions behind. Much of what remained was buried in a large pit.

Thirty years have now passed. The authorities say people will be able to live in Pripyat again one day; that's the good news. The bad news is that this day will not come for another 2700 years. Those not wanting to wait so long for a glimpse of their former lives can make a day trip back. The area is slowly opening up to small numbers of brave/stupid/insensitive/curious/macabre tourists who want to see what a modern-day Pompeii looks like—tourists who aren't satisfied just reading the Wikipedia pages of iconic events from the safety of their couches, and want to get closer to them; see them, touch them, feel them, take selfies in front of them.

Tourists like me.

The Fukushima disaster was nearing its fifth anniversary. Natural disasters were on the rise. As well as a blossoming interest in unusual places and the weird things humans did to each other in them, I also had a growing interest in how we treated (or mistreated) the natural world.

So I found myself in the back of a minibus from Kiev, Annett-less but not alone. I was joined by seven other tourists, two guides (only one ever said anything), and a driver (who almost never got out of the vehicle). When he did, he buffed said vehicle fastidiously, as if trying to make amends for where he had taken it.

Chernobyl is just 170 kilometres from Kiev, a journey along mostly empty roads. Exclusion zones do wonders for reducing road traffic. Door to door, you can go from the centre of bustling Kiev to the thirty-kilometre "exclusion zone" in just two-and-a-half hours. Although the accident is usually associated with the Ukraine, in many ways, Belarus suffered far worse: 20 percent of its land is still contaminated by fallout. Head north from the exclusion zone, instead of south, and it's a lot more than two hours before you reach a metropolis like Kiev.

Ivan, our guide, turned round from the front seat. He was a short, bald man with electric blue eyes that flirted with menace. "Just a year ago we had to pretend people were scientists," he said, his sentences delivered in a soft voice that shunned the word *the*, as is common for many native Russian speakers. "Now is okay, I think." His hypnotic eyes darted from side to side in a manner that didn't reassure. "If authorities ask, you scientists, okay?"

"Okay," we mumbled.

I've never been good at science. In fact, my high school science teacher had said he thought I'd probably end up "working in McDonald's all my life." While that sounds like a harsh thing for a moulder of young minds to proclaim, I bear no grudges. As a practitioner of the scientific method, he was merely forming a logical conclusion from the data at his disposal. That data said that I didn't know my neutrons from my neurons, my electrons from my electro. The only thing periodic was how often I handed in my homework. The ruse that I was a scientist would collapse under even the most cursory of questioning. I didn't tell Ivan this. He was busy speaking Russian with his colleagues, free of the tyranny of *the*.

There was great excitement in the minibus as we approached the exclusion zone. I think we were all secretly imagining visiting the Springfield Nuclear Power Plant from *The Simpsons*—we'd don biohazard suits and hold glowing green bars with long metal pincers. At lunchtime we'd wander nearby forests teeming with three-eyed or two-headed animals. The minibus passed the first security checkpoint and a sign you didn't have to be a scientist to understand: a large red triangle with a yellow-and-red radiation symbol within it.

Was this a good idea? Why go to a place so many had fled? Out of the window I saw a pack of wild dogs and two horses. Animal life was flourishing in our absence. At the next checkpoint, three men in Ukrainian-army uniforms stepped out of a brick hut and presented us with health and safety waivers to sign. We had to agree not to:

"Take any items outside the zone."

"Drink water from wells, rivers, and other open-water sources."

"Bring in/take out of the exclusion zone any animals (dogs, cats etc)."

On leaving, we'd have to "pass compulsory radiation control of clothes, foot wear, personal items." The waiver further stated: "If contamination exceeds the established control levels, personal clothes, foot wear, and items are subject to decontamination."

I gulped.

"It's fine," said Ivan. "You get more radiation on flight than today."

Well, he would say that, wouldn't he? It was his business to bring gullible people like me here. They certainly don't give out forms like this on Ryanair. Which is a surprise, actually. They could certainly make money offering a biohazard suit and BLT sandwich combo.

My pen hovered over the blank signature line. I looked up at the rest of the group members, who were waiting, having already handed their forms back. They didn't seem conflicted. I scrawled my name, dated it, and passed it back to the bored-looking guard. He checked our passports and waved us back onto the minibus.

A hundred metres down the road, we passed the real welcome sign—a white brick structure with a blue *Chernobyl* written in Cyrillic. The word was topped with the atomic symbol, a picture of the reactor, and the Soviet hammer and sickle. We stopped and took turns photographing each other in front of it. There were some apples lying around the sign in various stages of decay.

"I dare you five hundred euros to eat one," said Paul, a fellow tourist. I picked it up and looked for any obvious flaws, hoping it might glow. Then I wrapped my lips around my teeth and pretended to sink them in.

"Wait!" he said, in alarm.

I laughed and dropped the apple back on the ground.

We began our tour at what has became the poster child of the disaster—Pripyat, that Soviet ghost town. Current population: zero. We pulled into what was once its town square. In the distance, more wild dogs scavenged.

The driver began buffing the front of the van with a cloth, his face just a few inches from it, whispering it sweet nothings. Ivan had us form a circle. "First, rules. No wandering off." The group moaned. "Okay." Ivan smirked. "A little wandering off okay. But not too deep into woods, okay?"

We liked Ivan already. He played fast and loose with our health and safety.

"That's it? That's all the rules?" a Polish woman asked.

"Yes. I think. Oh, don't eat things."

I scanned the others' faces, looking for someone stupid enough.

"How long can we stay here?" A London stockbroker asked.

Ivan looked at the paved road we were standing on. "Here? Long time." He got his bright-yellow Geiger counter out of his padded jacket. He showed us the reading: 0.4 μSv/h.

"Radiation here safe, see? Radiation not spread evenly. Some surface absorb it and you find much. Other places nearby, little. Here, paved road, little." He turned around, pointing into the woods behind him, where four dogs were play-fighting. "There. Much. Come."

He stepped off the road and into the brush. It didn't seem like a very good idea. We did anyway. The Geiger counter began to click as we trampled over the leaves, moss, and mud that could better absorb that radioactive material. He held his meter up like a trophy to his adoring crowd. "Here is 8.1 μSv/h. See? Here we should not stay too long. One day only." It was unclear why he'd taken all of us into the brush to prove this. Personally, I would have been willing to believe him from the surer footing provided by the asphalt.

"Ingesting just a tiny amount can be fatal," he said, stomping back towards the road. I was learning so much. Not that it would be much use when I returned to my job at McDonald's.

He led us through the ruins of a gym, a cinema, and, most iconic of all, Pripyat Middle School. The town's structures still stood, but inside they were a mess of graffiti, broken glass, and signs of the looting that had gone on here over the years. In their cracks another battle was taking place between the human-made and the natural. Tree branches, weeds, and grass fought valiantly to reclaim spaces that used to belong to us. A sign warning of children crossing had been swallowed by overgrown foliage. No children crossed here anymore. Pripyat reminded me of the temples of Angkor Wat, Cambodia, where trees have so fused with the temples' ruins that it's hard to imagine that they weren't always there, weren't part of the architect's original designs.

There was a heaviness to the silence. Other than the sound of glass and debris cracking under our feet, all was calm, still, defeated. Because the citizens of Pripyat had had such a short time to evacuate, much of their lives were still here on display, in stasis, waiting for their return. In a school classroom, bright-yellow *Matematyka 3* workbooks lay atop wooden desks. The blackboard had remnants of a maths exercise scrawled upon it. Inside *Matematyka 3* was a picture of children putting flowers around a portrait of Lenin. Before the accident, Chernobyl had been a big part of the propaganda of Soviet superiority. It was possible that this classroom scene had been staged; it felt a little too perfect. Some gas masks were suspended on ropes hanging from the ceiling. Others lay in a heap on the floor amongst dolls' heads and the shell of an old television set. Why would there be dolls' heads here? And what had happened to their bodies and eyes? Also, why would you attach gas masks to the ceiling? You can't see radiation.

Perhaps people had simply staged this space to make it as creepy as possible. That didn't stop us from enthusiastically photographing it. Abandoned buildings, graffiti, gas masks, dolls' heads with eyes removed: Chernobyl. These were the money shots. The reason people came here. For the name, story, myth, and legend. Not the less-photogenic reality.

Next, we paid a visit to the town's former swimming pool. It was in a similarly dilapidated state, although it was actually used by the clean-up crews for recreation until ten years after the accident. There's dispute about how many of the clean-up crew lost their lives. "Officially, death toll below one hundred," said Ivan, with scepticism. "Unofficially, nearer million."

You can't get near to the reactor because of its still dangerously high radiation levels, so after the dolls' heads and gas masks, the most important sight for the few visitors who do make it here is Pripyat's amusement park. Coincidentally, the disaster occurred just before May Day. A celebration had been scheduled to take place, with rides and amusements set up to entertain the locals. Because of the accident, this celebration never took place. We found mildewed, faded, and ripped posters on doors and walls advertising the planned festivities. The bumper cars sat rusted to perfection, looking as if they'd crashed and skidded into retirement after having given humans thousands of hours of light, electric hedonism. In reality, they'd been turned on only very briefly, the morning after the accident, to calm and distract people while the authorities decided whether or not to evacuate them. There was just enough yellow and blue paint to imagine how they might have looked in their prime. Next to them stood an equally rusty Ferris wheel. Things aged quickly here, due to the radiation in the air. People had placed dolls and soft toys into the Ferris wheel's yellow carriages to amp up the bleakness. I found it impossible not to imagine people on that carousel—excited children, proud parents, all circling up into the sky to get a view of the power plant where they worked, just a few kilometres away. Very few got to ride on it. Like the bumper cars, it was in use for only an hour or two, and those lucky enough to experience it ended up exposing themselves to yet more of the air's toxicity.

On the way to the reactor we passed a few small settlements, clusters of five or six dilapidated-looking dwellings. "A few people have returned to live here," said Ivan.

"What? Inside the exclusion zone!"

"Yes. Babushkas, mostly."

"Do you think they're brave or crazy?"

"Most just old. They want left alone. We help them when we can."

We reached a good vantage point to view the sarcophagus covering the ruins of reactor #4. From this special viewing deck, some three-hundred metres away, we could get our all-important photographs. What we were seeing was still an active disaster zone, still had clean-up crews working on it each day to try to make it safe(r). While it's estimated that 10 tons of radioactive material escaped, another 190 tons remained here under the sarcophagus, covered in some 5000 tons of sand, boron, dolomite, clay, and lead, much of it dropped from helicopters that circled briefly overhead, just long enough to throw out their contents. Many of these brave pilots died shortly afterwards from the radiation they were exposed to. In the beginning, robots were used for the clean-up work, operated from a safe distance, but even their circuits were fried by the radiation. So the authorities turned to us: bio-robots.

"People ran in, stay for one minute, ran out," said Ivan.

"What could you do in one minute?" someone asked.

"Not much." He smirked. "In the end, even one minute too much. Almost all people died."

We could see the Ukrainian Government building an even bigger, thicker, new sarcophagus that was to be wheeled on top of the old one. "It's largest moving structure on earth. Five metres thick. Thirty-one thousand tonnes. One and half billion euros. They say it finished in 2018." Ivan chuckled. "We will see."

Would it last until this area was safe again? Bearing in mind that the current one was showing its age after just thirty years, and the area wouldn't be safe for almost three thousand, it seemed unlikely. But no one had a better idea. Nuclear really is the nuclear option. There's no going back, no undo; its scars are permanent.

"This was supposed to be the world's power station," said Ivan, staring towards the ill-fated reactor. "They had plan to make it biggest." He checked his Geiger counter. "We should only stay here fifteen minutes."

We were back on the minibus in five.

For tourists, Chernobyl is not that rewarding. All the things you want to see, you can't, because they're too dangerous. Yet that danger doesn't feel real, because it's just a number on the screen of a Geiger counter. This makes you bolder than you should be. Our group trampled off the paths, climbed onto the roofs of the abandoned buildings, and fussed the stomachs and backs of the friendly dogs that sloped around us hoping for food.

An awful tragedy happened here, one that changed the world and its opinion of nuclear energy. That's why it's so important to keep the memory of Chernobyl alive. At Pompeii, we were the innocent victims of the natural world. With Chernobyl, the lesson is much starker. It speaks to the arrogance that we used to have, that many of us still have; the belief that we are somehow separate from and in control of the natural world.

"We knew, with certainty, with arrogant certainty, that we were in control of the power we were playing with," said engineer Sergiy Parashy in an interview with The Christian Science Monitor. He'd been there that day. "We could make the forces of nature bend to our will. There was nothing we could not do. This was the day, of course, when we learned we were wrong."

Arrogant certainty. I thought back to Andrea, the man I'd met in the bar in Istanbul. He wanted to know why a country became North Korea, Yemen, or Eritrea. After seeing Chernobyl, I thought this seemed like the best explanation. The wrong group gets too certain about themselves, their beliefs, and their rights. They pull society's levers and inflict the repercussions upon everyone else. History is what happens when ego meets happenstance.

Seeing Chernobyl made me feel small, irrelevant, humble. I wasn't sure I wanted to be arrogantly certain about anything. There are far worse things than being a *Mitläufer*. Of course I wanted to contribute in some way to Project Humanity, however small and inconsequential, but maybe that contribution would be best if it grew out of feelings of uncertainty, weakness, and insecurity. I no longer considered these character traits as flaws I needed to fix. They seemed in keeping with the unfathomably messy, tangled, complex world in which we live. It's certainty we should be afraid of.

Chernobyl was a watershed moment in human hubris. The end of the rush to build bigger, better, bolder nuclear testaments to our own ego, majesty, and ideology. The disaster was large enough even to stop the beating heart of the Soviet Union. Five years after the tragedy of reactor #4, it too lay in ruins. A brutal regime, like so many before it. We could have learned something from its destruction and not rushed to simply cover over the damage and get busy repeating the same mistakes. Yet just thirty years later, Russia is back out from under its sarcophagus, marching once more through its former territories, reclaiming what it considers to be its own. Crimea has been annexed and people of the Ukraine are uneasy, expecting the rest of the country to be next. There are so many lessons to be learned at Chernobyl, and I'm not talking about those on offer in *Matematyka 3*. The question is whether anyone is paying attention.

I knew this wasn't going to be a problem at my next destination. It was getting a lot of attention. I hoped it would be less depressing.

10

LIBERLAND, CROATIA/SERBIA: "HITLER WAS ALSO DEMOCRATICALLY ELECTED. THERE IS NO VIRTUE IN DEMOCRACY."

Micronations, libertarians, cannabis shaman, THE DRIVER!

It certainly wasn't depressing, I decided, leaning against the front of the boat, looking out at the Danube, the sun warming my face. Seated behind me, in a similar state of excitement, wonder, and possibility, were five libertarians, a future diplomat to Liechtenstein, and a self-proclaimed cannabis shaman. We were going to the newest country in the world! To *Liberland.* Just a kilometre upstream.

The story of Liberland began one year earlier, in 2015, when Czech politician Vit Jedlička walked onto an abandoned piece of swampland on the shores of the Danube, the international border and waterway between Serbia and Croatia. Believing that a seven-square-kilometre piece of swampland there was *terra nullius*, available under international law, he placed a yellow flag into it and declared himself president of the Free Republic of Liberland.

A ridiculous story, right? You don't just get to create your own country, surely? Yet away from the scrutiny and glare of popular culture, people are doing just that. Micronations, they're usually called. Nations like Sealand (an oil rig off the coast of England), The Republic of New Atlantis (which was a bamboo-raft nation founded by Ernest Hemingway's brother), and the Kingdom of North Sudan (created so that the founder's seven-year-old daughter could become a princess. Disney has bought the movie rights). Much closer to my home (Wittenberg, to be precise) is Germany's Königreich Deutschland. Its eccentric founder, Peter Fitzek, presented his Königreich Deutschland ID when arrested for driving without a licence. "The jurisdiction of the Federal Republic of Germany does not apply to other heads of state," he claimed. It doesn't really work like that, a judge of the German legal system informed him, by way of a three-month prison sentence. "You have built a fantasy world with a fanciful political worldview," the judge said, making it sound like a bad thing.

I'd become hooked by the world of micronations. They offered so much promise and the chance to reinvent yourself. I was interested in reinventing myself. Maybe I was presidential.

Usually micronations' daft little flirtations with statehood don't get very far—a bombastic press release; quick bit of media attention; some memorabilia for sale—before everyone moves on to the next great potential sovereignty. Every time I checked in on Liberland, I expected their attempts to be fizzling out, but that never happened. The land they claimed became 50 percent less contentious when Serbia declared it wasn't theirs, leaving only Croatia to convince. Fifty thousand people applied online for Liberlandian citizenship, in case they managed it. The *New York Times* sent a reporter to spend ten days following Mr President around. They created Liberland Merits, their own currency. Ambassadors were appointed in forty countries. Four hundred thousand people applied for citizenship.

Were they serious about this? Might they even pull it off? Would they accept this pre-Renaissance man if they did? It was time to meet Mr President and find out.

～

My first email to the Presidential Office of the Free Republic of Liberland went unanswered. But then, on a wet Wednesday evening, I received the following message:

"Dear Adam, I am thinking about going for lunch with you on Tuesday. What do you think? Where do you suggest to go?"

It was President Vit himself, coming to Berlin. Not only was I in contact with a head of state, he wanted *me* to suggest where we could meet for lunch! I mostly ate at döner kebab stalls inside subway stations. These places were not presidential. So I broke into my piggy bank and suggested we meet at a Russian-themed restaurant in Berlin Mitte called Gorki Park. I thought the irony of taking a libertarian who despised government and taxation to a restaurant celebrating Soviet socialism was just too good of a chance to miss. A few days later, below murals of Russian peasants carrying apples and Sputnik memorabilia, I found three men in suits waiting for me. President Vit and his entourage were certainly dressing the part. I looked down at my creased blue shirt and dirty black jeans—I wasn't. I was dressed as if I'd just finished fixing some troublesome bathroom plumbing. To further undermine my credentials as a "journalist," which was what I was pretending to be, I'd also forgotten my wallet. While extremely embarrassing, this at least saved me from the inevitability of opening it to discover it had no money inside.

I found Mr President at a corner table, perusing the menu. He was heavyset, had a squishy, warm face, cheeks like pockets, and a neat blond goatee. His entourage moved to another table so we could talk privately. I began the interview by accidentally insulting him: I called Liberland a micronation.

"We've got four hundred thousand people applying for citizenship." He tilted his head. "If we accept them all, we'll be larger than Iceland. So are we still a micronation?"

We'd not even ordered drinks yet, drinks I couldn't actually pay for, and yet I'd already questioned the man's sovereignty. I tried to soften my approach. Not that he was being defensive or aggressive. He was calm, friendly, charismatic. I liked him.

I leaned forward. "Well, obviously you know this better than me. To me, it looks like there is a border dispute. Serbia is saying 'It's not ours' and Croatia is saying 'We're not sure whose it is, but it's certainly not yours.'"

He frowned. "Croatia says it's theirs. But then if it was, why would they stop us going there? Since we wouldn't have to leave Croatia to do so?"

I wasn't prepared enough to answer. I wasn't very well prepared, in general. I thought I was just meeting some crazy opportunist who wanted to get some press for himself, sell some T-shirts, and be able to travel the world introducing himself as Mr President. The intensity of his gaze and the size and professionalism of his entourage convinced me that this wasn't the case. They were serious.

Vit wasn't just some Internet chancer either; he knew his way around politics. He'd been an elected official in his native Czech Republic, but had grown disillusioned with public office there when a former KGB agent was democratically elected as the Czech finance minister. "People vote into power the people who steal the most from them through taxation," he lamented.

"But he was democratically elected, right?"

He scoffed. "Hitler was also democratically elected. There is no virtue in democracy."

I'd always assumed democracy was, as Winston Churchill had once quipped, "the worst form of government, except for all the others." People went to war to spread it, didn't they? Sacred cows were being slaughtered in front of my eyes.

The food arrived. Blini. It was delicious.

"The concept of one or two people attempting to create their own country, usually it never gets beyond those one or two people," I said. "Why do you think Liberland is so much more successful?"

He considered it between mouthfuls of his borscht, a typical Eastern European soup. "A lot of people believe in the ideals of Liberland. Any nation is only as strong as the people who believe in it.

When I was arrested for going there, the chief of the Croatian police came to the court to argue for a longer sentence for me. He said, 'Liberland is just in your head. It's just an imagination.'"

Vit laughed, as did his (not-listening) minders. "I told him, 'Croatia is also just in your head. It's just an imagination.' That really pissed him off, of course. But that's the reality."

Croatia—imaginary or not—had armies and courts and jails that could be used to convince the doubtful of its existence. Vit had a flag, a website, and a lot of emails from interested people. It didn't seem like a fair fight.

"Maybe it won't work." He shrugged. "Who knows? All we ask is that they let us try it." This sounded pretty reasonable to me.

My chance to visit came a few months later, during the country's first anniversary. They were holding a libertarian conference on the Croatian side of this controversial piece of marshland. After a three-and-a-half-hour bus ride from Belgrade, Serbia, I arrived in Osijek, Croatia, the nearest city to the conference and a very pretty historical one at that. Unfortunately, no one was waiting to meet me, as had been agreed. I called the organiser, Damir. I was angry. These people wanted to start a country? They couldn't even arrange a shuttle bus. They were kidding themselves. "Boris is waiting out front," Damir said. "He has curly hair and an estate car."

I doubted it. I doubted it very much. *Boris?* People aren't really called Boris. Characters in movies are called Boris. They're either good with IT, or they're hitmen. Out the front of the bus station, a man with tight black curls of hair to his shoulders approached me, his hand outstretched.

"Mr Fletcher?" he asked.

"Yes."

"I'm Boris, your driver."

He didn't look as if he would be good in IT, so I decided it best to behave myself. The other passenger in the back of the boxy grey car was a tall, lumbering man with puffy cheeks and floppy hair parted in the centre. His head sat atop his body like an overinflated balloon pinned to a lamp post. He introduced himself as Gregor. He smelt of alcohol. Perhaps unaware of the consequences of crossing a Boris, Gregor was not on his best behaviour. Over the thirty-minute journey, it became clear that Gregor was a man who enjoyed the sound of his own voice so much that he didn't deny himself any opportunity to hear it.

"I'm an investor," he said. "Real estate. You know, Guangzhou, New York, Korea, Florida. *Whatever*. No big deal."

It clearly was a big deal.

I smiled. "Are you a libertarian?"

"Well, you know, it would be good for some investments, but I'm aware there are some problems with it. I told Vit that when I met him one-and-a-half years ago. I met him, you know? Yeah, no big deal."

It really was.

He stuck out his chin. "He came to my house and everything. Sure. Have you met him?"

"Yes, in Berlin. He didn't come to my house though."

"Oh, well, whatever. Who cares? Right?" He patted me limply on the shoulder.

Gregor cared.

We stopped at the conference site, a hotel in the middle of nowhere, which seemed like such an inconvenient location for a hotel. I can only assume it was in the middle of something really tremendous that I never found because it was too well hidden. In the car park, a bombshell had just been dropped: *President Vit wasn't coming.* Damir was frantic. "They stopped him at the Croatian border! Which is obviously illegal since he's an EU citizen."

"What? *Fuck*," said Gregor. "I've got some big deals lined up."

"Yes," said Damir. "I'm sorry."

Gregor hung his head, kicking a stone out from under his shoe. "Man, Serbia is the Wild West, but Croatia isn't much better. Here, they just *pretend* at being diplomatic."

Inside, the buffet was underway. I got a plate of food and approached a table with one empty seat. "Can I sit here?" I asked. The two men already seated looked at each other, then laughed. "This is Liberland," one said. "Just take it." I took it, put my plate down, and headed to the bar to get a beer. When I returned, someone had taken the chair from me. He'd simply moved my plate of food into the middle of the table and sat himself down. Was this what it would be like in Liberland? Dog eat dog? The person didn't apologise, so I was left to awkwardly lean over him, pick up my plate, and move to another table. At the next one, I asked if I could take its empty seat.

"No, our friend is going to sit there," said a man in a flannel lumberjack's shirt.

Diplomacy was getting me nowhere. I needed to take a page out of President Vit's book and just put down a flag and declare any seat the Free Republic of Adam's Ass. The people at the third table did let me join. They were right in the middle of an impassioned conversation about gun rights, the main thrust of the argument being that there weren't enough. A two-man keyboard-and-acoustic-guitar band began playing classic rock covers at the other end of the hall. They began by strangling and setting fire to "Don't worry, Be Happy." I felt quite happy amongst this group of affable eccentrics. That might have been because I was drinking (liberally) Liberal Ale—Liberland's own beer. "I got it directly from Vit's apartment, this morning," said the squirrelly man who had presented it to me. All those I'd spoken to were keen to emphasise how they were Best Friends Forever with President Vit. The band molested "One Love" by Bob Marley next. At least I think that's what it was supposed to be. If there was love in this room, it was reserved for the president-in-exile. I turned to talk to a computer programmer from London. "How are you enjoying the conference so far?" I asked him.

"It's very low key," he said. "No one's even been arrested yet."

If anyone was going to get arrested, it would be Gregor. I found him a few tables over, wasted on red wine and flirting outrageously with a pretty Turkish woman eating birthday cake. They were discussing a private social network for rich people.

"My mother had money, so what, doesn't matter. I don't care about money." Gregor was balancing his chair precariously on its two rear legs. "I want to be with quality people. *Come on, let's go sailing?* You know? No big deal."

The woman looked bored. He ploughed on regardless. "Sometimes you eat tuna, sometimes caviar. You know?"

She smiled politely.

"Relax," he continued. "It's a joke anyway, right? Who cares?" The girl didn't appear to care.

"Envy, whatever," he continued. "It's been a big factor in my life. Probably in yours too. I don't care about other people."

She put down her fork. "Me neither. They can talk behind me, I don't care."

"I like you, you know," he said, reaching for her arm. "You're really great."

She pulled her hand back. "I'm going outside to smoke a cigarette."

"*Yes,* let's go," he said, jumping up enthusiastically after her, his chair crashing to the floor behind him. I picked it up. Gregor was like every bad real-estate investor cliché rolled into one. Yet, he was the only openly noxious person I'd met so far. The rest were smart, open, happy to talk about their beliefs. They bristled with conviction and certainty that all this—country, state, and governance nonsense—was about to collapse. When it did, well, they'd be there with their ideas. It would be their time. A time for libertarianism and something called anarcho-capitalism.

In the meantime, well, they were going to take turns kicking the current system while it was down. The band lynched "Stuck In The Middle With You." It was ten thirty. I made murmurings of my desire to leave. "No problem," said Damir. "I'll arrange a car for you. Five minutes." Thirty minutes later I wandered outside. I found Gregor in the car park, attempting to embrace the Turkish girl, who was attempting, mostly, to avoid said embrace. By now his eyes were bloodshot, and his puffy cheeks had taken on the soft pink hues of excess.

"Have you had fun?" I asked him.

He scoffed. "Here? With these Nazis and crazy guys and people with beards?" I hadn't met anyone who came even close to the accepted description of a Nazi. I can attest that there were several people in the room with beards, including me. I've always found people with beards quite agreeable. "*Pfft*, I'm not interested in that, man," Gregor added. "I'm here for *investments*."

An hour passed. We went back inside to find our own willing chauffeur. We failed. Gregor complained loudly about this until Anton, a calm, stoic Austrian with wild, unkempt hair stood up from his table. I think keen to spare everyone Gregor's loud, drunken blustering.

"Let's go," Anton said.

Unfortunately, Gregor came with us. "Fifty-five euros for two bottles of wine?" He ranted from the back seat of the red estate car. "*Fuck*. And I had to go *inside!* I mean, come on! I had to pay for it *and* go in there and get it? *Inside*? And pay for it? Seriously?"

I shot Anton a look of apology from the passenger seat. I was used to Gregor by now, but Anton's baptism of fire was happening in an enclosed space that he couldn't escape. Anton smiled back calmly. He was the anti-Gregor.

"My best friend is the prime minister of Croatia!" Gregor growled, a hand on the back of each of our seats. "I mean, come on." There were a few seconds of silence. I hoped he'd fallen asleep. No such luck. "So you know Vit then, do you?" he barked. Neither of us answered because we didn't know to whom the "you" of the question was aimed. "THE DRIVER," Gregor added, impatiently, having forgotten Anton's name. "I'm asking THE DRIVER."

Anton, THE DRIVER, breathed in deeply. "Yes. I know him." His voice was that of meditation tapes. Of summer BBQs with friends. Of apple orchards. Of first loves. Of a world that made sense. A Gregor-less world. "Oh, do you?" said Gregor sarcastically, "Well, I think my relationship to him is a bit closer, no offence. He was at my house and everything."

There was a pause. "Okay," Anton said, stoically.

Gregor started up again. "He wants my embassy? *Pff.* Whatever.

I'm going to give it to him. For money, of course. *A lot of money.* He was at my house once. No big deal."

I'd prided myself on liking nearly everybody. Sometimes it took some creative mental accounting, and moral-flaw overlooking, but everyone had at least one redeeming feature. Until Gregor. Gregor defeated me. I'd have to be saving a lot of tax to be his neighbour.

The next day the conference would begin. I had thrown off my social-democratic shackles and was frolicking with a new world view —libertarianism. I found it much less taxing. *Fuck the system! Fight The Man! Burn it all down!*

I went to bed excited. The 9am pickup came exactly *as* expected, just not *when*. In many ways I thought it had been falsely advertised, being that it arrived not at 9am, but at 10:30. As Damir pulled into the car park of the conference hotel, we found a Croatian police car and two men in suit jackets (wearing plastic earpieces that disappeared into their collars) flanking the building's entrance.

"Croatian secret police," said Damir. "Here to try and intimidate us."

We took our seats inside. "I will now give the floor to Mr President, the founding father and president of Liberland," said our host, only an hour later than the advertised start time. Above us, on the wall, the face of President Vit Jedlička appeared. "Hell—ooo," it said. The video froze. "Ev—vvvvv—errry—one." The sound dropped out, came back, dropped out. "I'm ve—rrrrry happy to seeeeee—"

"Please everyone disconnect from the Wi-Fi. We need the bandwidth for Mr President," said the stressed-out moderator. *A whole country? Seriously? From scratch? These people?*

Sure, this was rural Croatia's fault, not Liberland's, but rural Croatia had a twenty-five-year head start over Liberland, and look how rubbish it was at providing simple services such as Internet connections speedy enough for Skype. Once the conference did get going, the content was extremely interesting, despite its shabby and chaotic wrapping. We learned more about the area, and why the local government had such a problem with Liberland. We heard from a Croatian politician who summarised it well: "My grandmother has never moved and yet has lived in five or six different countries. It's no surprise people fear change around here."

He wasn't exaggerating. The region, called Slavonia, has a very troubled past and has often found itself as the subject of disputes between nations, including the brutal four-year war of the early nineties, fought against Serbia following the collapse of Yugoslavia. Today its struggles continue, evidenced by the new direct bus line to Germany—the region's population decreases by fourteen people per day. There are few jobs, few opportunities, and, from the conversations I had with locals, little hope. Remarkable, considering it's a place of such abundant natural beauty and resources. It is still Croatia's main wine-producing region.

Between conference sessions, everyone mingled on the large sun terrace. It was surprising how many of the hundred attendees were in suits and had given themselves fancy-sounding bureaucratic titles. They dispensed business cards to each other as children might stickers. For a group who wanted to overthrow the system, they were dressed and behaving remarkably like that system. Which made me wonder if they truly did want to overthrow it or just recreate it somewhere new where they could have its power and make its rules. I was suddenly having doubts. The anarcho-capitalist utopia of my imagination would be stubbornly business-card and Executive-Vice-President-to-the-Ambassador-of-the-Attaché-Investment-Management-Consultant free.

A large, fluffy white dog had been sloping about the terrace and sidled up to the gun-loving Brit from the previous night's dinner. It jumped up and latched on to the man's leg, which he began humping furiously. The man tried to remove the excited mutt, but he was a big dog and so sprung immediately back up, pinning him against the wall. The man knocked him down and tried to walk away, but the dog chased him across the terrace. People laughed and cheered. This would have been a funny scene anywhere, but at a libertarian's conference it was somehow more comical, as if the dog had got caught up in the spirit of the event and was indulging his own sexual liberty. I'd heard the word *freedom* so many times that day, and this was a very visual reminder that one person's freedom can directly inhibit someone else's.

The conference was good, but the conference was talk. We wanted action. We wanted to go to the promised land. To squelch our feet in its soils. To be bitten by its libertarian mosquitoes. To tell people we'd visited a country that they hadn't, a country so new they didn't even know it (sort of) existed.

That night in the hotel, I sent Annett some pictures from the conference, which were greeted lukewarmly. I think we were both aware a relationship time bomb was ticking, but neither of us knew the length of its fuse.

The following day, a warm Sunday, thirty libertarians and I climbed into a silver double-decker bus and headed for the Croatian border. We were going to Liberland!

"Borders remind us that we're all slaves," said Susanne Tarkowski Tempelhof, the conference's keynote speaker and creator of something called Bitnation, a tool to replace governments with the blockchain technology used by Bitcoin.

"Yeah. This will all come crashing down soon enough," said the gun-loving Brit who'd had the romantic encounter with the large white dog.

"Right, because the state doesn't exist. It's a collective fiction," said Susanne's husband.

I looked out at the barriers, security fencing, barbed wire, and people with guns. It looked both secure and non-fictional to me. All the concerns we'd had about leaving Croatia's collective fiction proved unfounded. We were waved through their border with a minimum of fuss. They were probably happy to get rid of us. On the other side of it, an affable border guard from the collective fiction known as Serbia got on and collected up our passports. He was a squat man with a small blond moustache. "Where are you going?" he asked.

"We're going to the other side of the water, to the restaurant," answered Paul, an English journalist now living in Croatia.

"Oh, it's very nice," the official replied. "They have a new chef. His name is Vitrovich. He's very good. Well, enjoy," he said, leaving the bus.

Wait, were we all still slaves?

After a quick lunch, and the arrival of Mr President himself, the big moment had arrived: it was time for our voyage to Liberland. We'd all come to the Serbian side to make our attempt so that Vit could join us, being as he was now barred from Croatia. Would we make it onto Liberlandian soil? Would we be detained en route? No one had set foot on Liberland without getting arrested for months. Unfortunately, the three boats that had been planned had become just one boat. I'm sure this shocked many people. I was not one of them. The boat we did have was large enough for just eight people. Liberland was a forty-five-minute journey upriver. We were fifty people. "It's going to take at least three hours," warned President Vit, and that was with a shorter route, using an off-road vehicle to take the rest as close to the land as possible.

Fortunately, I managed to wrangle a spot on that first boat. Calm, heroic, stoic Anton was at the helm, and as I watched his wild hair blow in the breeze, I was distracted from the fact that we had only three life jackets. If he could drive a drunk Gregor for thirty minutes and resist the urge to crash and kill us all, forty-five minutes in a boat with me and a few fellow libertarians would be child's play. The engine spluttered into life, filling the boat with diesel fumes. There was a palpable excitement. The only things that could have made it better were eyepatches, a parrot, and, maybe, a few more life jackets. Sat next to me was a shabby, dreadlocked Czech man called Štefan. His T-shirt had a large hole under the armpit. He set about rigging the bright-yellow Liberland flag to a stick, which he tethered to the back of the boat. Once he'd finished, we cheered. We meant business: deregulated business. Since he looked the subversive type, I asked him if he'd ever tried to found his own country.

"No," he said, a mad glint in his eye. "I did help create a church once, though."

Of course you did, Štefan. Nothing surprised me with these people. They were doers. They had life by the balls.

"It was called the Cannabis Church. I was a shaman. We were small, but we had a lot of believers." He mimicked the smoking of an imaginary spliff. "Not just believers. *Practising* believers. Very devout they were." He winked. "I'm also planning to create a Procrastination Party. I just didn't quite get around to it yet."

About twenty-five minutes into our journey upriver, our yellow Liberland flag flapping triumphantly in the breeze, we found a Croatian police border-patrol boat waiting for us.

"Damn," said Anton. "I guess they won't let us pass."

He accelerated towards them.

"Let's wave to them," said the Turkish girl who'd spent the evening avoiding Gregor's advances and was obviously still high on birthday cake. We waved at them. We smiled at them. We tried to will these sad vestiges of the broken nationalist system to let us pass and approach the shores of Liberland.

The two Croatian policemen aboard did not wave back. Nor did they smile.

"The system has made their hearts cold," said Štefan.

Their boats and cold, dead hearts drew closer to us, at speed, creating waves that rocked our little, pitiful sea vessel.

"They're not trying to tip us over, are they?" I asked.

"They wouldn't dare," said the future ambassador to Liechtenstein. I think exaggerating his present importance.

Anton surveyed the scene. Inhaled. Steered us closer to them. "Maybe..." he said. I did feel like a slave in that moment.

Their boat stayed in line with ours, on our right-hand side, stopping us from turning and getting any closer to the shores of Liberland. They kept their boat in this position, flanking us all the way up the river. We stared at them, they stared back at us. They were much better at it, being professional intimidation operatives of the military industrial complex. They also had uniform, guns, and a real boat, all of which helped immensely. By comparison, we were a ramshackle group of hedonists, libertarians, a cannabis shaman, and a bald writer. We were equipped for anarcho-capitalism, not confrontation. Unless that was the same thing. I still wasn't quite sure.

"Oh, come on," the Turkish girl said. "Let us pass."

They did not.

"Can you see that no-mooring sign?" Anton asked. We squinted. Ah, there it was—a small white-and-red sign, possibly hand-painted, some hundred metres ahead.

"That's the start of Liberland," he said, proudly.

As borders went it was inauspicious. Anton narrowed the gap between us and the police boat to just two metres. We passed parallel to the sign, our path to shore still blocked. But we'd reached Liberland. We were alongside it. Were looking at it, round the edges of a police boat, anyway. As promised, it was full of trees, marsh, and mosquitoes, but it was also clearly a handsome piece of land with a three-hundred-and-fifty-metre-long white-sand beachfront.

"I'm going to open a cafe there," said Štefan, pointing towards the beach.

"The good kind of cafe, right?" asked the Turkish girl. Štefan didn't need to answer; the man was a cannabis shaman. After the island, Liberland continued for another hundred metres along the shoreline that Serbia said was probably Croatian, Croatia said was definitely Croatian, President Vit said was Liberland, and I said was handsome. Then, just as subtly as it had started, it ended. We were still thirty metres from the Liberland shore, still being blocked by the police boat. Unable to get any closer to the promised land without getting rammed by a boat, wet, arrested, and having to endure a few days in a Croatian jail, we turned around and headed back. Could we really say we'd been there? The boat's passengers were uncertain. I decided we could, for the bragging rights alone.

At the shore, President Vit was waiting. "How do you like Liberland?" he asked.

"It's very beautiful," I answered, and at that moment, as just an idea, and a barren patch of land, it was.

∽

It's certainly easy to dismiss the whole Liberland project as ridiculous. I know I did at the beginning, and during the middle. In fact, I wasn't sure I was totally free of ridicule for it now, at the end of my weekend in its inner circle. Yet the romance of it had me smitten. Every country that now exists began in just the same way as Liberland, with a group of radicals chasing something other people said was impossible. Creating something out of nothing. Countries might feel sacred or as if they've always been there and yet they're created; divided; reunited. They change their names; have their borders drawn and redrawn; change their capitals; change currencies; and elect new governments all the time. Ask the citizens of Rhodesia, Burma, Ceylon, South Sudan, Yugoslavia, or, closer to home, the German Democratic Republic about the sanctity of borders and the longevity of regimes. The libertarians are right—countries really are collective fictions. They're also right about the potential of new technology to change those fictions, to create better, fairer stories. It's already happening. Look around next time you're in a bar or restaurant or on the subway. How many people are checking out of that physical place and into a virtual one, a digital no-man's land. Physical location is just not as important as it used to be. Long gone are the days where we are damned to grow up, work, find a partner, raise children, and then die within a hundred kilometres of where we are born. As an immigrant, I've experienced the benefits of free movement first-hand.

Does that mean Liberland is going to get its voluntary-taxation, anti-government, cannabis-shaman paradise any time soon? I've no idea. The project is in good shape and the brand is well known and attracts more followers with each passing day. Not that this project is exclusively about politics. It's also about fun, adventure, rebellion, and spending the short time we have here on this big spinning rock being part of something bigger, chasing down an impossible dream —indulging in the romance of creating your own country. My little taster of that life convinced me it's a good one. Superior to the one where you actually get what you wish for, and then have to try to turn a bit of marshland into a society, armed with only the free market's invisible hand, and Gregor.

The world's a much more interesting place because of radicals like the people behind the Liberland project. They have imagination and conviction and that's more than most. I hope they make it, and I can place my feet on the sandy beach of a real Liberland one day. Their project also helped me understand my own a little better. I was challenging the establishment. Only the difference was that my establishment was, mostly, myself. It was the responsibilities and expectations of the life I had built in Berlin. It's a weird thing to admit that you've become bored of yourself. But I knew now that I had been. That had ended in Istanbul. That was what travel was for. The unfamiliarity of being where you don't belong frees you from any expectations about how things there are supposed to work, and, in turn, how you will react to them. A childlike naivety takes over. I enjoyed that feeling immensely. I knew that like Liberland, it might not come to anything. But waiting at Belgrade Airport, feeding my growing dictator fetish with a book about Slobodan Milošević, I realised I was enjoying my journey regardless.

After landing at Tegel Airport, I sent Annett a message letting her know I'd be home shortly. Usually she'd reply with a "nice to have you back," or a "looking forward to seeing you." This time I got no reply at all. Arriving at the front door, I put my key inside the lock. I tried to turn it. Nothing happened.

11

INTERLUDE #2: REAL LIFE, REAL PROBLEMS

After I rang the doorbell and waited impatiently with visions of heartbreak, flat-hunting, and several months spent sitting in my underwear eating Ben & Jerry's Phish Food, Annett opened the door from inside. She hadn't changed the locks, merely left her key inside it. We had a discussion in the hallway that an observer might have described as "somewhat heated."

In order to make peace, I agreed to attend a number of upcoming events, giving the confident impression I had some idea where I was going to be in the next months, and that that place would certainly be Berlin.

While there, I did my best to open postal mail, pay taxes, swap light bulbs, and look interested when Annett bitched about colleagues who kept, repeatedly, egregiously, unfathomably, failing to recognise her genius.

I listened, mostly. I empathised, often. I went to the shops to buy us cheer-up chocolate. I washed up. Then I washed up some more. Then I washed up again.

Daily life is kind of boring, I realised, standing at the sink, wiping soup from a bowl. It's full of obligations to be met, bills to be paid, and washing up to be... *washed(?)*, and if that's not bad enough, if you do just one teeny tiny little inconsequential thing wrong—like, oh, I don't know, forget to pay a few years of tax—*they put you in prison.*

It's not to be recommended, really, any of it.

Unlike running away. Running away is great. It lets you escape from the prison of routine. So while pretending to be happy to be home, I was secretly researching a trip to Transnistria—a weird, Soviet throwback country I'd discovered while in Belgrade. There would be no washing up waiting for me there, of that I was sure.

It would also be the perfect follow-up to Liberland. Because while the Liberlandians and I were trying to change, trying to reinvent ourselves, rushing towards the new, Transnistria was doing the opposite. It was trying to go backwards.

Transnistria is a tiny, wonky, narrow strip of land squashed from either side by Moldova and the Ukraine. When the rusty Iron Curtain finally collapsed, many Eastern European countries sought to regain their previous autonomy and form new national identities. The tiny, wonky, narrow strip of land now called Transnistria found itself sitting in what was now calling itself Moldova. A Moldova that had decreed its official language would be Moldovan. A linguistic inconvenience for the mainly Russian-speaking Transnistria. As Moldova looked west, Transnistria glanced forlornly east, towards Mother Russia. A cultural tug of war ensued. The white arts of diplomacy tried to fix it. They failed. The dark arts of war stepped in. Bearing in mind that Transnistria only had a population of half a million, and is, at some points, just a few kilometres wide, it was a war that should have ended by lunchtime of that same day, with Transnistria waving white flags and issuing humble apologies for having got ideas well above its station.

That was not what happened. Instead, those half a million plucky Leninists called home to Moscow. Moscow was probably flattered. No one else wanted to play with its ideologies anymore. Russia's former territories were all flying their own flags now, and reaching for the shiny baubles of capitalism. All except this tiny, wonky, narrow strip of land squashed from either side by Moldova and the Ukraine.

Of course Moscow would send weapons. Lots of weapons.

There were skirmishes, on and off, from November 1990, and by 1992 things really began to escalate. The war continued intensively until July of that same year, at a cost of some seven hundred lives, before Russia managed to broker a peace deal between the two, perhaps neglecting to mention that they'd been arming one of them all the way through. As part of this deal, Moldova didn't admit that it had "lost," nor did it accept that Transnistria was a real country. It just decided the cost of proving itself right was too high. A truce was agreed. A truce that still exists. The people of Transnistria think they have their own country; no one else does, yet no one is willing to call their bluff and try to take it from them because... Russia.

Unlike Liberland, someone can visit Transnistria without getting arrested. Or, so I hoped. Because I'd decided to do just that.

12

TIRASPOL, TRANSNISTRIA: "IT'S LIKE THE TRUMAN SHOW FUCKED THE TWILIGHT ZONE."

Boredom, the hammer and sickle, the sheriff, corruption

Getting to Transnistria is not particularly difficult, but understanding what you are seeing there, and having someone to discuss it with, is. I decided to join a group tour. The group was twelve people, seven of them fellow Brits, regretfully. Even more regretfully, its two guides, Chris and Jack, were Irish. The tour company they worked for specialised in unusual destinations. I'd begun by spending a few days with them in the Ukraine. Sober they were a lovely bunch; while drunk, they were awful.

They were always drunk.

They were especially inebriated as we stepped off the otherwise empty train from Odessa and onto the platform of Tiraspol's central (and only) station. Tiraspol is the capital (and only) city in Transnistria. Depending on your definitions of *capital* and *city*.

It became clear how few tourists Transnistria receives when we found an immigration officer waiting on the platform just for us. He was a doughy, middle-aged man warming his hands in the deep pockets of his official Transnistrian immigration officer's jacket. He held his chin at an elevated height that suggested nobility. Carbohydrates and hedonism had swollen his broad face.

Stood next to him was Sergei, the local student the tour company had hired to show us around. He was a young, blond, baby-faced, born-and-bred Transnistrian. He held his chin at a depressed height that suggested humility. Humility he wore like a cape.

"Welcome to Transnistria," the official said. "Delete that photo!" he barked at Mike, an American sneakily photographing the back of the train station. "This is an official building. No photos."

We strolled towards the station. Perhaps detecting a certain intimate, jovial glow emanating from the group, he asked, "Have you all been drinking?"

With the exception of me, everyone had been drinking. A lot. As per usual. Jack, in his misbuttoned yellow duffel coat, staggered forward to shake the man's hand. "How you doing, chief. Lovely to see ya." Officially, Jack was employed as one of our two guides. In practice, he was only qualified to lead a tour through a liquor cabinet. He knew his way around liquor cabinets. Or he knew the way in, anyway.

The immigration officer squinted at Jack. He didn't seem to know what to do with a *Jack*. "I heard reports of loudness on train. Of wvhisky and beer?" A wry smile escaped from the edges of his mouth. "You will fit in well in Transnistria, comrades!"

At the front of the station we found a rectangular sliding window. Behind it sat a bored woman on a swivel chair. It missed a wheel.

"Hello, darling. Lovely to see ya. You having a good night?" said Jack, crudely balancing his forearm on the frame of her window, his legs swaying beneath it. She said nothing. She didn't seem to know what to do with a *Jack* either.

The immigration officer seemed delighted to have an audience. He strutted around like a small child given a badge and told to patrol the sandpit. We huddled in front of the window while immigration forms were dispensed. Forms he didn't care if we filled in; he just wanted to talk.

"Is there anyone here from France?" he asked first. It was three days after the Bataclan terror attack in Paris. Anne-Sophie, from Paris, raised her hand.

The man raised his fist to the sky, shook it, brought it back down, and kissed its knuckles. "France, *very* beautiful country..."

"Thank you," she replied.

"I hear you have been having some..." He paused, trying to find the correct word. "*Problems* there?"

Anne-Sophie leaned back, seemingly surprised to hear the loss of 130 lives being described about as trivially as getting a bicycle puncture. "The attacks, you mean?"

"*Yez. Problems.* In your Paris. Terrible. Terrible." The man put his fist to his heart. "Transnistria stands with you!"

This was both nice and unexpected, and would come, no doubt, as a great relief to France. His voice grew solemn. "Are you refugee?"

Her mouth opened. Nothing came out. She looked at the rest of us for reassurance that her ears were hearing what her brain was reporting. They were. "A... refugee?"

"Yes, you apply for asylum?"

"*In... Transnistria?*"

The public official puffed out his already inflated chest. "Yes, in Transnistria. Transnistria is great country!"

I guess that depends on your definitions of *great* and *country*.

"Erm... well..." She suppressed a smile. "No. I'm just here as a tourist."

The man lowered his head and closed his eyes. "Tourist, I see. Well, you are welcome."

"He's probably never left Transnistria," whispered Sergei. "This may have coloured his understanding of world. Play along otherwise we won't get our forms stamped."

It took some time to fill out our forms because the immigration department only had three pens, and our group had forgone packing anything useful, such as pens, in order to create more space for transporting alcohol.

It was a farcical scene. Twelve people from countries that do exist, being drunk and raucous and disrespectful to a man in an oversized coat and hat and a woman on a broken swivel chair, asking for a visa to a country that didn't.

"Is there anyone here from America?" the border guard asked next. Mike, with the itchy camera-trigger finger stepped into the centre of our huddle. "I've been reading about your America," the man said.

Mike nodded, trying not to laugh.

"I've been reading about *Detroit*." He said the word *Detroit* as if it were *Atlantis*, his eyes wide with wonder. "A lot of wolves!"

"In Detroit?"

"Yes. In Detroit. A lot of *wolves*."

"Okay..." said Mike, tilting his head.

"Also," the man continued, "a lot of crime. In your Detroit."

That made more sense. We were back on track, conversationally.

"Yes, a lot of crime," Mike answered with a sharp nod. *Detroit. Crime. Fine.*

"Maybe," the man added, stroking his beard contemplatively. He might not have been a travelled man, but he still knew a thing or two about the world. "It's... because of all the niggers?"

Oh...

Slowly our visas were approved. Generously we'd been granted permission to remain in this non-country for twenty-four hours. "It used to be twelve hours," said Sergei, his arms hanging limply at his sides.

At the taxi rank, opposite the train station entrance, we found just one solitary taxi. "I'm not sure where the others are," Sergei said, discussing our predicament with the solitary taxi's driver, whose downcast expression suggested he had also just arrived here and found it as ridiculous as we did. The rest of the group, having pickled their brains in alcohol, couldn't manage this level of emotional nuance and so wore the stupid, wide, happy grins of indulgence.

Fifteen minutes later two cars turned, far faster than necessary, into the station's empty car park. These two dented, dejected vehicles appeared to have just finished a banger race in which they'd placed well outside the medal positions. They were the unofficial taxi drivers called by the perturbed real one. Sergei told them all that we wanted to go to the AIST hotel. "It has closed down," the official taxi driver said flatly.

"Oh," said Sergei.

With no better ideas, we decided to go there anyway. I ended up in one of the two unofficial taxis. It was driven by a lanky, clean-shaven, middle-aged man. We'd not yet seen any young people, other than Sergei. The man's cheekbones protruded out from below sunken, sad eyes. I wanted to buy him a warm meal, then several more. He popped the boot of his small car so we could put our luggage inside.

"Thank you," I said, moving nearer to it with my sports holdall. Looking down into the boot I saw that it contained just one giant speaker and no space for bags.

"Oh," I said, the group's new motto. The man nodded at the speaker, breathed in deeply, then slammed the boot closed. That was settled. Four of us piled into the small car, luggage clutched tightly to our chests. I got the plum seat in the front because of my obnoxiously long legs. The driver climbed in next to me, made himself comfortable, turned to me, winked, and spun the volume dial on the stereo to DEAFEN. House music began to play at a loudness and intensity that surpassed common decency. We were suffocated by bass. The man cackled loudly as he hit the accelerator, the tyres screeched, and we spurted out into the (otherwise silent) Tiraspol night.

The journey was painful, aurally, due to the oppressive volume of this maniac's music. I self-medicated by imagining how awesome it was going to be here if Transnistria continued to pack as much entertainment into the next day as it had the first forty-five minutes at the train station. It was spoiling us. I decided never to leave, which was going to be difficult since I had to in just twenty-three hours and change.

The journey took no more than five minutes. The city we passed was surprisingly modern, built in a grid fashion, with large, imposing Soviet buildings that all seemed to have been freshly painted and spruced up for something. The streets were empty. We saw no more than ten humans and not a single wolf.

The tiny car screeched to a stop in front of a huge, drab, concrete, Death Star of a building. The driver switched off the engine, turned to me, and cut the air with a sharp nod. *We did it*, that nod seemed to say. *They doubted us, but we did it.* I scrambled for the door handle and tripped and fell onto the tarmac, my ears ringing as if punched by Soviet Russia's finest pugilists. Getting back to my feet, I looked up at the monolith before us. All of its lights were off. It didn't look like a hotel. It looked like the sort of place hope went to die, had its corpse been dragged out the back and buried, before being dug back up and shot again, just to be sure. What had its architect been thinking? And, perhaps more importantly, had he or she been adequately punished for those thoughts?

In front of what might have once been the entrance, five gigantic male humans stood in a row, all silhouetted in the moonlight as if they were posing for an album cover.

Trance-nistria: So you want to (Communist) Party?

They looked down at this flash flood of foreigners like patients given a long-feared terminal prognosis. "What's their job?" asked Pierre, a French Canadian who had the useless talent of always looking as if he'd just woken up.

"Menacing?" someone answered.

"Ya' right boys?" Jack shouted up at them, climbing unsteadily up the few steps to the entrance. "How the devil 'r ya? Lovely night for it, aye?"

The men said nothing, their arms crossed. One turned and unlocked the building's front door. Its hinges creaked ominously. Inside the lobby we found a graveyard of things that used to be: a smashed-up vending machine covered in a dirty sheet; an eclectic collection of earthenware pots without plants; mismatched furniture thrown together in a heap and left to rust or dust. Sergei talked to one of the men. He confirmed what we were thinking: "Apparently, you're the only guests."

"Tonight or in the last decade?" asked Pierre.

Behind the reception desk sat an implausibly old woman, almost certainly the oldest person who has ever lived, surrounded by dust and cobwebs. Possibly she'd been sitting there since the last guests checked out, back in 1967.

"'ello darlin'," said Jack. *Burp.* "Lovely to see ya."

She said nothing. Perhaps because she was mummified.

But then, to my surprise, slowly, she rose from her seat and stepped gingerly out from behind reception clutching a great cluster of keys like a medieval jailer. One elevator was out of order, as indicated by the potted plant blocking its entrance, but she gestured to the other elevator before turning her head to us slowly, like a thoughtful, injured owl.

"I'm not sure about this," said Mads, as we stepped in. Mads was an affable Dane, a student of law, and my roommate-to-be. The elevator was carpeted. The colour was puke. We held our breath. It groaned its ascent up to the ninth and final floor.

Relieved at having not plunged to our death, we swiftly stepped out into a dark hallway. The AIST had prepared a welcome committee for us here in the form of several piles of awning, pipes, and other things that used to be attached to a building, probably this building, in 1967. A light flickered overhead.

"Blimey," said Jack. "It's like *Bates Motel* fucked *The Shining*." The old lady shuffled, as if walking was something she'd read about but not got around to trying just yet, wordlessly towards the corridor's first bedroom. The beds in it were bare. She gestured towards a chest of drawers. There we found blankets and pillows. "I don't think we're the first people to use these," said Mads.

I fluffed a pillow. It made a cracking sound like breaking glass.

"We'll take it!" said Mads.

The woman nodded very, very slowly, perhaps unsure of its effect upon her aged spine. She creaked back out into the hallway and on to the next room. That room was to be Jen and Anne-Sophie's, the only two girls in our otherwise testosterone-heavy group. We heard laughter emanating from the hallway. We found the old lady standing with their doorknob in her hand. It was no longer attached to the door.

"Feckin' hell," said Jack, scratching at the stubble on his neck. A light further down the corridor had seen enough; it flicked one final time and quit the business of illumination. The AIST was a place of wonders. If this was the past, I was more than happy in the present, I realised.

After dropping our stuff, we regrouped in the lobby, keen to explore Tiraspol's nightlife, not yet aware that it didn't exist. We found the city's streets quiet. Very quiet. A dropping pin would have been shushed, had there been anyone around to do so. Two streets later, we did see something moving, when a midnight-blue police car crawled past us. Its driver looked at us as though we were exotic fruit he didn't know how to eat yet. The police car was a comically small Lada. It looked as if it were made of Lego. Ladas, while beautiful, lack authority. They're like monkeys dressed as firemen. Ladas are the sort of car eight clowns tumble out of at the circus, one playing the trumpet. It seemed impossible that this could be the vehicle the Transnistrian police used to inspire the respect, awe, and co-operation of the local populace. There must be no crime here. Or no crime committed by people over 1.6 metres. They'd never have fit into the back—well, unless they were clowns.

I hurried my step so I could get closer to Sergei.

"Is there a lot of crime here, Sergei?"

He chuckled. "Seriously? This place is one big smuggler's den. There are some towns I can't take you to. They're just big outposts for Soviet weapons."

"Is it always this quiet?" Chris asked.

"No." He shrugged. "It used to be quieter."

"It's beautiful, though," Anne-Sophie said.

"Yes. The new prime minister is on a painting offensive, for the election. Paint is cheap. You don't have to do anything with the insides of the buildings."

"Is he a good guy?"

"No, not really, same like others."

On the fifteen-minute walk to the restaurant we passed ten pedestrians, about a dozen cars, and two police Ladas. We kept seeing the same word again and again: *Sheriff*.

Sheriff Supermarket, Sheriff Hotel, Sheriff Bakery.

"What is this *sheriff*?" I asked Sergei between mouthfuls of spicy pepperoni pizza at the only open restaurant.

"The sheriff is the richest man in Transnistria," he said, taking a swig of beer. "He used to be the police chief, back in the nineties. Apparently he was the only person who could give out business licences, so gave himself all the business licences. Now he owns almost everything. He gets rid of any competition."

I imagined dissidents being whisked away to remote forests, their hands and feet tied, their faces squashed against Lada windows. The sheriff sounded like a malignant Transnistrian Bruce Wayne, with Tiraspol as his Gotham City.

"I'm surprised that one person can control that much," said Mads. Sergei lowered his shoulders, his face emotionless. "You shouldn't be. This is a country that no one knows exists. You can do what you want here."

"How bad is the corruption then?" I asked.

"Hmm... Let me think..." Sergei's eyes twinkled. "Ah, I remember. It's all day, every day. For example, next week I will have my driver's test." He took another sip of beer. "I'm going to pass."

"How do you know that?"

"The guy told me when I booked it. If I want to pass I need to pay him fifty dollars."

Our mouths tumbled open. "This is why I didn't go to university. You can only pass if you pay the bribe before each test. I don't have money. So now I stay home. I go to University of Google."

As sad as this was, Sergei seemed totally unaffected by it. There was no hint of emotion or resentment in his voice, as if he were reading the weather forecast for a country he knew he'd never visit.

"In hospital," he continued, seeing he had an enraptured audience, "if you want to get treatment, you bribe doctor. With bribe you get treated today; without it, in eighteen months."

"Do you think Transnistrian culture will change over time?"

"There is no Transnistrian culture," he said, forcefully. "We're Russian. That's it."

After dinner, the group wanted to go "drinking." A novel idea and a nice change of pace from all the drinking they'd done earlier in the day, and all the previous days.

"I know a place," Sergei assured us.

"Will it be busier than the restaurant?" Chris asked, scanning the empty seats around us. Three parallel streets of the Tiraspol grid later, we entered a karaoke bar and got the answer: *No.*

Upon entering, as if on strings activated by the door, two staff members popped up from behind the bar. There were no other guests. "It's like *The Truman Show* fucked *The Twilight Zone*," Jack said.

The bar staff was composed of a short, stocky woman in her mid-thirties with gritted teeth and the demeanour of someone sucking on a thousand lemons and a younger man with ghostly white, almost translucent skin who appeared, at all times, to be apologising for his own existence. The group warbled their way through some terrible Oasis covers followed by some terrible Beatles covers then some terrible eighties covers and then, just when I thought it couldn't get any worse, it rained men.

In between, alcohol flowed. I yawned and pinched myself to stay awake. The same two or three exhibitionists traded turns at the microphone. After an hour, an argument broke out. It was between the female bartender and our guide, Chris. "Stop trying to rip me off," he said, waving his receipt.

The woman adopted a power pose, dropping her hands to her hips. "You said you vanted big one."

"When did I say that? What's a 'big one'?"

She looked him up and down. "You look like you like big one."

"What the hell does that mean?" He waved his receipt. "I asked for a double. You've charged me for a quadruple!"

"You asked for qwadruple," she said, squinting out from under her furrowed eyebrows.

"Who orders a quadruple rum and coke? That's not a thing."

"In Transnistria it is thing."

He gestured to the empty bar. "If you stopped trying to rip your customers off you might have a few more of them."

Her eyes narrowed further. "How dare you talk to me this way."

The woman sent her meek male colleague—who had pinned himself against the wall in an unsuccessful attempt to make himself invisible—outside to wake up the bouncer. The bouncer was sleeping in a chair, his head leaning against the wall. It was a slow night, after all. Possibly it was always a slow night.

The bouncer came inside rubbing sleep from heavy eyes. The barwoman talked to him in Russian. He blinked, slowly, seemingly unaware what any of this had to do with him. He let out a loud yawn. The woman removed one hand from her hip and began waving it in Chris's direction. The bouncer scratched at patches of his bald head.

"Since I know you like them big, I gave you bigger one."

Chris tutted. "You can't charge me for things I don't order. It doesn't work like that."

I was pretty sure it did work like that, just as long as the sheriff said so. Eventually she backed down but only after Sergei stepped in and worked some of his calm, rational, diplomatic magic. Chris's money was returned to him. She spent the rest of the evening scowling at him, and anyone else foolish enough to enter her eyeline.

At 3am, lights were switched off. We were still the only customers. "I fucking love y's all," said Jack, propping himself uneasily against the bar. I'd wanted to go home hours ago but had toughed it out so as not to look like a stick in the mud. We began putting on coats and thinking of sleep. Two of the group had wandered outside together, thinking of something else. There was a lot of hugging, singing, some wobbling.

Mrs Quadruple pushed a piece of paper across the bar to Jack. It was a bill. We were not expecting a bill. The drinks had been paid for as we'd ordered them, sometimes for more than we'd ordered, even. An extraordinary amount of swearing then occurred, most of it from Jack. I'll censor it now, for those of a sensitive nature.

"I don't love you, you f***** charlatans," said Jack, after scrutinising the bill. "They're trying to fleece us f***** two dollars per f***** song. They're taking the p*** is what they are, c***s."

Jack's outrage was understandable. Two dollars went far in this country. The average wage was just two hundred dollars a month. Our karaoke bill was $110. "Two dollars per f***** song? Are ye having a laugh? I could buy the song for less, and sing it as much as I want," added Chris, standing next to Jack, shoving the bill back across the bar. "Where does it say it costs that much?" He looked around the bar for a price list or menu. Nothing in the woman's face moved. Her hands were stuck firm to her hips.

"You never asked," she said. "I vould have told."

The life-averse male barman had discovered some very important dusting and bottle rearrangement work to be done in the far corner. He was summoned back and told to rouse the slumbering security guard once more. The guard took even longer to gift us with his dopey presence, which he announced with a loud yawn and some lead-footed shuffling. He looked as if he were being asked to referee a game he'd not read the rules of. The woman squared up to Chris, across the bar, her finger within swatting distance of his nose. "Who are you to give me advice on running business?" she said.

"I'm the punter. F*** this s***hole. Let's go, I'm not paying it."

She threw her arms up in the air. "I don't set the prices. It's nothing to do with me."

"Yeah, well, you don't communicate them either, do you, love?" an irate Jack fired back at her. I thought midnight-blue Ladas were going to be called. Sergei stepped tactfully back in and convinced the three people who had held the microphone hostage all night to pitch in and pay. It was strongly recommended, he said, without saying why. Group tours can be nice, but they depend heavily on the group. In this one, I was a fifth wheel on a party Lada. I already wanted out.

The next day was a beauty. I found the main street approaching a light bustle (by Transnistrian standards). Almost all the people in the broad streets were advanced in age, huddled against the strong wind as they walked over whitewashed pavement. Decrepit Soviet trolley-buses rattled by; commuters pushed up against dirty windows covered in propaganda art showcasing a time of prosperity long gone.

After breakfast, Sergei led a tour of the city. It held my original positive impression of it—calm, unabashedly Soviet, favouring brutalist architecture, not unfriendly or hostile to outsiders, just confused by their existence. Sergei explained that the country's current president had got elected on an anti-sheriff ticket. The city had only one supermarket, imaginatively called Sheriff Supermarket, but this man, Yevgeny Vasylyevich Shevchuk, had promised that if he was elected, he'd open a second one. As political promises went it was certainly less ambitious than "no taxation without representation," "better dead than red," or "make Transnistria great once," but it had worked nonetheless. His new supermarket had just opened. "Take a look inside," Sergei said. It looked like any other supermarket, anywhere in the world.

"So is it cheaper than the sheriff's?" Mads asked.

"No, I think it's pretty much the same. Probably it's really the sheriff who owns it anyway," Sergei added, with his usual portion of nonchalance. "Or a friend of his."

A taxi passed us. Inside, riding next to the driver, was a person of colour. Given the immigration officer's comments, I found this as unexpected as passing a wolf in downtown Detroit.

"You have black people here?" I asked.

"Of course," he said, running a hand slowly through his cropped hair. "We have two."

My head jerked backwards. "What do you mean *two*? Like two in the whole country?"

"Yeah. They play for the basketball team."

"Wait, *there's a basketball team?*"

"Yeah." He nodded. "It's called Sheriff."

Of course it was. On the way to a flea market we passed several Lenin statues, including one outside of the government offices. Lenin statues were being removed from the Ukraine now, as it began airbrushing its history. Transnistria was fighting progress. Sergei showed me an election poster of the sheriff's son. "Do you think things will change if the sheriff's son gets elected? Will Transnistria become a real country?"

"No." He laughed. "They say every day in the paper that they're *working on becoming recognised*. It's bullshit. Nothing ever happens. They don't want anything that would threaten their monopoly."

After lunch we drove out towards an abandoned brick factory. I told Sergei about Chernobyl. He furrowed his brow. "Why would anyone want to go there? Transnistria is full of abandoned buildings! When I travel abroad, I like to visit things like Starbucks, McDonald's, or shopping malls. Things we don't have here."

On the way, we stopped at a supermarket in a town outside of Tiraspol. It may or may not have been owned by the sheriff. Sergei returned from it clutching a plastic bag containing a bottle of vodka, an onion, a loaf of bread, and some cheese. At the abandoned factory's gates he told us to stay put, and disappeared inside with his loot. He returned empty-handed. "You can go in now," he said. "I've bribed the guard."

We passed the guard's house. He lived in the derelict building nearest to the complex's rusty iron gates. Outside his hovel was a bathtub full of junk and scrap metal. He came out to take a cursory look at us. "Hello there, captain. How you been keeping?" said Jack. The man didn't reply. He was wearing a beanie hat, and had a thick, unkempt black beard. He didn't smell of roses. He did smell of regret. Sergei said he'd probably been in prison and with nowhere else to go after his release, the government had posted him here to guard what was left of the facility. After we'd been exploring for ten or fifteen minutes, an expensive off-road truck pulled up. A fat man got out and whistled to Sergei. They had an intense conversation. It sounded like war was imminent. But it looked, from Sergei's face, as if they were old friends inquiring about the health of each other's mothers. Everything was a negotiation here, everyone wanted to be bribed, yet Sergei never seemed fazed or flustered by the chaos and uncertainty within which he was forced to live. I found him extremely impressive. He was perfectly adapted to his surroundings, like a chameleon, but a chameleon who understood that his surroundings were nonsense and he really shouldn't keep being asked to blend into them. He wore his stoicism like a shield. The stranger got back into his truck and drove away leaving a cloud of dust.

"Who was that?" we asked.

"Some guy," said Sergei, flatly. "He says we have to leave, and that the other guy I bribed is not in charge and so I should have bribed *him* instead."

Just then the security guard with the wild beard appeared from a different entrance to the hangar we were exploring. He and Sergei had a similarly threatening-sounding conversation.

"It's okay, we can stay," Sergei said, afterwards. "The boss man talked to that normal security guard guy and he gave him my number and now everything is okay."

"So you have to bribe them both in future?" I asked.

"Yeah. Or, I told Mr Truck I would, anyway. I'll just call the normal guy I bribed today and ask him if the other guy is around. If he's not then I'll come."

"You're very calm about all this," I said, sitting on some metal piping.

He shrugged. "Why wouldn't I be?"

"I don't know. You don't get tired of everyone trying to exploit each other?"

"Sure I get tired of it," he said, like a tortoise about its shell. "But what am I going to do?" I might have tried getting really angry, or having a little cry, or moving to Moscow.

I sat next to Sergei on the ride back to town. "Do you think there's any ideology here?" I asked. "Do you think people want to go back to Communism?"

He scratched his chin. "No. That's just what the government says.

This is a cowboy country. It doesn't stand for anything, except money."

"What do you think is going to happen? Do the people want to have another revolution?"

He laughed. "I'm not sure they wanted the last one. No, I think the people just want to be left alone, mostly."

I frowned.

"Why did you want to come here, Adam?"

"I don't know. I thought there was something different happening here."

"Do you think that now?"

"No." I sighed.

"Do you regret coming then?"

"Not really. For some reason I'd still rather be here than in Berlin."

His eyes widened. "Why? *I'd* rather be in Berlin."

"I don't know. Everything just sort of functions there, you know? It's boring."

We passed a Soviet tank that was now a memorial of their war of independence. Sergei's dad had fought in it. "Boredom is a luxury good," he said.

I gasped. *Boredom is a luxury good.* This simple statement dug its claws into me and didn't let go. Of course. I'd lost sight of the extraordinary privilege inherent within boredom. Most people in the world don't get to decide whether or not to engage in politics. Don't feel so safe and secure and bored that they actively go out looking for danger, just to feel more alive.

Having a life like that didn't make me normal—it made me special. I was the unusual one. The weirdo. The outlier. Boredom was not the enemy. My ingratitude of it was. I'd been looking at it wrong. Writing it off as a commodity, when for most of the world it would be impossibly luxurious. "I'd happily swap your boring normal life for mine." Sergei smirked.

I cleared my throat. "Yeah, perhaps not right now."

13

CHIŞINĂU, MOLDOVA: "I AM THE DEVIL INCARNATE!"

A billion lions, windsocks, bountiful harvests

Our group's next destination, Moldova, was one of the ten least-visited countries in the world, and so largely unused to tourists. The short train ride from Tiraspol, Transnistria, to Chişinău, Moldova, was passing smoothly for my group of intrepid, roving alcoholics, lubricated as they were by the liquid charms of Transnistrian cognac. I was staying on with them through Moldova to Bucharest.

"So, like," shouted David, over the music coming from his portable speaker, "who do you think would win in a fight between a billion lions and the sun?" He was an English history student openly hostile to silence.

I groaned. "A billion lions?" said Mike.

The carriage's attendant appeared at the door. Each carriage of the train had its own personal attendant. Perhaps a throwback to socialism's drive for full employment. It was unclear what exactly our attendant was supposed to be doing, beyond tightly filling out an official-looking uniform. The group was endeavouring to keep him as busy as possible by spilling things, breaking things, and shouting things.

"SSHHHH. Too loud." The man pointed at the speaker. David turned it down. The man left. David turned it up again. Mike fell back in his seat. "It's actually quite hard to imagine a billion lions."

"I know, right," said David. "Now imagine the sun, and have them fight."

Chins were scratched. Brows furrowed. "How would that, like, work?" asked Chris.

David shrugged. "I don't know. But it's a lot of lions, right? They could, like, bite the sun?"

Mike took another swig of cognac from the bottle being passed round. "Yeah, my money's on the lions."

The song "Sweet Home Alabama" played. We were a long way from both. The group sang along, collapsing over each other affectionately like a litter of idiot puppies. At the start of the journey our carriage had been full. A woman with dyed blonde hair and knee-high leather boots was the last to break. She lasted twenty minutes. I found this impressive. She snarled something under her breath as she stomped past us. I apologised with my eyes. I don't think it worked.

"Lovely to see ya," Jack shouted at her. "Thanks for stopping by. Have fun in the next carriage, you tool."

I felt her pain but couldn't find the courage to abandon my tour-mates altogether. Were they so totally beyond redemption? Possibly. Probably. Yes. As a compromise quasi-rebellion, I moved a few seats away from them, where I kept myself busy quietly seething.

I was relieved when we reached Chişinău's central station, for it meant I was closer to being away from the group. I'd leave them in a few days, in Bucharest. Waiting on the platform, we found a confused-looking man staring vacantly at his shoes—a thin, lanky individual who appeared stretched against his will. His head was shaved around the sides, leaving just one central hair clump: a Mohawk, but brushed forward and prone to flapping, giving him both the appearance and function of a windsock. He was our local guide, Marius.

In keeping with the tour company's philosophy of frugality,

Marius was not a real tour guide, just a local student impersonating one. Unfortunately, he possessed neither Sergei's knowledge nor charm. "This is a pretty station. When was it built?" asked Paul, an IT consultant. He tripped as he walked, no longer in a state to consult on anything except poor life choices.

Marius's eyes darted upwards. "Erm," he said. "Yes, it's quite old." With outstretched arms he turned and tried to get the group into a flock that could be led towards our accommodation. At present, they were a mishmash of competing geographies scattered over the station's entrance hall, some singing, some dancing. David and Anne-Sophie were embracing in a dark corner.

"Everyone," he shouted. No one responded. He found two people on the periphery, inspecting a phone box, and tried to nudge them back towards the group's centre, near some ATMs. "Hello. *Hello!*" he shouted. "Everyone. Attention, please."

It didn't work. The second he loosened his grip on the arm of one straggler, to try to corral another, the first would become distracted by something shiny or alcoholic, and wander off. It was an entertaining scene, for everyone but Marius. It was going to be a long three days for him, I think he now realised. He tried whistling. No one responded. He grimaced, and massaged the duster on the centre of his head. Ten minutes in and he already looked exasperated.

"Who wants to go to a club?" he yelled.

The group snapped to attention. People emerged from the shadows, alert and responsive. A loose huddle formed around him. *Had someone mentioned a club? Yes, the group wanted to go to a club. Why had the possibility not been mentioned sooner? Where was this club and why were we not already in it?*

He didn't take us to a club, the liar. Instead, we walked for ten minutes to the entrance of an enormous high-rise hotel. The sort of hotel that markets itself primarily on its size using clever marketing slogans such as "Size *does* matter" and "Chișinău's *biggest* party."

After the AIST hotel of Tiraspol, this one seemed impossibly luxurious. Nothing fell off the wall, even. You sank into the bed, rather than being repelled by it. We had bedside lamps.

Lamps. Plural.

It was almost too much.

After a warm shower I was back down in the lobby waiting for the rest of the group. Weary from having spent another day with twelve people who thought restraint was ordering a beer without a chaser, and that intercultural awareness was knowing how to swear in six languages. Something had happened in Transnistria, although I guess it had been building slowly since Chernobyl. It was a new, poorly defined feeling manifesting in the centre of my chest. I was investigating it cautiously. So far I'd concluded it was homesickness iced with guilt, lightly dusted with regret, and then wrapped in a growing realisation that what I needed next was there, not here. It was a complex emotion. I liked that I was capable of them now. That I was decreasingly apathetic about the human experience.

At the lobby bar, attempting to locate The Mood and get into it, I ordered my first beer of the day. I was excited to learn more about Moldova. It wouldn't be hard, since I knew nothing, other than that it had once had a war with Transnistria, which it was in denial about having lost.

The barmaid returned from the fridge with my beer and change, a wad of leu banknotes of some heft. After I squeezed them into my pockets, it looked as though I'd taken part in a successful heist. The bar was empty save for an older gentleman two barstools over. He was hunched over an identical beer and wore a lilac linen shirt, the first two buttons of which were undone, revealing tufts of thick, white hair. His face was dimpled but possessed a quiet dignity, like a rusting but seaworthy boat.

"Do you know the exchange rate to euro?" I asked him.

He rotated towards me on his stool. "I'm not sure, my boy. But I think you've plenty there for a good few tipples yet." I'd not been called "my boy" for some time, possibly my entire life, in fact. I detected a slight accent.

"Irish?"

"Welsh." He smiled. "But that's another lifetime now."

I took the first pull of cold beer. "How long since you lived there?"

He scratched at his neck. "Well, erm... It w
paused, observing something on the bar. "I had 1
That was in, ah..." His voice faded out. Not as if he w
forgotten, but as if he had such an abundance of pa
that it would be like trying to drink the ocean arm
straw. "And then I sold that, and then it was, well, ce   , ᴀ ᴛ least
twenty years now, lad."

"What did your company do?"

"Well, that's an equally long story, isn't it." His tone sauntered upwards at the "isn't it," as though he'd been considering making this a question but then thought better of it, presumably because only he knew its answer. "I made my money in logistics, shipping and trucking and so on. Yeah, made a man of me it did. Then I sold it all and hit the road. That made more of a man of me. What are you doing in Chișinău, my boy?"

I gestured behind me with my thumb to the few freshly showered members of our group, who had draped themselves over the lobby's sofas, red-eyed and staring into their phones. It was a rare moment of Wi-Fi and they intended to indulge. "I'm on a group tour," I said.

He rolled his eyes. "Oh, a group tour. I see."

There was a pause in which I think I was supposed to defend the merits of group tours, but didn't. He took another sip of his beer. "I'll give you a piece of advice now, laddie—get yourself down to Africa. Forget all this group-tour nonsense." He flapped a wrist back in the direction of the others. "Buy yourself a ticket to Africa, anywhere there, doesn't matter. One way, naturally. Then just go-o-o." He paused. "Africa will sort you out. Make a man of you."

He'd quickly deduced that I wasn't a man. I'd have to get better at hiding it. I felt the grip on my beer bottle tighten. "Spent a lot of time there, have you?"

"Yes, before I started my, what was it now... second company. In Africa there's, well, a certain spirit that's lacking where we are from. There, you can be anything. Can make anything happen. It's far better than being out of your skull here with your group-tour buddies."

I flinched. "I've been to Africa."

"Oh, have you now." He smirked. "Group tour, I suppose?"

I looked back at my travelling companions. They were shambolic, disrespectful. Many of them were low-functioning alcoholics. Yet they struck me as honest. They knew who they were. They were without pretence. They just wanted to have a good time. Tomorrow? Tomorrow's problem. They didn't lecture people they didn't know, at bars, on how they should be living. The man saw that I was slipping from his grasp. "You think you need it, I know. But trust me, I've been around the block once or twice now. And then a few times more. *You don't*. Just throw yourself out there, and it'll be fine. You seem to have a good head on your shoulders. Why not use it?"

"You don't know anything about me," I said, standing up from my stool.

"Well, you live as long as me, you get an idea for these things."

I dug my nails into the soft flesh of my palms. I didn't want to show him I was annoyed. I was annoyed. "Thanks for the advice," I said, passing him to return to my tour friends. The older man continued drinking alone. This man knew nothing about me. I knew nothing about him. Regardless, based on the fact that I was on a group tour, he'd felt comfortable giving me condescending life advice that reduced Africa, a continent of fifty-four countries and 1.1 billion diverse people, into a giant shortcut to a purer, more noble existence.

It seemed very obvious to me in this moment that, of course, you could "find yourself" in Africa, just as you could find yourself in Bolivia, or rocking in front of the Wailing Wall, or in your home town while out walking the dog. People who aren't self-reflective in their everyday lives don't magically uncover new modes of thought or hidden depths of understanding just because they swap Home for Rome or Gloucester for Gabon.

I reflected on my current quest, if that's what it was. I knew I didn't want it to end with my sitting on a barstool, in my seventies, in Chișinău's biggest hotel, giving life advice to people I'd just met.

∽

The next morning, the old man was sitting alone in the breakfast room. He smiled at me as I entered, gesturing at the empty seat opposite. I smiled back and then sat on my own, on the other side of the room. It was far too early for life advice. Just an hour later than agreed, Marius appeared to show us around the city. Chişinău turned out to be an interesting place, in an under-construction way. Everything in it seemed to be either really new and so not quite finished or really old and so about to be knocked down to become something new again, probably a shopping mall. Marius took us to see a church and the parliament buildings.

"Is this the Măzărache?" asked Paul, looking up from his Central Europe guidebook.

Marius's eyes darted around as he bit his bottom lip. A look fast becoming his signature.

"And what's that building in the background?"

Marius pulled at his hair and pivoted onto the back of his feet. Mike threw him a lifeline. "Is it the opera house, perhaps?"

He relaxed his shoulders. "Y-e-s, that's right, the opera house." He said *opera house* as if hearing the words for the first time.

For lunch he took us to a shopping mall's food court. I thought back to Sergei, and his love of international shopping malls. Is this what they thought Western Europe was like? What they thought we liked? Shopping malls, luxury brands, McDonald's? *Is it?* Maybe they were on to something. But that didn't mean they had to stay on it, riding it through all our mistakes of modernisation.

Growing tired of Marius and the group, that afternoon, I elected to wander around the city on my own. It was very pleasant, with a number of nice parks and the wide, flat streets I now associated with the Soviet Union. I strolled through the central park with its Triumphal Arch, Nativity Cathedral, and monument to Ştefan Cel Mare, the city's most revered son for having defeated Turkish invaders in the fifteenth century. Today, about eight hundred thousand people call Chişinău home, although from their expressions, not all seemed happy about this—many preferred the poker faces I'd grown used to seeing in the Ukraine and Transnistria. Much of

Chişinău was destroyed in the Second World War and rebuilt in the favoured, imposing, Soviet style of the time.

It felt as if the city was still trying to form its own identity, even though it had been independent since 1991. Outside the parliament were two separate protest groups, just a hundred metres from each other. One wanted to go West, and join the EU; the other was pro-Russian, and like Transnistria, wanted to pull East. The most striking thing about the city's streets, like in Tiraspol, was that an entire demographic felt absent: people between the ages of eighteen and thirty. I've always been passionately pro-European. A world with fewer borders has to be a better world, right? A world where people are free to overcome the shortcomings of their birth and move, visa free, somewhere that might offer them greater prosperity. But then, I'd only ever lived in two prosperous European countries—the countries people went to, not the countries people left. Here, it became clear to me for the first time that there might be losers in the European experiment. Already so many of the young people here had left. What would happen if suddenly those people were offered twenty economically stronger places to relocate to, visa free? Sure, it's possible that those people would send money back to their families, or would return one day, when ready to create their own. But they were not in Chişinău today, and as those two protester camps showed, they were needed. There was a country to build, a national identity to create. An important demographic, the one famous for its ideas and energy, had already voted with its feet.

Moldova had its freedom, but it didn't seem to know what to do with it yet.

After two days' exploring the shopping malls of Chişinău, it was time to move on to Romania, where the tour would end, or at least my part in it. I was counting down the hours but, first, there was the tricky proposition of an overnight train from Chişinău to Bucharest. I knew what that meant. I'd done two train rides with the group already. They were suitably excited about the proposition of a third. Since we'd arrived in Chişinău, during lulls in the conversation, someone would shout "Champagne Train!" Another would respond

"Choo choo," or make a crude train impersonation with circling arms, followed by a champagne-cork-popping motion.

This good-natured joviality was shattered when Chris returned from the train station to inform us the overnight train had been cancelled. Instead, we'd have to take an overnight bus to Bucharest. Twelve hours, no beds. I immediately thought of the night bus from Wuhan. The group greeted this news as though hearing about the death of a relative they'd met once at a BBQ—someone who had seemed pleasant enough but whose loss would not linger.

"Boozebus?" someone tried, after a quiet moment of mourning. There were some murmurs, one half-hearted honking sound. It was okay, but certainly no Champagne Train.

That afternoon there was to be a wine-tasting trip to Mileștii Mici, the world's largest wine cellar housing an incredible 1.5 million bottles of plonk. I decided to skip it. I'd spent enough time in the company of this group and alcohol to know how poorly they mixed. They were like a quadruple gin and stupid (in Transnistria it is thing). Probably Mileștii Mici would lose its world record by the time the group had plundered its vaults.

Predictably, creatures of habits that they were, the group returned from the wine tasting in a dishevelled state best described as sozzled. I found them rosy cheeked and rolling over each other on the couches in the hotel lobby.

"Boozebus!" shouted Jen.

"Boozebus," the others replied, in unison. The Moldovan wine had certainly raised the spirits. I looked around. Two people were missing. "Where's Anne-Sophie and David?"

"We still have an hour to the bus," said Pierre, with a wink.

"Boozebus," Jack corrected.

"Boozebus, thank you, Jack."

Jack burped. "Pleasure."

I took a seat next to Pierre. "How was the wine tasting?"

Pierre blinked, slowly. It looked as if he'd recently teleported into this body and wasn't sure yet how to operate it. "It was. Good. The guy." He paused for a blink break. "Said. We were supposed to spit it out. Though."

"Idiot," added Mike.

"I'm guessing you didn't though?"

Jack chuckled. "Too fucking right we didn't."

We arrived at the bus a few minutes early. The group found the nearest off-licence and enthusiastically loaded up on essential provisions: beer, wine, and vodka. Just one more bus ride and it would be over for me. I couldn't wait. They weren't horrible people, but they were horrible to travel with for more than a few hours. They didn't want to travel, just drink in front of increasingly exotic backdrops.

The bus driver was a broad-faced, hostile man with lightly pockmarked cheeks and a nose trying to compensate in breadth for what it lacked in depth. He didn't speak English and so had to try to stop the group from bringing their alcohol on board wordlessly—with defiant, open-palmed, cross-shaped-arm gestures that made it clear the bathroom was out of use, and no alcohol was permitted. In short, that this bus was to be, in no way, a *Boozebus*. Jack brushed passed him, a bottle of red wine hidden inside his puffy coat. "Whatever you say, chief. No problem."

The driver returned to his seat, satisfied he'd been listened to. More smuggled bottles appeared from the innards of coats and bags. "Anyone got some cups?" Jack asked, relieving the bottle of its screw cap, which bounced to the floor. No one had any cups. "Oh well, fuck it," he said, raising the bottle in the air. "To the Boozebus!"

We were seated at the back of the bus, spread left and right across the aisle. The bus filled up. The singing got louder. More secret stashes of alcohol were raided and the driver came back several times to try to confiscate it. He didn't succeed, and then it was time to depart. The vehicle was now nearly full with locals, most a few decades older than we were. I felt sorry for both them and myself. I knew what was coming, what had already started, actually. If they thought they were going to get any sleep, they'd have plenty of hours ahead, awake, to realise how wrong they'd been.

Thirty minutes into the journey and midway through a group

rendition of Rick Astley's 1987 hit "Never Gonna Give You Up," one of the locals, a squat man in a brown flat cap, rose from his seat at the front of the bus, turned to us, and gave impassioned, shouted pleas: "Shhhh" and "No!"

The group jeered. "Sit down, you chump," yelled Jack. The driver stopped the bus and came to the back again, in search of bottles the group were never going to give up, either.

"Hello, boss," said Jack. "Lovely driving up there. Lovely."

"Really great," Chris added. "Sterling work. *Stay up there.*"

The driver reached across Chris and tried to remove the bottle Jack had nestled between his right arm and the window.

"Oi! What you doing?"

"No," the driver said, red in the face. "No!"

The scene degenerated into a light farce of amateur wrestling as the two grappled over the bottle. Unsuccessful, the driver climbed off Jack, stood up, and smoothed the creases in his shirt.

Jack raised his palms. "Easy, fella." He freed the bottle from the nook to the right of his hip. "You can have her. I'm just not quite done with her yet." He unscrewed the cap and downed what was left, then handed the empty bottle to the driver. The driver began groping around our seats. As soon as he reached for a bottle, it would disappear, passed to another group member under or over the seat, leaving him shouting, grappling, and out of breath. After a few minutes, to placate him, Chris rounded up some empties. "There you are. That's the last of them." He winked.

The driver sloped back to the front. He'd made his point but knew it wasn't very sharp. A few locals clapped him sympathetically anyway. In retaliation for his treatment, he turned the heating up to maximum. The bus became a furnace. I put my hand up to the nozzle above my head and felt enough heat escaping to cook meat. I stuffed the hole with some tissues.

The group re-retaliated, if that's a word, with an even louder drinking song, about a highwayman, and the passing around of the last bottle of Transnistrian cognac. "Boozebus, Boozebus," they shouted.

The locals were horrified but powerless. Sitting in my row, in the opposite window seat, was a Romanian man in a tight, striped blazer far too smart for a Boozebus. He'd been slurping generously from a metal flask hidden in his inside pocket. He rose from his seat.

"I AM THE DEVIL INCARNATE," he shouted, in perfect English.

The bus fell silent. The group turned to observe this strange man, now singing in Romanian.

"Boozebus!" Jack roared at him.

He swayed, nearly fell, steadied himself with one arm on the headrest in front, took a swig from his flask with the other, met Jack's gaze, and let out a primal howl of "BOOZEBUS!"

Music to their ears. "Boozebus, Boozebus, Boozebus," the group chanted in response. He was in.

Two hours into the journey, the bus stopped by a large corn field. Four men waited there by the side of the road. They took the only vacant seats, in the back row, behind us. They were speckled with mud and wearing heavy work shoes. They looked to have just finished a day's hard labouring. Now, they had been thrust, unwittingly, into the back of a Boozebus warm enough to fry eggs, behind a man claiming to be THE DEVIL INCARNATE, and surrounded on all sides by eleven drunk, offensive foreigners singing Irish drinking songs (and one with his earplugs in, quietly seething).

"I AM LUCIFER, HEAR ME ROAR!" said the devil incarnate. I groaned like a wounded animal. So it was moments like *this* that they made Ghanaian moonshine to forget. "Do you have any drugs?" I asked my neighbour, Paul. "I'd kill for some sleeping pills."

"I have some Valium. It's a muscle relaxant. That might help."

Anything was worth a go at this point. My muscles were feeling extremely tense. As was my brain. Possibly because it was being cooked by the rotisserie oven above my head.

The devil incarnate rose to his feet once more. "I WILL KILL YOU. I WILL KILL YOU ALL!" he shouted.

Chris raised his can of beer. "Cheers to that, pal."

Another rendition of "Boozebus, Boozebus, Boozebus," rang out. Jack got up to use the out-of-order toilet. Collapsing back into his seat, he reached for what was left of his red wine. "Well, boys, if she wasn't out of order, she is now!"

David's head appeared from the row in front of me. "Gang, I've got another one. Who would, like, win in a fight between a Mongol horde and four hundred bears?"

The local man from the middle of the bus, who had become a quasi-spokesman for the locals, despite not being able to speak the language of the people he was negotiating with, stood up for another stab at diplomacy. "Shhhh. No!" he shouted loudly, one finger in front of his mouth. "Shhhhhhhhhhhhhhhhhhhhhh!"

"Sit down, you wanker," said Jack with a sneer. The group jeered and booed him until he sat down. Eight hours of suffering to go. It was a good thing Old Master Traveller wasn't here to see this. I knocked my head repeatedly against the window, hoping I might pass out.

Suddenly, the bus stopped. We were going to be thrown off. I'd been waiting for it ever since we got on. Through the window I could just make out the dark shape of a recently ploughed field. There wasn't a building in sight. This would be a bad place to be stranded. The door halfway down the bus opened. The four farmers rose from their seats, collected up their things, and headed for the door. I was happy they could escape. As they passed I made eye contact with the first of them. He smiled and said something to our row in Romanian. "The man wishes you a good life," the devil incarnate said. The row in front of us got, "May your harvest be bountiful."

The absurdity of the scene was too much. I was in hysterics, both captivated and appalled and waiting to feel some effect from the Valium. The farmers stepped down onto the empty road. They were angels too good and pure for this world.

"Lovely boys," said Jack. "I had a lot of time for them."

"AND THE FIRES OF HELL BURN HOT TONIGHT," said the devil incarnate, rising once more from his seat. It was a scene that I would probably have enjoyed, if I were reading about it in a book and not stuck in the middle of it, sweat dripping down my back, concentrating on not getting motion sick. I thought back to Old Master Traveller. Was that my future? More importantly, why was this bus my present? My life was already full of great people, back in Berlin. Berlin, where I had a girlfriend who loved me and was waiting, sometimes even patiently, for me while I continued on some kind of quest, to, well, I wasn't sure any more. I think, mostly, as she'd suggested at the ashram, to try to outrun my fate. To not admit that I was getting older, that my friends were buying houses, starting families, having careers, moving on with their lives while I was on Valium, on a night bus with THE DEVIL INCARNATE to Bucharest, where I wanted to learn about yet another dictator (Ceauşescu). I'd been in a rut, and rediscovering a passion for travelling had, albeit temporarily, helped me escape it. But then without noticing it, the pendulum had swung too far the other way. The solution had morphed into a new problem.

I wasn't normal. I had been given everything I wanted—security, love, recognition, money, time—and yet didn't appreciate any of it. *I was the weirdo.*

I put my head against the window into a patch of condensation. Something needed to change. Suddenly, I knew the next trip I needed to make. The last trip for a while. One I'd been putting off for a decade.

14

THETFORD, ENGLAND: "WHAT ARE YOU DOING HERE?"

Legal highs, funerals, homecomings

The drizzle of rain against the train window perfectly matched my brooding, sombre mood. I was more apprehensive about this trip than all those that had come before it. Here, it was not the unknown that concerned me; it was the known but not liked. I was heading to my home town: Thetford.

Thetford is part of East Anglia, a large, possibly tumorous lump sticking out on England's hip. Thetford is cloaked tightly in forest, as if someone is trying to hide it. Having lived there for the first eighteen years of my life, I don't rule the possibility out. The only reputation it had in the local area was for being "a bit rough," which is like describing a kangaroo as "a bit jumpy."

To my knowledge, Thetford has only ever made the national news on three occasions. The first was when *The Sun*, England's most popular daily waste of tree, outed the town on its front page as the country's "dogging" capital. Dogging is the practice of meeting strangers in car parks for anonymous sex. The second time Thetford made the news was when the book *Crap Towns* shortlisted it as one of the worst places in England. Now that was a party to remember. It was almost better than learning we were the nation's dogging capital, although perhaps less good for the town's car park revenues. The final time we had a brush with stardom was in 2004, when England played Portugal in the European football championship and lost on penalties. A riot took place in the town centre, as English hooligans attacked one of the Portuguese-owned pubs. By this point the Schengen Area had encouraged ten thousand mostly Portuguese and Polish immigrants to come work in the town's factories, increasing the town's population by 50 percent and its xenophobia by 1000 percent.

When I turned sixteen, I got a job in the town's Turkish delight factory, where I was remunerated at a generous 2.80 pounds per hour. A pittance anywhere else, but quite ample in Thetford—chip butties cost only eighty pence, after all. It was a job that consisted, largely, of putting paper lids on boxes of sweets for nine hours a day. The training for it took less than a minute. A former pimp worked there and recognised in me an impressionable young virgin whom he could, and did, corrupt with his depraved stories. He had a particular fetish for lying under glass coffee tables and looking up... Actually, I'll stop there. Sadly, my factory-production-line career ended late one night at the end of an arsonist's lit match. The factory was burnt down. It wasn't just dogging we excelled at—we could more than hold our own at arson. A few years before, someone had even managed to burn down the town's swimming pool. No, I never got my head around that one either. Not everything in Thetford is explainable, but absolutely everything is flammable.

Walking home from school was like running a public shame and bullying gauntlet. I spent my childhood looking, with pangs of envy, at adults and thinking how I couldn't wait to be them. They could just get in a car, or on a train, and never have to be in Thetford again. It looked magical.

At nineteen, I got my wish. I left for university. Since that day, all I've done is try to forget about Thetford. I've boxed up all my memories of it and shoved them into the racks at the far back of my mind. The boxes are marked "Childhood Trauma—Do Not Open!!!"

Which, of course, raises the question as to why a decade after my last proper visit to the town, I was stepping off a train into it. I wasn't there in search of a neat, feel-good ending but because of a nagging feeling that if that ending did exist somewhere out in the future, the route would almost certainly pass through Thetford. After all, most of my coping strategies—not showing emotion, hiding behind jokes, running away when things got tough, treating my past like bones to be buried—had been learned there. Thetford was ground zero for my personality flaws, for patterns of behaviour that had seen me churn through friendships, jobs, and responsibilities.

The small station looked identical to my memories of it. As did The Railway, the pub next to it, as did the newsagents down the road that I'd been to many times as a kid, just past the same red postboxes, at the same pedestrian crossing. If this was all the same, surely everything here would be? The rain increased in severity. So did my apprehension. I tried to hide my head in my shoulders. Heavy-footed, I trudged towards the town's pedestrianised centre, and my hotel. I was shocked to be reacquainted with Star OK Kebab, a Thetford institution. Every night out of my youth, as a jangly, spotty fifteen-year-old in brightly coloured Ben Sherman shirts, had ended at Star OK, an eating establishment whose name made as much sense as our decision to go there, i.e., no sense at all. It was a place I'd forgotten existed, but as soon as I saw it again, the lids from boxes of long-neglected memories flipped off and out jumped dozens of long-suppressed experiences: throwing up in front of it, watching the regular fights there, sitting with school friends against the church wall opposite while a man threw chips at my head. It seemed to have exactly the same sign, layout, interior decor, menu—as if frozen in time.

My hotel room looked out onto a building site that the receptionist informed me, with barely suppressed pride, would become a new retail complex and "three-screen cinema." Star OK might have been in stasis, but other things in Thetford were progressing. Another memory bubbled to the surface: the town had briefly had a cinema in the mid-nineties. A month after its opening (to much fanfare), I visited it, with my friend Kevin, to watch the movie *Beverly Hillbillies*, which is now almost certainly a cult classic. Upon arrival, we found the doors and windows boarded up. How a business could lose enough money that it has to shutter just weeks after it opens is still a mystery to me. Perhaps someone had threatened to burn the cinema down, or the mayor feared that we'd lose our "crap town" status.

After lunch I took a walk. Outside Poundland, two drunks embraced and swore affectionately at each other. *Here we go*, I thought. *They'll be fighting soon enough. Classic Thetford.* But they didn't; they just sat quietly together on a bench, a can of Special Brew in hand, whistling. I bristled as a group of teenagers passed me, forgetting that because of my age, all that petty tribalism and bullying I'd had to endure in my youth didn't apply anymore. I was anonymous to them now, just another boring adult.

To my surprise, evidence of creeping gentrification was everywhere. The bus station had been knocked down, moved a few hundred metres, and renamed the grander-sounding Bus Interchange. The high school had also been rebranded, earning the more prestigious nomenclature of "Academy." An important TV show called *Dad's Army* had been filmed there, and the show now had its own small museum. Thomas Paine was born here, and had his own statue. I walked the banks of the river Little Ouse, which flowed lazily behind my hotel. Following it out of town, I expected to find toxic sludge, rusting shopping trolleys, mutant fish, and heroin addicts. Instead, I discovered ducks, swans, thick curtains of weeping willows, thatched roofs, unspoilt woodlands, and traditional English pubs.

It was, dare I say it, *pretty*. I guess it always had been. That just hadn't fit the narrative of my being better than it, of it being this ugly thing I'd endured, escaped, rubbed myself clean of, like Andy Dufraine emerging from the gutter before heading to live my prosperous, middle-class, exotic, international life. That was a nice story, but it was a story. I'd always prided myself on being someone willing to change his opinion when presented with compelling evidence to the contrary. Here was that evidence. Thetford was not crap. It was my imagination that had distorted it into something ugly. Therefore, I'd been unnecessarily slandering and avoiding it for years.

During that walk, just like in meditation, whenever I felt my thoughts wandering to the future I would take them gently by the collar and pull them back into the past. I walked to the newsagent that had employed me as a paperboy. I'd spent four years getting up at 6:30am, seven days a week, three hundred and sixty-four days a year to earn thirty-two pounds a month. With the benefit of hind-sight: clearly child exploitation. The shop was an Indian restaurant now. ~~Karma~~. Korma.

I was staring at this shop, thinking about the pungent, cheap aftershave of Malcolm, its terrible and erratic manager, when I heard a car horn and turned around to see that its owner was my auntie, on her way back from work. Although my parents and siblings have long since left the town, I do still have some family in Thetford—family I didn't see often for that very reason. "I thought that was you," she said, through the open passenger door. "I had no idea why it would have been. What are you doing here?"

I didn't have a very good answer.

We drove to her house, just a few streets away, and she told me, in rapid-fire, stories about the more distant branches of our shared family tree—of births, marriages, and deaths. Families are like icebergs: there's always way more going on under the surface. I learned that my Uncle Graham, whom I hadn't seen in twenty years, was now a member of the right-wing UK Independence Party. "He's got some horrible views. I switch off whenever he starts talking." My auntie is a benefits adviser at the local council and had endured a rough day at work taking calls from the general public. "If only you knew what was going on out there, Ad. The system is kind to all the wrong people."

My Uncle Paul was dozing on the sofa. He's been practically housebound for the past seventeen years as a result of fibromyalgia, chronic muscle pain. He passes his time with history books and the simulated warfare of computer games. "You have to keep your mind active. That's the hard part," he said, when I asked how he managed to stay so upbeat about his house arrest. "The loneliness, well, you get used to it." He was similarly positive about Thetford's progress. "The Premier Inn is expanding again. Your old high school, well, you wouldn't recognise it. Thetford's really looking up." He said this with the sort of satisfaction you'd expect from someone playing a more active role in it—a manager, perhaps, or consultant. Or a management consultant. "You've heard about the new cinema, right?"

Everyone was excited about the new cinema, which meant it would almost certainly be a massive disappointment.

My grandma lived one estate over, and my auntie visited her every day. On the walk I learned that it was the eve of my grandma's ninety-fifth birthday. We found her in the living room of her small bungalow reading *Gone Girl* under a thick green woollen blanket. Not expecting to see me, she made an exaggerated *oooh* sound to mask the fact she was struggling to locate my name. It's never a nice feeling when your grandma sees you so rarely she's uncertain if you're an Adam or an Anthony. "What are *you* doing here?" she asked. Like most elderly people, my grandma has no problem spending time with her past. She immediately began regaling me with stories of people I'd never met, and who were possibly fictional, dead, or both. The stories ran into each other and collapsed dizzy in conclusion-less heaps. "Did Granddad tell you how he had his heart restarted on the operating table?"

I groaned. "Yes, Grandma. Only every time I saw him." He also told it to the man who brought the free paper, and sometimes even passing pedestrians. With the aid of her Zimmer frame, my grandma got to her feet and headed for her bedroom in a sprightly manner for someone her age. I could now say this, as I now knew her age. I found her rummaging through the drawers by her bed. "Last time I saw you, you asked me for Granddad's funeral thingy."

"I did?" I had no memory of that. How did she? Or was she making it up?

"It's in here, I think, if I haven't lost it. Ah, here it is." She handed me a leather-bound book. It was the programme for my granddad's funeral. We looked through it together, on the couch.

"Not bad for eighty-nine, was he?" she said, staring down at the grainy black-and-white photo on its first page.

"No, Grandma, he was very handsome."

I didn't go to his funeral, because, predictably, I was travelling at the time. Another thing I now regretted. Another chance for sentimentality I'd forsaken in my pursuit of the new and exotic. The service had featured a lot of Christian hymns. "Was Granddad a Christian?" I asked.

She inhaled. "Yes. *I* think he was."

Out of my grandma's eyeline, my auntie shook her head vigorously.

"I've never heard a Christian swear like your granddad," my auntie said, on the walk back to her house. "Your grandma's one, so she wants to think he was. She's rewriting history now. Granddad was the same towards the end." She paused as an excited dog bounded past us and across the field. "Actually, he was always like that."

This sounded eerily familiar. I realised how much of it I did, too. I guess we all do—recast ourselves in the stories of our lives, giving ourselves starring roles in our successes and minimising the role we play in our failures, working back from our actions to justifications, not the other way round. In my imaginative, directorial hands, my coming-of-age-in-Thetford tale had slipped genre and become a slasher movie with me running from a zombie army of the proletariat.

I'd agreed to meet my old best friend, Dan, the next day. It was his wedding some three years earlier I'd elected not to attend, to Annett's chagrin. Not only that, I'd also defriended him at the same time, letting him know I felt our relationship had run its course. I could think of eight or nine people I'd defriended via email when they'd become a little bit too much work, or I felt our relationship had peaked. There'd been no reason to. I had time for them. I was mostly just sitting around the house googling myself and eating chocolate. I just didn't want the effort and commitment of them. Or the guilty feeling they gave me when they complained how little I called, wrote, or visited them.

I hadn't realised then that the only way you know that something has value is if you find yourself willing to make sacrifices for it. That's what elevates it, helps you separate life's noise from its signal. Just as monogamy gives a relationship one sacred act you agree to do with each other and no one else. This should have been obvious from the time I spent with the protesters in Istanbul, the Orthodox Jews in Israel, and the Hare Krishnas in Argentina. An obligation-less life *is* a selfish life.

Somehow I'd missed the lesson.

I'd had no contact with Dan since he'd been defriended. We'd agreed to meet in the pub that had been attacked after England lost to Portugal. Dan strolled in ten minutes late. We recognised each other instantly, even though he'd bulked up since I last saw him, when he visited me in Leipzig, some eight years earlier. He had made the effort. I hadn't. And *I* was the one who'd moved country. A stiff handshake didn't feel enough, and morphed into a stilted hug. "It's good to see you, Fletch," he said, sitting on his high barstool. "But why now?"

I didn't have a very good answer.

I told him about my recent trips and that I was taking a stroll down memory lane. I could see he remained unconvinced, and so I paddled us to the calmer waters of his job. For the past twelve years he'd worked as a prison guard. The last three had been particularly harrowing, he said, because of a loophole in the law regarding legal highs. While throwing *illegal* highs over the prison fence was a very quick way of ending up incarcerated yourself, throwing legal highs was like, well, throwing chips over the fence. A legal high was a psychoactive substance that was, ostensibly, just an illegal high (drug) with a molecule or two changed and thus would be sold until the law caught up with criminalising it. It had been raining legal highs in the prison yard, Dan said. The prisoners didn't know what they were taking, and many got indebted to those dealing the drugs. Some reacted okay to the substances, others got violent or simply over-dosed and died. Dan tilted his head to show the sides of his nose, recently reset after an inmate punched him, breaking it in three places. A brave inmate. "He was off his head on something."

"Is that the first time one took a swing at you?"

He sniggered. "No, happens all the time. It's the first time someone connected that well, though. Nah, mate, they do all sorts to try and get a rise out of you: pee in a cup and throw it through the crack in the door; throw shit at you. Recently, one prisoner came up to a colleague of mine and said 'I've been paid to assault you.' Then he pulled a razor blade from his pocket and slashed the poor bastard diagonally across the face. Usually it's because they want to be reclassified and moved nearer their families. A lot of them are nice, though. It's not, like, all bad."

The first hour and a half of conversation was a little frosty, although, just like the prison population, not all bad. Dan's guard was up—I'm going to sidestep any obvious puns here—but by the third beer he seemed to relax, slouching into his stool, I think convinced I wasn't there with any kind of nefarious intent and that even after all these years apart we still got on just fine. We teased each other in that uniquely English way that is simultaneously offensive and affectionate as we leapfrogged from topic to topic.

"Fletch," he said, adopting a more serious tone. "I'm sorry, but I've got to put it out there—what happened with the wedding?"

I squirmed on my stool, which seemed suddenly prickly. "I... I don't know," I stammered, looking down at the table. "I thought it was for the best. A friendship can't only be based on the past, right?"

He leaned back on his stool. "Why would ours be? I know I'm still here, and I've got the same job, but I've changed, too."

I'd never met someone who'd been on the other side of my defriending. Not only that, because of my talent for living only in the future tense, I'd never given the people I'd cut so surgically out of my life a second thought. Yet here was one of those people, on the next stool, obviously still resentful. "I know. I'm sorry. I'm sure that message came across much blunter than I intended it."

"Well." He hesitated. "I know what you're like. You always were very direct. I guess that's why you like Germany so much. I think other people found it very blunt, though."

I squirmed a bit more; it seemed the least I could do. He necked the last of his beer. "We had a good connection, and I thought it was sad that you just closed it off."

I nodded, drank faster to try to keep up, made some murmuring noises that hinted at wrongdoing and guilt without actually admitting any. He was right, he had changed. So had Thetford. I'd forgotten that. Because I'd hit pause on it the day I left, that was how it had remained in my mind, but really, it had long since run on without me.

"Come on," Dan said, getting up from his stool. "There's some people I'd like you to meet."

Dan and his wife owned a house just a few estates over from the ones in which Dan and I had grown up. We found his son Noah in the lounge watching cartoons. He was just eleven months old but huge for his age. He had the delightfully wrinkled appearance of an elderly man, so that when he proudly took a few unsteady steps towards us, it looked more like walking was something he was slowly forgetting than a talent he was just acquiring. We had dinner, sat in the garden, and drank too much vodka and cranberry (our old drink, something else I'd long forgotten but that Dan had prepared especially). Amy worked at the prison as well, and they passed the evening telling stories just as varied and wacky and entertaining as those I'd travelled thousands of miles to collect—not just of the prison but also of the people Dan and I knew: stories of one-night stands that had resulted in pregnancies, of marriages cut short by infidelity, of out-of-control gambling and drinking. Stories of people who'd grown up, and of people who'd remained stubbornly the same; of sociopaths and soccer mums and kids, so many kids. The past was sprinkled in there too, but only as a minor, supporting character. They mentioned their wedding at least six times, teasing me as much as they thought I could bear.

"I'm sorry, Dan," I said, finally, my face flushed crimson with embarrassment. "I regret it. I should have been there."

Dan looked at Amy. "Yeah, you should have, you big idiot. What you reckon, Ames? Shall we let him off the hook?"

Amy smiled. "Nah, let him grovel a bit yet." They laughed.

At eleven, we stood to hug once again, this time with genuine warmth. "It's been great," Dan said. "Don't leave it so long next time, okay?"

"I won't," I said, and meant it.

The next morning, I waited at the Bus Interchange for a bus to Newmarket, some thirty miles away, where my parents and sister now live. The two days in Thetford had been extremely enjoyable, full of interesting characters and humorous tales. Revisiting them hadn't depressed me, as I'd thought it would. I was no longer that spotty, confused teenager. Nor was Thetford the awful, depraved place I'd pretended it to be, probably to assuage any guilt I'd had at not wanting to visit it. It was a somewhat generic market town, not the best that England had to offer, but hardly the crappiest either. Is it a strange place? Certainly. Because all places are strange places, I was coming to realise. Strange because people are, fundamentally, strange. We're odd ramshackle collections of confusions, delusions, hopes, dreams, neuroses, unrequited loves, repressed traumas, magical thinking, denial, honesty, humour, earnestness, and kindness. For some reason, I'd thought that because the people here had chosen to live in the same place in which they were born, resisting the urge to flee to some big, anonymous, polluted city, their stories were uninteresting. That had been stupid. In the end, the only thing that had really stopped me from coming here was me. I'd had a story about Thetford, and I'd told that story so often I'd started to believe it was true.

As humans, we're constantly working to try to make sense of ourselves, to try to neaten our histories. We're our stories, nothing more. I'd gotten stuck in an incorrect narrative of my own life, a story that said I was normal, that my life was boring, and that there was some greater nobility in the struggles I saw playing out in Taksim Square, Hebron, Chișinău, Tiraspol, and other places.

Here I was on yet another trip, alone, while Annett was back in

Berlin. The last year of our relationship had been our worst. Where we'd needed to work harder to understand each other, and to stay interested in each other after all these years, I hadn't been pulling my weight. It had gotten hard, and I'd reacted as I usually did, by running away from it in a spiral of counterproductive behaviour that only exacerbated the original problem and thus increased my urge to do a little more fleeing. I had gotten so focused on what was out there, on the next weird country, the next great anecdote, the next despot, that I'd stopped appreciating the life I had. Travel is wonderful. A near-perfect state of surprise, wonder, and excitement. A chance to challenge your assumptions, defeat your prejudices, and write a new story for yourself. As a traveller. An exile. An adventurer. An explorer. As someone with great stories of struggle, survival, curiosity, courage, and reinvention. But the pursuit of those narratives can be harmful, too.

Everything in life is about dosage. I'd gotten the dosage wrong. I felt ready to reprioritise, to commit to Berlin, to Annett, to my job as a writer, to staying when things got hard, instead of running away to some romanticised, mirage, wanderlust new. I wanted to change my story.

To show Annett this, on the way back to Berlin, I bought her something I thought I'd never buy.

15

INTERLUDE #3: A GIFT

I seated myself at the kitchen table, facing the front door, waiting for Annett to return home from work. A small rectangular box sat in front of me, on the table. I drummed two fingers impatiently next to it.

She should have been home by now.

Then came the sound of jangling keys in the lock, followed by a thud as the door slammed into the wall. That poor wall. It wasn't Annett-proof. Five steps later she stood in the doorway to our kitchen-diner scrutinising the mail in her hand. She caught a glimpse of me from the corner of her eye and yelped.

"You made me jump. What are you doing sitting there like some kind of weird, bald statue?"

Her gaze moved down to the table. A look of alarm flashed across her face. "What's that?" she said, pointing at the wrapped box in front of me.

I adopted a calm, authoritative tone. "Sit down, Annett."

"Oh God. You are even using my name now? Why? What's going on?"

"We need to have a talk." I betrayed no emotion.

She dropped her backpack on the floor. "Right now?"

"Right now."

Her breath was shallow and rapid. "Oh God. What is that? It's not—"

She sat, continuing to breathe as if she'd never done it before. "You fucker," she muttered. We tended to treat our relationship like a toaster we'd won in a prize draw we couldn't remember entering— not necessarily what we'd been looking for, but now that it was here, well, a toaster could certainly be useful. It wasn't a normal approach to a relationship, to not think you'd always be together, to not have that as a goal even, but it worked for us. Took the pressure off having to chase Happy Ever After.

I put my hands on the box. "I know things between us haven't been great lately," I began. "And you've been asking me where this relationship is going."

I took a theatrically large breath. I was milking the moment. "But I think it's time for us to take the next step..."

Annett was trying to meet my gaze but couldn't. She angled her face away but peeked back, like someone watching a horror film. "Oh God, oh God, oh God. ARRRGH. No. Why?" Annett was the product of divorce and strongly opposed to involving the state in her love life.

With two hands, I pushed the box across the table to her.

She was squirming in her seat, as if every word I spoke raised its temperature five degrees. I was certain. I was ready. "I want us to take the next step. Open it."

She reached hesitantly for the box, wrapped in silver paper. "I can't believe you're doing this," she said, as the paper fell away. A few tears streaked her cheeks.

She read the words on the box slowly. "*Pet rock?*" It was not the jewellery box nor the ring she'd been expecting.

I nodded. "Pet rock."

She opened that box to find not the sort of rock you put on your finger, but the sort you might find in the garden. A small smooth grey rock. Pet Rock was a smash-hit novelty Christmas gift back in the seventies. It really was just a rock. It came with a lead (for taking Pet Rock out on walks) and a book that explained how to look after it.

"Our first-ever pet!" I gushed. "I think we're ready to take the next step, to be responsible for something." I was laughing now, enjoying the meanness of my prank.

She picked up the rock and pretended to throw it at me. "You son of a bitch. Why did you do that to me? I thought you were going to propose. Oh God," she said, wiping her eyes with the back of her sleeve. "That would have been awful. Oh, wow, what a relief."

"I know," I said. "But..." I hesitated here because, again, I was going to say my least favourite words in any language. "There is a point to this. *You were right.* You usually are. Going to Thetford was good for me," I continued. "I'm not saying I've changed, and that you were right about *everything*. Travelling's great and I'll always want to see as much of this odd global Human Experiment as I can. But I realise now that those stories I've been chasing, in all the places that weren't here, well, there are also great ones right here, too. I've also realised that it's good to make sacrifices for the things that are important to you."

She put Pet Rock back in its box. "I like that you're wired for novelty. You have been since I met you—you just lost it there somehow. That curiosity is what makes it interesting to be in a relationship with you. Every time you read a book you suddenly have a whole new world view, even if you forget it after a week."

I nodded. "I'm hoping to try to keep this new one for quite a bit longer. Somehow I lost sight of how lucky, special, and in no way normal my life is. I'm going to work on that. Say yes to any weddings, family events, or social engagements you want us to go to. I always enjoy them in the end no matter how much I complain beforehand. In the meantime I'm going to be here, trying to keep a grip on myself, and reinvesting in my relationships."

"Okay," she said. "I can do that." I got up to go to the fridge, moved a magnet, and returned with the itinerary she'd created for the Italy trip we'd cancelled for China. It had been pinned, unloved, to the fridge for a long time. "Our next trip," I said, pushing it towards her, "once we decide to take another, is your pick."

She scrunched up her nose. "Nah. Italy's okay but it peaked like five hundred years ago already. And I've kind of missed the trips like Istanbul, Israel, and Ghana."

"And China and the Hare Krishnas?" I winked.

"Don't push your luck." She slid the paper back across the table. "No. For my pick, I've a much better idea where we should go."

16

PYONGYANG, NORTH KOREA: "HE PRAISED IT FOR ITS REVOLUTIONARY SPIRIT."

North Korean kebabs, mass dances, dem two bruddas

With not a minute to spare, Annett and I arrived at the tour company's orientation session, in Beijing. The room was above a restaurant, had no air conditioning, and was sweltering in the August heat. Inside were fifty fellow tourists and six Western tour guides. It was a bumper group, since we would be in North Korea during the seventieth anniversary of their liberation from Japanese colonial rule. There were rumours of military parades and mass games. "The insanity will be turned up to eleven," said a tall, Australian guide called Tristan. The group clapped and whooped enthusiastically. We were here for insanity. We were here for eleven.

We were going to the collective fiction known as North Korea, one of the least-visited and most-secretive places on earth, a dictatorship ruled by the iron will of one family of legendary, malevolent megalomaniacs: the Kims. North Korea, or the Democratic People's Republic of Korea, to use its official (flagrantly inaccurate) name, has been ruled by just three of them: Eternal President Kim Il-Sung (1948–1994); his son, Supreme Leader Kim Jong-il (1994–2011); and his son, the chubby-cheeked Marshal Kim Jong-un (since 2012).

Backpacks were slung onto backs and suitcases were rolled in the direction of Beijing Central Station for our overnight train to the border.

"I can't believe we're doing this," Annett said. "We've been reading about North Korea for years. Now we're finally going."

"I'm really glad you pushed for us to do this," I said. "It's the perfect way to wrap up all those trips I've been doing. North Korea has a bit of all of them, somehow."

"Yeah, but on a totally different scale."

Inside the station we found about four million people all jostling each other in a space for four thousand.

"Ah, China," I said. "It's good to be back."

Annett jutted her elbows out in an attack posture and looked at the gauntlet we would need to run. "Bring it on."

When it comes to tourists, North Korea works a little differently from other countries. You have to enter via China. You must have a guide at all times. You can have a personal one, which is extremely expensive, or join a tour, which is merely very. Our tour would last ten days. After a few weeks of nerves and extra forms to complete to convince the Koreans to let a writer in, I got a Skype call from the agency to say it was all done and very much dusted.

I looked at Annett, making use of her boxing training, more than holding her own in the scrum. It was nice to have her with me again. I had someone to talk to, and reassuringly, that person was always better informed and organised than I was. It was like travelling with a real-life Google that you could also hug.

Aboard the train, our group spread out across several carriages and swapped stories. None of us could quite believe it was happening; we really were going to North Korea. For some it was a whim, a lark, a good story for the pub, while for others it was the culmination of years of fevered interest in and study of what is undoubtedly one of the planet's oddest little nooks. Everyone wanted to know why everyone else had decided to visit North Korea, or the DPRK, as our Western guides kept encouraging us to call it. It would be disrespectful to call the country North Korea in front of our Korean handlers. As far as they were concerned, North Korea was the only Korea. The centre. Not the *north* of anything.

A cart of alcohol and snacks was wheeled through the carriage. After it passed us it contained neither. Soon one of the guides, a short Englishman called Rob, was tipsy. We crowded around him like children at Grandpa's knee.

"So I know this guy, a Canadian, right," he said. "Speaks fluent Korean, works as a translator. He's met Kim Jong-un many times."

There were murmurs of disbelief. The marshal himself?

"Anyway. No big deal." I had a sudden flashback to Gregor. "So he says the last time he met Kim Jong-un, at some sports event, right, he called him aside and said he wanted to make the country more open, to make it better for the people."

"Do you think Kim Jong-un is as bad as the media makes out?" asked an Australian, called Simon.

Rob scoffed loudly. "You can't trust the media, man." He flattened his empty can under his foot. "I think he's quite misunderstood. I don't think he's a bad guy, really." As long as you didn't question his deforestation strategy, anyway. Reports in the (untrustworthy) media were saying Kim Jong-un had just had one of his senior advisers killed by firing squad for doing just that.

"Wasps?" Rob said next. "Any of you ever eaten wasps?"

We looked around at each other. *No.*

"They're great. Not chewy. They're crispy all the way through. Delicious. I'm more Chinese than most Chinese people, man. I know what I'm talking about. Have any of you ever heard about the North Korean kebab?"

We hadn't heard about that either. We were such amateurs...

"So I'm in Rason, which is in the north-east. I'm trashed on beer and soju. We're just standing there, me and this North Korean handler, in the kitchen of this bar. Great guy, I know him really well..." *Burp.* "Where was I? Oh, yeah."

He might have known what he was talking about, but he was having trouble talking about it.

Hiccup. "Erm. What? Ah. So... suddenly, the guy reaches up and takes down two raw eggs from a shelf. He thrusts a chopstick in one, puts the egg to his mouth, and then makes this elaborate loud sucking sound."

We expressed audible disbelief.

"So I'm like, is this guy serious? Oh well, what the hell. I dig a chopstick in the other egg and try it. *The North Korean kebab.*"

The disbelief amplified.

"Hey, don't knock it until you've tried it. It was good enough for Rocky."

I was afraid that the train journey might degenerate into a Champagne Train. Not only was this another group tour, it was also through the same company that had hosted my Transnistria/Moldova debacle. Annett and I had only had a choice of five tours, and this one had been half the price of the others. Fortunately, this was a different group of people, with an average age of thirty; they were more mature, more knowledgeable about where we were going, more excited to get there.

The next morning, by the time the first rays of light pierced the carriage's flimsy blue curtains, we'd reached the Chinese side of the border. "Just to warn you, security here is a shitshow," said Jack, our Irish guide. Yep, that Jack. Fast-talking, heavy-drinking, potty-mouthed Jack. I wasn't overjoyed to be reunited with him, but so far he'd been behaving much better on this trip. North Korea was his normal route; Transnistria had been a one-off, almost a holiday for him. Here, he had to be responsible. One transgression and he'd be banned from the country, or worse. Otto Warmbier had spent a year here doing hard labour just for stealing a poster, before dying on his return to the US, his body showing signs of torture.

The door to our train's carriage opened.

"Here we go," said Jack.

A mob of DPRK border guards entered, each wearing increasingly impractically large hats denoting their rank. They began going through the luggage of the North Korean and Chinese passengers amongst us. Thirty minutes later, one reached our set of bunks, where seven of us sat sharing the bottom two beds.

"Good morning, sunshine," said Jack. "Lovely day for it, aye?"

The man smiled and removed his enormous hat. It was at least thirty-five degrees outside; more in the cramped train. He wiped the sweat from his forehead with his sleeve before exhaling loudly and putting his hat back on. He looked done with this national-border-protecting nonsense.

"Flwetcher?" he said, reading my name from the top of his stack of passports.

"Yes."

"Phwone?"

I showed him my phone.

"Beebley?"

This threw me. I looked at Jack.

"Bible."

"Ah! No, no Bible."

"Bookey?"

I showed him my Kindle. He turned it over in his hands as if it were something I'd smuggled out of Chernobyl before handing it cautiously back. This was easy so far.

"Bag?"

I got my bag out from under the bunk I was sitting on.

He patted it as though it were a dog he distrusted.

"What in? Clotheses?"

I was pretty sure he wasn't supposed to be giving me the answers. "Yes, clotheses."

He put the bag back under the seat. This was absurd. The most paranoid place on earth? Israel had treated me so much worse. Sighing under the weight of his hat, he turned and took the next immigration form from the pile.

Clotheses really was the magic immigration word. After the guards checked our bags, without opening our bags, the only things that lay separate, on the middle bunk, were our laptops. They awaited a

DPRK technology expert, who, based on what we'd read online, would promptly wipe all the drives and then set the whole lot on fire, like they were medieval witches. This person arrived, and I was curious as to how he was going to search seven laptops thoroughly, on a congested train that probably contained another hundred. We got the answer quite quickly. He wasn't. He began by opening the laptop of a Filipino travelling in our group. "The Philippines having a good relationship with the US," said Jack, "they usually check them boys more than us."

I watched over the DPRK technology expert's shoulder. He went to Start then Search, and typed "Interview." Of all things they wanted to stop getting in from the outside world, what they were most afraid of was *The Interview*, a bad movie, in English, starring Seth Rogan and James Franco. A movie that features the execution of Kim Jong-un, and, if the Internet conspiracies were right, a movie that had so incensed the regime that they'd hacked into Sony and released lots of embarrassing personal documents as revenge for its mere existence. North Korea's regime was not famed for its sense of humour, but then, neither was the movie *The Interview*.

The IT expert's search didn't uncover that movie. However, predictably, it did find some interview-related documents. He flicked through them then closed the laptop.

"That's it?" Annett asked Jack.

"That's it," said Jack. "The poor bastards don't have time to do anything more."

Forty-five minutes of opaque bureaucratic tomfoolery later, our elaborately hatted friends all bade us adieu and stepped off the train, which groaned in apology as it trundled into the Hermit Kingdom. Another trolley came through with alcohol. It left just a trolley. The train accelerated to an impressive thirty-five kilometres an hour. "Is the train going slow so that we can better see everything?" the Filipino asked. Jack laughed. He seemed to enjoy his job. And his beer.

Looking out of the train's windows, we were treated to a lush landscape of bright, almost neon, green. A land seemingly unspoilt by the usual human malevolences of power stations, shopping malls, and Irish bars. There was palpable excitement amongst us. Anything was considered photo worthy at this point, merely because it was North Korean.

Annett high-fived me. "We did it!"

"We sure did." Although what we'd done was unclear. Would it really be like what we'd read? A giant Kim family personality cult? There were plenty of North Koreans on the train, returning home. They all wore the red pin badges of the dear leaders on their hearts, a requirement for every adult, every day of his or her life. If that part was true, maybe it was all true?

Then... *they appeared*. In the third town we passed, atop a hill sat a giant white mural depicting Eternal President Kim Il-sung (K1 for short), his arm outstretched paternally, and Supreme Leader Kim Jong-il (K2) standing in a field, looking down at the town below.

It was all true. Here was the evidence! Look!

Jong, a half-Swedish half-Chinese member of our group, failed to get his camera out in time, and was furious at having missed this photo opportunity. Jack laughed once more. "That's not going to be a problem, lad. Once you get out of this place you'll check your photos and realise 99 percent of your pics feature dem two bruddas."

I sat back in the bunk. "Why do you call them brothers? They're not brothers."

He winked and opened a new beer. "Very perceptive. It's just a bit of a nickname we have for them."

Jack then told us where this nickname had come from. It involved the worst two tourists the company had ever hosted—American rappers, called *Pacman* and *Pe$o*, who'd raised the money to visit via a Kickstarter campaign that promised to create the first-ever North Korean rap video.

"They'd never left the USA before," said Jack, between swigs. "And they only had one outfit each with them, these cheap tailored suits they'd got made in China. They were freezing their asses off the whole time, they were. They never wanted to get off the buses and they knew nut'ing about the country. On the third day, we'd stopped at a monument of the dear leaders, probably like the twentieth of the trip, right, and one sidled up to me and said, no word of a lie now, 'So whose dem two bruddas?'"

"Really?"

"*Really.*"

"Wow," I said. "That's like going to Egypt, pointing at the pyramids, and asking if it's a sandcastle."

He laughed. "Yeah, or going to Italy thinking Mussolini is a type of pasta."

Annett shared round a packet of barbeque-flavoured crisps. "Did they make the video?"

"Aye. It's called *Escape to North Korea*." He rocked back in laughter. "The opposite direction of all previous escape attempts involving North Korea. Idiots."

After four hours, and a dozen more murals and statues of dem two bruddas, the landscape began to change: fields and paddies surrendered to longer and longer stretches of paved roads and houses until finally, the glass facade of a gleaming new airport came into view. We were approaching the capital, Pyongyang.

Jack pointed at it. "Apparently Kim Jong-un visited the airport and gave on-the-spot guidance that arrivals and departures should be separated. They tell you this like it was very innovative, bless 'em."

This was the first time we'd heard the phrase "on-the-spot guidance." It would not be the last...

North Korea's dilapidated train network had managed to turn a 160-kilometre trip into five hours of slow-paced sightseeing pleasure ending in Pyongyang's impressively Soviet central station. We were giddy. We'd made it to the centre of the most secretive place on earth, and so had all our clotheses.

Outside the station, we were divided into groups across four smart, new air-conditioned buses. Jack said a few words of welcome then passed us over to our North Korean handlers. Conveniently for the absent-minded, our guides were called Mr and Mrs Park who welcomed us over the P.A. system as we pulled out into Pyongyang as harried-looking pedestrians scurried around the city like ants. Many wore military uniforms and marched in formation. For civilians, since all the clothing is supplied by the government, there is only one style of dress; it almost looks as though people are wearing uniforms. The men wear silk shirts and suit trousers, and the women wear loose-fitting blouses and skirts. It seemed as if everything was required to be two sizes too large, maybe to help with the heat.

Pyongyang seemed a reasonably attractive city let down by a little too much concrete and brutalist Soviet high-rise pomp. The atmosphere was a mixture of hubris and the Cold War. Most striking to me in this showpiece city was the complete absence of graffiti.

"It's spotless," Annett said, photographing from the seat next to me.

"I know. Part of me wants to go and drop a wrapper just to see what happens."

Almost every tourist in Pyongyang stays at the same hotel, Yang-gakdo, because it's situated on a small island, making overthrowing the government very impractical. During dinner, in the hotel's top-floor revolving restaurant that wasn't revolving, over a buffet of rice, vegetables, and mystery meats, we met one final member of our group: a lanky Croatian called Kir. Kir had arrived a day earlier than the rest of us to visit an attraction in the north. "Can you keep a secret?" he asked, four seconds after introducing himself.

"Yes," I lied.

"Last night I was in another hotel, in Pyongyang's centre, and I sneaked out for a walk. I thought they'd stop me, of course. But the guard was distracted with something and so I just kept on walking and suddenly I was alone... on the streets of Pyongyang."

This was strictly forbidden. He showed us a video on his phone. "It was incredible," he said, his shifty eyes darting around to check that none of the handlers were listening. "I walked around for about ten minutes." The video showed him walking along a street. The buildings he passed were dark, lit only in their stairwells. "Then a car pulled up and the driver gave me a strange look and so I ran back to the hotel."

After dinner, Annett and I headed down to the hotel's basement, where we found a bar with some pool tables and a karaoke lounge. As we'd be unable to leave the hotel each evening, these were to be our only entertainment options. I found Kir in a corner of the pool room, his phone in his hand, asking people if they could keep a secret. He certainly couldn't. At the bar, instead of the change I was expecting from the purchase of a beer, I was handed four sticks of Wrigley chewing gum.

The barmaid smiled apologetically. "No change."

A few of my tour group were nearby playing pool. They laughed at my confusion, and waved their own chewing gum change at me. Money is based mostly on belief, so chewing gum makes about as much sense as rectangular pieces of dead tree with the queen's face on them. I decided to be a believer, and pocketed the gum. Later, when I returned to the bar for another beer, I took these chewy sticks of legal tender with me and attempted to exchange them for more alcohol. The woman simply laughed as I presented them, and pushed them back across the bar. She was no longer a believer.

The next morning, at the extremely antisocial hour of 6:30am, Annett and I trudged up to the revolving restaurant for a breakfast of rice, vegetables, mystery meats, and eggs. Last night's meal plus egg. We had a perfect view of the city. Where we'd expected it to be slowly shaking off the previous night and yawning lazily into the new work-day, we found it already abuzz. There were groups everywhere moving with a commendable sense of hurry and purpose. I got (even more) tired just watching them.

"Can you believe we're in North Korea?" Annett asked.

"Nope. And I think it might even be weirder than I expected."

It was 7:30am when we climbed onto the tour bus for the first packed day of sightseeing. Our first stop was a collective farm. There to meet us was a beautiful woman with a beehive hairstyle. She wore a pink-and-red floral-patterned traditional dress. "Welcome, comrades," she said. Behind her was the entrance and to the left of that, two large marble statues of dem two bruddas.

"Welcome to the Kim Il-sung collective farm, where under the expert tutelage of the dear leaders, the people work to grow food for our great nation."

A few people moved in the direction of the farm's gates. "Wait, comrades!" She ushered them back to the group. She wasn't finished yet. "The collective farm was first visited by Eternal President Kim Il-sung in 1957."

Okay, fine, nice, good.

"Only the fiftieth time we've heard this name so far this morning," Annett whispered in my ear.

The woman turned and swept her arms in the direction of the statues. "In honour of his visit, we presented him this statue."

Of himself. Humble.

She bowed her head slightly. "He praised it for its revolutionary spirit."

Is it important how often Kim Il-sung was here and what he thought of his statue?

"He next visited the collective farm in 1971."

I guess so.

"Where he gave on-the-spot guidance to local farmers that significantly increased harvest yields."

On-the-spot guidance again. Apparently the dear leaders were true Renaissance men and could give on-the-spot guidance on an incredible range of matters, from running the economy to the engineering of buildings, the design of school desks, and harvesting techniques. They were certainly not *Mitläufer*, like me. Someone sighed, eager to get inside. The nice lady in the traditional dress still wasn't finished yet, though.

"Supreme Leader Kim Jong-il first visited the collective farm in 1984, where he praised it for its architectural beauty."

Ah, K2. We haven't heard his name in five minutes. A veritable drought.

"Supreme Leader Kim Jong-il visited the collective farm again in 1997, when..."

I was on the edge of my feet.

"I feel on-the-spot guidance coming on," Annett whispered.

The woman turned to the statues again. "...we presented him with his own matching statue!"

"Damn, so close," I said.

What do you buy the dictator who has everything? Another big-ass statue of himself, that's what. The country has forty thousand statues of dem two bruddas.

"He praised the statue for its artistic integrity."

"Hurrah," said Kir, sarcastically.

The woman turned and beckoned us in the direction of the statues. "Now, please show your respect."

We lined up in rows of fours, behind each other, facing the statues before bowing together to the dear leaders. Our Western tour guides laid a bouquet of flowers at the statues' feet. We didn't know it yet, but this same scene would play out at every attraction, all day long. On the bus, off the bus, pretty woman in traditional dresses, an explanation from her of how often the dear leaders had been to the thing we were seeing, some bowing, then we would finally be given permission to enter it. This for up to fifteen hours a day. It got tedious.

However, there were occasional, fleeting moments where it felt like, just maybe, we'd smashed through the facade of utter nonsense and experienced something real. The first was during a visit to Pyongyang's enormous new water-park complex. Until then we'd had no meaningful contact with the city's people. How could we? Our Korean handlers never left our sides. Yet as we pulled into this enormous new complex, Mr and Mrs Park informed us that they would be waiting outside. We'd be free to mingle unsupervised amongst the thousands of bathing, swimming, and splashing locals.

I ran inside giddy with new-found freedom. It didn't last long. Inside the lobby I skidded to a stop in front of a familiar face—KI. It certainly takes some chutzpah to put a three-metre-high bronze statue of yourself in the lobby of a swimming pool complex. Kɪ was all chutzpah.

A quick bow later, sufficient respect displayed, we headed to the changing rooms. It was strange to be surrounded by locals in such an intimate setting of mutual nakedness. We'd been told that North Koreans had been told that all foreigners were enemies—prisoners of capitalism living in inferior, miserable countries—who wanted nothing more than the destruction of the *real* Korea. Whereas we'd been told that they were all just brainwashed lemmings. Whether or not either of these things were true, as we undressed together, saw each other naked and failing at the same basic human things like not falling over while taking off our socks, we seemed pretty similar to me.

Stepping out of the changing rooms and into the complex reminded me of the scene in every Western where the stranger enters the rowdy saloon. We were still in Asia, so no one stared blatantly. However, they would steal quick glances at us before quickly looking at something else, usually the floor. No wonder they were looking—we were unusually shaped. Tall, lumbering, chubby, bearded. Some might have never seen a Westerner in the flesh before; certainly not this much flesh, anyway. I also understood now why Annett and the group's other women had elected to wait in the coffee shop instead. If our bodies were getting this much attention, in a country where few had seen white foreigners, the arrival of a sudden wave of Western women in swimsuits would surely have raised more than eyebrows.

The park had at least ten giant slides, some of which required the use of rubber rings or inflatable dinghies, and the whole complex was connected by a network of rapids. Thousands of locals were cooling off in the water during the hottest month of the year. It was really exciting to be in such close proximity to them.

"Actors," said Kir, dismissively, as we walked around. "Splashing around and pretending everything is fine here."

I sighed. "As if they would go to these lengths just to show a few white people everything is fine in North Korea."

He blinked slowly. "Oh come on. Don't be so naive."

The idea that there might be a swimming complex and that the hardworking, loyal, elite party members might get to go there at the weekend didn't seem ridiculous to me. It couldn't be tyranny all the time, could it? If there is a Hell, I'm sure even it would have the odd bank holiday.

Unfortunately, we had only two hours at the water park because while there were limited hours in our days, there were unlimited numbers of statues of the dear leaders to bow in front of. Kevin, a confident, outspoken American with wild curly hair bounded up to us. "You *need* to go on the diving boards," he said, pointing at a structure about fifty metres away. "It's so awesome."

The diving boards had attracted about a hundred spectators, who surrounded a rectangular diving pool. The tallest board was a lofty fifteen metres up into the clouds. "When we go on," said Kevin, "they go wild."

Being clapped for by a large crowd of excited North Koreans? That seemed like too good an opportunity to pass up. The only problem was that I didn't know how to dive. I didn't even really know how to swim. Annett mocked me mercilessly for my one swimming stroke, which she'd coined "the drowning monkey." I don't think anyone on earth expends more energy, to go less distance, than my monkey and I. I looked up at the highest board. Could anything go wrong if I jumped from it? Was it worth it for the risk, to have had the experience?

I decided it was.

So up I went.

About halfway up I peeped over the side.

I decided it wasn't.

I came back down again.

It was high up there.

I guess that's the point.

I was going to walk away, but then I passed the lowest diving board, suspended one solitary metre in the air. I could just walk to the end and fall off. No harm would befall me, would it? How could it? I would do it and find out. But if I was going to do it, I wanted to be loved. I wanted applause. So I decided I'd really ham up my dive for the crowd, give them a show.

I stepped confidently up onto the board, as if I'd been diving all my life. I bowed slightly in a greeting to the audience. This got a laugh. It felt great. I edged further out onto the board. I looked out at the audience. I bowed. I looked down at the board. I twisted my face into one of shock and horror. I faked losing my balance. I opened my mouth as wide as I could. I screamed and trembled. A second laugh. I pretended to be stuck, afraid of a fall of just one metre. Then I punched the air defiantly, my fears suddenly conquered, dropped my weight, and made the board shake below me. This was where things got confusing. I wasn't exactly sure what to do next to get off the board. I'd never dived before. So I bounced a few times more than anyone was expecting, panicked, pretended that was part of the act, and fell sideward into the water. I landed horizontally with a loud slap.

The crowd went wild. Cheers, clapping, some light whooping—I was huge in North Korea! In fact, I was pretty much the Bono of slapstick North Korean water-park diving. Some doubted my methods, sure, but I got results, entertained. This was international relations done right. My head swelled. An Australian called Tim had been watching and decided to lance it. "You can't dive for shit," he said, as I climbed out the end of the pool.

I puffed my chest out. "What? I was just working the crowd. Did you hear that reaction?" I considered telling him I was the Bono of slapstick North Korean water-park entertainment, but it seemed as though the moment had passed.

Back in the changing rooms, Bono couldn't get his locker open. Bono was embarrassed, and wet, and unable to get dry because his towel was in his locker, which, as Bono mentioned, Bono couldn't get open. Luckily, a few lockers down from Bono stood a tall, muscular, naked North Korean. He saw Bono struggling, put on a T-shirt, and came to help. Why the man had picked just a T-shirt, to cover only the top part of his torso, Bono had no idea.

"It is not working when wet," he said.

This was a surprise. "You can speak English?"

"Yes. Little. I student at Kim Il-sung University."

Under his expert tutelage and on-the-spot guidance, the locker door sprung open. I had so many questions. None of them about the locker. "What are you studying?" I asked.

He smiled, revealing a set of wonky front teeth, then stepped gingerly back across the wet floor to his locker, to continue changing.

After everyone had finished swimming, we visited a Starbucks-style coffee shop in the swimming complex. The friction between the tourists intensified. "Maybe this table is bugged?" said an absurdly tall man from Belgium, peering under the coffee table, presumably in search of covert recording devices.

"I don't think that," replied a Dutch girl, "but I think that they are sort of required to be at places we go to, to show us the good side of the country." She looked out through the glass and into the water park, at the thousands of people enjoying it below us. "Maybe they were all invited here today? Did you notice how no one pays for anything anywhere?"

This stopped us in our tracks. We thought back to all the places we'd been thus far—restaurants, coffee shops, museums, the circus. None of the locals had paid for anything, at least not that any of us had seen.

"Proof!" said the Belgian, high-fiving a paranoid German student who was backing his photos up each night across seven hidden SD cards. "Also, in the park, I forget the name—"

"Kim Il-sung Park probably?" the Dutch girl suggested. Everyone laughed. The naming of things was easy in the DPRK; they just picked a Kim and then added the appropriate noun to the end: *park, square, stadium, flower.*

"Anyway, at that park," the German continued, "did you see that guy with the expensive camera? How did he afford that? Why does no one else have one like it?"

He looked around at us one by one, provoking us to find holes in the cheese of his logic. No one dared. We were on a roll. We had answers. *It was all fake...*

"Yes! I saw that too," said the Dutch girl. "And... and... did you see those young guys playing volleyball?"

A few people nodded.

"Well... as soon as we left, I managed to sneak back behind the group and away from the handlers."

We sat up a little higher in our seats. "Guess what?" she said. "They'd stopped playing and left! I think they were actors."

I cleared my throat. I didn't want to be the one contrarian; however, I'd always been a big believer in Occam's razor, in favouring explanations that were simpler, that required fewer presumptions. Since we'd arrived in North Korea, I'd felt trapped in an episode of *The X-Files*, as the only Scully amongst fifty tourist Mulders. They wanted to believe. I wanted to know, and if that wasn't possible, to err on the side of caution. All the other weird places I'd visited had only reassured me there isn't all that much New out there. The wrapping changes, but underneath are the same flawed humans muddling through as best they can, getting to be either the ones who give the orders, the ones who have to obey them, or something in between. The stories we'd been told about North Korea in the media were sensationalist, but so were the stories I'd been telling of Thetford. Sensationalism sells. Not that North Korea was ordinary, but that didn't mean it used three thousand actors to stage a play of leisure normality for fifty tourists.

"Guys," I said, "it's a fun theory, but the sheer logistics involved in it are just baffling. Look how many people are out there. All for us? And, I mean, perhaps more importantly, *why*? Why would they care enough to stage all this?" I swept an arm in the direction of the water park below.

The Belgian tutted. "Because they want us to think everything is normal here."

"Okay, but *why*?"

"So we go home and tell people it's normal."

"Okay, but *why*?" I had become a five-year-old.

He sighed. "So that other people will come here."

I clenched my jaw. "But *why* would they come here, then? It would just be a boring normal country full of statues, a place where you can't talk to anyone, and have to spend eight hours each day on a bus, and all your time off it bowing. If it truly were normal, there would be no reason to come here. It's not fun. It's almost certainly one of the worst places on earth, in fact."

We sipped quietly at our coffees. People looked out at the water park and the actors pretending to enjoy themselves within it. I wasn't invited to further conspiratorial discussions.

The following day was, well, so many things. It was clear from what we'd seen so far that the DPRK had a pretty tenuous relationship with modesty. Nowhere was this more evident than our next stop: Kumsusan Palace of the Sun, K1 and K2's mausoleum. Every North Korean is required to visit it once. Some come much more often. Many were there that day, dressed, like us, in their finest formal wear.

The building itself was typically North Korean, which meant it was typically Stalinist, which meant it was eight times larger than it needed to be and probably took Herculean efforts to heat. Inside we found opulences of marble and gold at scales dizzying and awe-inspiring (oh, and bragging).

"Apparently it took a hundred million dollars to build the bugger," said Jack. The interior was a collection of travelators, wide moving walkways. We were not allowed to walk on them, despite the very slow speed they were set to. Instead, we had to simply stand on them and be carried along. This was so we'd have enough time to enjoy the countless numbers of propaganda pictures of the dear leaders adorning the walls and ceiling: K1 and K2 visiting factories; inspecting military hardware; being entertained by smiling children playing miniature musical instruments; giving on-the-spot guidance. Many of the photos were obviously Photoshopped—colours didn't match, and shadows suggested our planet is actually heated by *two* suns. Sweeping, lamenting orchestral music was pumped out of hidden speakers. It set the sombre tone.

It was simply absurd. The oddest thing my two eyes had ever seen. "I'm struggling for words," I said to Annett. "Since you never have that problem, can you help?"

She smiled, staring at an enormous picture of K1 holding a baby. "You've got to give it to them. They know how to do pomp."

"Yeah, it's kinda like Madame Tussauds on acid at the end of the world," said Jack, the best summary so far.

Finally, after an hour of being shuffled through this maze of indoctrination and having adequately mulled over the extraordinary, monumental achievements of the dear leaders, we came to an air-blowing, shoe-cleaning station. Relieved of our external impurities, we passed into a dark room illuminated by only the faintest red strip lighting. In front of us, in the room's centre, surrounded by columns of red marble, lay, embalmed in an elevated glass sarcophagus, the body of demigod Eternal President Kim Il-sung. A red Workers' Party of Korea flag covered him to his chest. He wore a dark suit jacket, his arms resting at his sides. Around the casket were dozens of pink Kimilsungia flowers. Did I mention K1 and K2 have their own flowers? I didn't? I take it you're not surprised?

Good. Because we're just getting started.

Annett and I followed the row of four in front of us and approached the casket. We bowed to three sides of it, but not to the top, as that would imply we were above the great man and could look down upon him. *As if.* The room was perfectly quiet except for the high-pitched squeaking of one pair of shoes. *My shoes.* I'd only ever worn them once. Where did I have to go that might require smart shoes? A guard clutching an automatic weapon to his chest frowned.

"Dude," said Tristan, another of our Western guides, "do something about those shoes." I wasn't sure what I was supposed to do about the shoes. Nor when and where I was supposed to do it. A few minutes later, we reached the second room, the resting place of K2. He lay wearing his trademark, iconic, olive zip-up suit.

Squeak. Squeak. Bow. *Squeak.* Frown. Bow. *Squeak. Squeak.* Frown. Bow.

Around him, predictably, were dozens of bright red Kimjongilia flowers. The next room was equally absurd. It was the awards room of K1, and contained every trophy, medal, key, and plaque presented to him in his distinguished life of gangster kingpindom. The walls were adorned with pictures of him posing with world leaders. K1 fraternised with a select crowd of despots and dictators: Stalin, Honecker, Mubarak, Ceaușescu, Gaddafi—the room was a shrine to history's assholes.

The final chamber was the same, only for K2. I knew modesty had finally died, been embalmed, and given its own Kumsusan Palace of the Sun when I saw a photo of K1 awarding K2 the "hero of Korea" medal.

Kumsusan was North Korea at its most ridiculous, absurd, offensive, gaudy, and shameful. The exhibits spoke for themselves. They said, "Can you believe we got away with this? That now, even in death, we're still getting away with this?" I couldn't. At the exit, shellshocked, disorientated, depressed, we stumbled back out into the torching sun.

"I've never seen anything like that," I said to Kir.

He nodded. "Yeah, they really turned the propaganda to eleven."

As mentioned, the reason we'd picked this specific tour was that *Juche 105* (the North Korean calendar is based, of course, on K1's date of birth) was the seventieth anniversary of the end of Japanese Imperial rule. To celebrate this, that evening, there would be a mass dance held in the city's main square. Would you like to have a guess at the name of that square? That's right, Kim Il-sung Square.

Shortly before 8pm, we stepped down from our tour buses and were led up into a pavilion. What we saw from that pavilion, well, if there were words for it, none of us could locate them. I got so dizzy that I had to sit down.

"Wow," said Annett. "It's..." But nothing further came.

"I can't," said Kir. "It's. Jesus."

Even Jack was humbled. "It's like the Bermuda Triangle fucked..." He faded out, defeated by the grandiosity of the spectacle.

Below us were ten thousand adults all staring straight ahead and standing perfectly still in blocks of thirty. The blocks covered the entire square and continued all the way to the banks of the Taedong River several hundred metres in the distance. The men wore formal shirts and ties, while the women wore their brightly coloured traditional dresses. We fumbled hungrily at the buttons of our cameras: it was pointless. There was no way to capture the beauty and absurdity of the spectacle. Of so many people standing stiffly, in formation, like marionettes awaiting their puppeteer.

"They're like the terracotta warriors of Xi'an," I said to Annett.

"Yeah, only these people are alive."

The music began to play. The people raised their heads and pumped their fists to it, in near-perfect synchrony. How many nights had been lost choreographing this? After that first song had finished, a more upbeat one began, and the men and women turned, faced one another, bowed, and began to dance.

They danced beautifully. No one bumped anyone else. No one tripped. No one arrived late, drunk, or in the wrong clothes. Who had coordinated this remarkable feat of logistics? Although the visuals overwhelmed, it was the logistics that baffled me most.

"Look at their faces," said Dennis, a Swiss lawyer.

They were completely devoid of emotion. "I'd call them robotic, but that would be a little offensive to robots," said Jong. This was supposed to be a joyous occasion, the celebration of seventy years of "freedom."

"They look so bored," said Annett

Jack lowered the enormous lens of his camera. "You would be too if you'd been dancing to the same half dozen songs since childhood."

My mouth dropped open. "What do you mean? There are only six official songs?"

"Yep. This song will loop again in a few minutes, just you wait. And there are only a few officially sanctioned dancing numbers. They learn all the steps in kindergarten, the poor bastards."

"Ah," I said. "That's why no one makes mistakes."

Four songs in, the handlers beckoned us down from the pavilion. My pulse raced as I skipped down the wide steps to the square. With so few tourists and so many groups, it was easy for all of us to spread out and have a block of thirty DPRK dancers to ourselves. Annett and I looked at the group in front of us. So perfect, structured, flawless.

"I don't know if I can do it," I said, one hand on my hip. "Do you think they'll mind?"

Annett shook her head and stepped towards them. "Nah. I think these people could use some spontaneity."

I picked a woman at random. She wore a pink-and-white traditional dress, puffy around the sleeves. She looked to be in her mid-twenties. In the short break between songs, I motioned to her male partner, pointed at Annett, motioned to myself, and then pointed at the young lady. He nodded and politely stepped aside. The whole group shuffled a little bit to create space for us, and we entered. The next song began. Annett and I exchanged mutual looks of terror as the perfectly synchronised mob began swirling around us; we attempted to keep up, learning the steps as we went, in real time.

For the dance I needed to hold my partner's hands—one in front of her body, one behind. Then we would take one step forward and two steps back (just like my literary career). Next we would turn and face each other, and link arms and circle each other, one way, and then the other, before resuming our original formation, and repeating.

It is, of course, very easy to explain all that now because I've watched the video of me doing it several times, and in slow motion. At that moment, however, in the tyranny of real time, I was hopeless. I dance like concrete swims. Actually, I dance like I swim. When the group turned left, I turned right; when they went two steps forward and one step back, I shuffled back and out. Fortunately I had a patient, pretty partner who smiled politely at me throughout. She didn't seem shy, nor to mind that the song involved so much touching. As the song ended, I bowed to her and, out of a feeling of guilt over what I had made her endure, I stepped away.

Annett did the same. We regrouped in a gap between dancers to swap notes.

I was giddy. "That was awesome!"

"I know. I was terrible at it though."

"Me too," I said, trying to make her feel better.

"You don't need to tell me that. I was right behind you."

I spotted Mrs Park just a few metres away, by a pole holding the country's flag. One of six thousand in my eyeline.

"Mrs Park." I bowed. "May I have the honour of this dance?"

"Dance?"

"Yes. Me and you."

She giggled nervously. "I'm not really a dancer."

"You haven't not seen anything yet," I said, trying to reassure her but just confusing her with a double negative. She handed her bag to her fellow guide. Her arm in mine, I led her into a small gap in the nearest formation of dancers.

"Do you know the steps?" I asked.

"I know the steps."

"Good. Teach me."

The song began. The beat was faster this time. The people in front of us began to swirl. I tried to follow. I tripped, recovered my balance, turned (out of time). They clapped. I tried to mimic Mrs Park. The group swirled back the other way. I followed, but forgot to spin back when they did, and bumped noses with Mrs Park. Next came the kicking of the leg, then a high-five. After a rocky start, I felt, by the time the song was fading out, that I had been only mostly awful.

We stepped out of the group. "What was that?" Mrs Park asked.

"What do you mean?"

She crossed her arms. "Was that supposed to be dancing?"

My pride bruised, I retreated to the pavilion to watch the rest of the spectacle from a distance. As Jack had predicted, there really were just six songs on a loop. The event ended exactly one hour after it started. Just a few minutes later, ten thousand people had filed neatly out of the square.

The group reassembled at the entrance to the pavilion.

"WOOO," said Kevin. He jumped on a couple of his friends. "THAT WAS AMAZING!"

"What did you think?" I asked Annett. She looked out at the empty square. "I don't know. I think I'm going to need some time with this."

I needed it too. I had this heavy, tense feeling in my stomach. Sadness, I decided, at having watched ten thousand intelligent, creative, imaginative people reduced to arriving at a set time, in a set pattern, in set clothing, to dance to a set number of songs, for a set duration, before doing some final (set) fist-pumping and then heading home again, in a set order. What if these people were actually allowed to do what they wanted? To create their own dance moves? To write their own songs? "Free" will still has value.

Having had one of my most treasured experiences, one I'll never forget, I left the square elated and baffled yet feeling deeply sorry for everyone involved in giving it to us.

A few days of bowing later, it was all over. At 5:45am we boarded the tour bus for the final time and headed to the airport where arrivals and departures were (oh wonder of wonders) separated. Jack snoozed in his seat at the front. I was going to miss these people. Friendships were built quickly and deeply in the DPRK. You have so much time with each other and you bond over the madness you're subjected to. I was even going to miss Jack. Maybe. A little bit.

At the airport, I asked him why he'd bothered to get up so early to see us off. "I only didn't come once," he said. "It was the time that one of the guests, a sixty-year-old American, freaked out at the airport and started screaming and shouting and trying to convince his handlers that they were living in a lie, that the regime was composed of dictators, that North Korea had started the Korean war. They arrested the goon. He burst into tears. Scribbled a quick letter of apology and they let him back on the flight. He later described the experience as 'the scariest of his life.'" Jack chuckled to himself. "No shit."

Nothing dramatic happened at the airport. We hugged our handlers, Mr and Mrs Park, and took some final group photos. A few people were tearful. This place got under your skin. But then, mosquitoes also get under your skin. We were getting out. We were the lucky ones. One day, this regime will collapse and we'll learn just how callous it has been to its people. Until then, I'll remember that the people we met in North Korea were extremely nice and offered what meagre scraps of honesty, doubt, and curiosity they could get away with. I have no doubt that they have doubts about the regime but that the cost of expressing these is simply too high. They aren't brainless zombies. It would have been easier to stomach if they were.

"Would you recommend other people come here on holiday?" I asked Annett on the flight to Beijing. We were flying Air Koryo, the country's national (and only) airline, voted in one poll as the worst in the world. "It's the most memorable place I've ever been," she said, then frowned. "But it's hard work. They really tour the crap out of you."

I touched the base of my spine. "I think I strained something with all that bowing."

The attendant handed us our in-flight food. A mysteriously nondescript burger-shaped spongy object. It had ingredients but we couldn't name them. Other than kimchi. We hadn't had a meal without it in ten days. "Do you think it's different from other dictatorships you've seen?" Annett asked, between bites.

I jerked my head back. "God yeah! Just the scale of it. The omnipresence of those same two faces, day in and day out. They were seriously needy, those two. Forty thousand statues? Every adult having to wear their faces on their heart each day?"

"Yeah, they made vanity into an art. The whole place was kind of like a dystopian, terror, misery, kimchi theme park."

I sighed. "I feel incredibly lucky to be going back to Germany."

17

BERLIN, GERMANY: THE END

I checked my phone as I walked up the stairs to our first-floor apartment. It was 6:10pm. Annett would be home soon. Inside the hallway, I dropped my yoga gear in a heap by the door. I glanced at the whiteboard, where I'd scrawled "Boredom is a luxury good" in green pen. I took a deep breath. It was good to be home. Wait, wasn't there something I was supposed to do? I did some mental accounting.

I'm fully dressed. Nothing is on fire. The fridge has food. I paid all my taxes. I did the washing up this morning.

Everything seemed fine. Ah, I'd wanted to email Dan. That was it. I'd get to that later. I hadn't heard from them in ages. I groped for the light switch. I flicked it. Nothing happened.

Change the light bulb. That's it.

I took one of our cheap IKEA chairs from the kitchen and opened the dedicated light-bulb-and-battery drawer Annett had created. I smiled as I looked down at bulbs sorted by wattage and batteries sorted by size. All annotated with brightly coloured Post-it notes. It was both deeply impressive and absolutely terrifying. A pretty good summary of Annett, I concluded.

I dragged the chair out into the hallway, stood on it, and reached up for the light socket. The chair groaned under my weight. I heard a key jangle in the lock. The door flew open, slamming into the wall with a dull thud.

"Hey," Annett said, slamming it closed again. That poor door. "I don't know why I bother getting the postal mail. No good news ever comes via postal mail. Did you ever notice that?"

Our hallway was L-shaped. She came round its corner and stopped to look up at me on the chair. "You're changing the bulb? Wow, I only had to ask you what, like three times? That's twelve fewer than normal."

I screwed the new bulb in. "You're welcome. Give it a try."

She disappeared back round the corner. "And God, said let there be...'"

Our dark, narrow hallway became, well, slightly less dark. "Good enough," I said, as she squeezed past me en route to the living room. I returned the chair to its home in the kitchen.

Back in the living room, I found her spread across the couch, as if shot by the relaxation gun. She smiled up at me. "How was your day then, my little *Mitläufer*?"

I crossed the room and sat, demurely, on the small slither of couch she hadn't claimed for herself. "Good. I went to the co-working place. I think that's making a difference. I almost feel like I have a job and colleagues again."

"Did you do some work or just eat chocolate and do vanity searches?"

"I did some work. Not much. But some. I think I'm going to try to write that book about unusual countries. Probably nothing will come of it, but let's see. How was your day? Anyone fail to notice your genius?"

She wafted a wrist in front of her face, like a slighted movie starlet. "Only just about everyone, as per freaking usual. It was crazy out there. That stupid woman from HR. Doesn't know her ass from her elbow. What do you want to do later? I was thinking maybe—"

"Sure."

She sat up. "I didn't even say what it was yet."

"I know. Doesn't matter."

She tilted her head. "What if it involves leaving the house again?"

"Especially if it involves leaving the house."

"And meeting other humans? Maybe humans who might want something from you, like your caring a teeny tiny bit about their lives, maybe? Or at least remembering something about them?"

"Sounds pretty good to me."

She grinned. "I could get used to this."

"Try not to," I said, looking round the room. "That was my mistake."

The next book in the series...

The end. You made it. Thank you. You're a wonderful human. I'm extremely grateful you took a chance on me (there's a song in that, I think).

If you want to support me in writing more books:

1. Join my newsletter and get two older (non-travel) books for free *http://adam-fletcher. co.uk/newsletter*

2. Buy *Don't Come Back* the award-winning second book in the series.

Adam Fletcher's life hates him...

That's how it feels since he lost his girlfriend of nine years, his confidence, home, and hair.

But then he gets an email from a mysterious stranger offering him the trip of a lifetime. Is it too good to be true? Can you outrun your problems?

He says yes and is catapulted on an unforgettable adventure of black magic, angry baboons, buffalo sacrifice, Komodo dragons, coffee-drinking dead Grandmas, late-night speedboat rescues, sky graves, love potions, dates with a princess, and the strangest funeral in the world.

A lot of really weird things are about to happen to him. He's not ready for any of them...

Winner of the Writer's Digest Memoir of the Year Award!
Available at Amazon

Need further convincing? Here's a sample chapter to whet your appetite...

A PREVIEW CHAPTER FROM DON'T COME BACK

I sat, opened my laptop, and stared at a clunker of a sentence. Who had written this sentence? I had written this sentence. I'd have to hide it deep within a paragraph of outstanding natural beauty. But where?

I tapped my foot in time to the blinking cursor and noticed movement at the periphery of my vision. I turned slightly to see a man striding towards me, his back ramrod straight, his gaze firm, his legs clad in tight maroon shorts just the wrong side of indecent. He was carrying a small leather satchel and a large sense of entitlement.

This man was my friend Nick.

"'ello, 'ello," he said, holding out a fist to bump. Unable to leave my ugly sentence, I wafted a fist in his general direction but missed.

"Smoooooth." He dropped his satchel onto the neighbouring desk. I guess the good thing about hugs is that with that much surface area it's hard to miss. Not that you'd hug Nick. Or do anything to Nick. He might do things to you, if he wanted. He was *control,* you were the *freak*.

"Wot you doin'? Checking your spam again?" He chuckled at his own joke. I was paranoid that if I didn't check my spam eighteen times a day, fantastic digital opportunities would slip past me out into the Internet night.

"Laugh away, Nicky baby, but a lot of good stuff goes in there."

"Yeah, well. I guess *you* need t' enlarge your penis."

Nick was from the north of England. I understood, at best, 82 percent of the things he said. The Germans around us were always delighted to land anywhere over the halfway mark.

I laughed sarcastically. "You been talking to my girlfriends?"

"That would be difficult since they don't exist. You just had one, forever. Before you screwed that up. You're basically a man-swan."

He sat and began doing whatever it was someone paid him far too much to do. I looked across at him, at his smug head all covered in hair. At his handsome face twinkling in all its stupid symmetry. At his muscular legs poking out from maroon shorts just the wrong side of indecent.

Someone needed to take this man down.

I opened my spam folder: 412 new messages.

I rubbed my hands together in anticipation. This folder was obviously full of fantastic, unmissable, point-making opportunities. I scanned the first: debt recovery. The second: an "aroused Asian woman keen to chat." The third: a lottery I'd won without entering. The fourth: another aroused Asian woman keen to chat. The fifth: a clinic promising to enlarge my "member"—I forwarded it to Nick.

Hope faded. Did anything good ever arrive in spam? Would I plumb the dark, depressing depths of page two to find out?

Yes, I would.

There I found the same sorry electronic cocktail of lies, damned lies, and statistically improbable lottery wins.

Nick was right.

Nick was always right.

And handsome.

And good at things.

I sighed. I was just about to tab back to my elephant man of a sentence when the following collection of human words caught my eye:

. . .

Urgent: Speaking opportunity in South Africa.

A bolt of adrenaline surged up my neck. I read the message. Then I re-read it. Then I re-re-read it. Then I read it too many more times to hyphenate. Then I did a little inner Macarena.

"Nick."

"Wot?"

"You know I'm not the sort of person to say 'I told you so,' right? Some people are like that. They like to be right. And when they are right, they lord it over people. I remember this one time, right, I played this German guy at table football. You know how Germans are at table football?"

"Yeah, I only made that mistake once."

"They're brutal. Sadists. Well, this guy gave me the thrashing of my life, and yet every time he scored—7-0, 8-0, 9-0—he still celebrated like he'd won Estonia a World Cup in extra time, with just his nose."

"Is this going somewhere?"

"I'm just not that sort of person, is what I'm saying." I pointed at my screen. "However. Come give this little missive the once-over, will you?"

With a swift thrust of his heels, he glided over to my desk. He tapped his fingers as he read. "This was in your spam, was it?"

"It was."

"You found it *right now*, did you?"

"I did."

"This"—he cleared his throat—"*very minute.* That's what you're telling me?"

"Uh-huh."

"Right. And you're expecting"—he pointed both thumbs at his chest—"young Nicky here to believe that, are you?"

"Yeah. Is it saying what I think it's saying?"

"Do you think it's saying that someone is inviting you on a last-minute, expenses-paid trip to South Africa? If so, yeah, it's saying exactly that."

"This has to be one of those too-good-to-be-true situations, doesn't it? I mean, not only am I right, which is, of course, not a point I will belabour, because I'm not one of those people, but I'm also being offered a free holiday?"

"Yeah. I'm googling the woman who sent it."

"Good idea. Check she's not 'Asian and aroused.' In the meantime, I think I'll just do a little I-told-you-so victory dance!" I got up and wiggled my ass in Nick's face. "Take that! You know what that is? That's being wrong."

He groaned.

"Yeah, you groan. Groan all you want. Groan like a man who's wrong. Then go check your spam."

"She's real," Nick said, unable to hide his disappointment. He returned to his desk. "First time I've seen you dance."

I sat back down. Someone wanted to pay me to go somewhere I would have gladly paid to go. And, crucially, if I was there, I couldn't also be here—that was physics 101. If I wasn't here, I'd be further from my problems—Adam logic 101. Running away had always worked wonders in the past.

Sure, this woman wanted me to deliver a one-hour keynote talk to 160 of the country's German teachers, in German, a language I spoke with all the grace of a donkey on roller skates tumbling off a cliff. But that was Future Me's problem. Present Me—the me I'd always liked best—leaned back into his swivel chair, gave his scalp a good scratch, and ushered his imagination out to play.

SOUTH AFRICA!

A burnt-orange sun illuminates a thirsty savanna.

Tribal drums pound rhythmically.

Men sing in an exotic language of clicks.

Animals emerge from bushes and wiggle their tushes.

A lion lifts a cub into the air . . .

I realised my imagination was ripping off the opening scene of *The Lion King*. I called it back and grounded it in the Here and Now.

"You going to go?" Nick asked.

"Damn right I'm going," I said, without hesitation. A smug silence fell between us. I'd been right. My prize was a holiday and an escape from the uncertainties of my life in Berlin. And if I was far away anyway, why not go further still? I could make it a proper trip, add a couple of other countries from the bucket list, there were a few really weird ones this would be the perfect excuse to visit. I could think of two that might even help me work out what to do to next with my shambles of a life.

My mind crackled with possibility. I could go *find myself*. That was a thing, wasn't it? It could be like *Eat, Pray, Love*, only I was kind of fat, and an atheist, and lightly heartbroken, so I'd need a new title: *Diet, Death, Celibacy*?

The title needed some work, but there'd be plenty of time for that. I sighed contentedly. While my problems weren't over, they could be the next best thing: indefinitely paused.

"I'm coming too," Nick said.

Wait, what?

Winner of the Writer's Digest Memoir of the Year Award!

Available at Amazon

Printed in Great Britain
by Amazon

43121919R00147